Selective Solidarity

CONTEMPORARY ETHNOGRAPHY

Alma Gottlieb, Series Editor

A complete list of books in the series
is available from the publisher.

# SELECTIVE SOLIDARITY

Children and Middle-Class Moralities
in Transnational Senegal

## Chelsie Yount

**PENN**

UNIVERSITY OF PENNSYLVANIA PRESS

PHILADELPHIA

Copyright © 2025 University of Pennsylvania Press

Published by
University of Pennsylvania Press
Philadelphia, Pennsylvania 19104–4112
www.pennpress.org

Printed in the United States of America on acid-free paper

10 9 8 7 6 5 4 3 2 1

A Cataloging-in-Publication record is available from the
Library of Congress.

Hardcover ISBN 978-1-5128-2757-6
Paperback ISBN 978-1-5128-2756-9
Ebook ISBN 978-1-5128-2758-3

*To Marguerite*

# CONTENTS

n Senegal, French is the official language of government and education, but Wolof is the lingua franca of the population. The Wolof spoken in Dakar includes "massive lexical borrowing from French" (McLaughlin 2001: 153), which linguists refer to as "urban Wolof" (Swigart 1992). My representations of the two languages reflect my interlocutors' blended usage of the two codes in France and in Dakar alike.

The transcriptions of Wolof terms used here are based on the orthographic standards developed by the Centre de Linguistique Appliqué de Dakar (CLAD), which were officially adopted by the Senegalese state in 1971. Middle-class Senegalese, like those described in this book, often consider themselves native speakers of both Wolof and French but are likely to master only official written French. When writing WhatsApp messages in Wolof or searching on Google, they use a mixture of spellings, usually based on French phonetic conventions. For instance, to purchase *cuuraay* incense online (/ʧuraɪ/, sounds like "choo-rye" in English), it is more useful to search "*thiouraye*," a transliteration based on French phonetics, than the official spelling.

For the most part, I have used the official CLAD orthography. However, I depart from this standard on the words "*tubab*" (white person) and "*teranga*" (hospitality). These terms have come into regular usage, spelled with a single "a," in written Wolof, French, and English. I conform to this generalized usage, rather than the CLAD spellings ("tubaab" and "teraanga"), which have a double "a" to reflect the long vowel sound. Phrases and initial uses of individual words in both French and Wolof are indicated throughout the book in Italics, accompanied by an English translation. Unless otherwise noted, all translations are mine (for Wolof translations I am grateful for the help of Ndeye Oulimata Diop and Oumoul Sow). The table represents Wolof orthography, using the International Phonetic Alphabet and English pronunciation examples.

Table 1. Wolof Orthography and Pronunciation Guide

| Orthography | IPA and English example |
| --- | --- |
| a | /a/ as in "father" |
| b | /b/ as in "bed" |
| c | /ʧ/ as in "church" |
| d | /d/ as in "dog" |
| e | /e/ as in "bed" |
| é | /eɪ/ as in "café" |
| f | /f/ as in "fun" |
| g | /g/ as in "go" |
| i | /i/ as in "machine" |
| j | /ʤ/ as in "judge" |
| k | /k/ as in "kite" |
| l | /l/ as in "lip" |
| m | /m/ as in "man" |
| n | /n/ as in "nose" |
| ñ | /ɲ/ as in "canyon" |
| o | /o/ as in "more" |
| p | /p/ as in "pen" |
| r | /r/ as in "roll" |
| s | /s/ as in "snake" |
| t | /t/ as in "top" |
| u | /u/ as in "rule" |
| w | /w/ as in "water" |
| x | /x/ as in Scottish "loch" |
| y | /j/ as in "yes" |

Source: Adapted from Croff 2019.

# Introduction

## Talk in Transnational Families: Economic Moralities of Belonging

May ma ci, Awa [Wolof]. *Et tata?*
*Donne un peu à tata, mon bébé* [French].
Give me some, *Awa*. And auntie? Give
a little to auntie, baby.
　　—Mouna Diallo, Malakoff (suburb of Paris)

n her apartment on the outskirts of Paris, Mouna Diallo[1] coaxed her daughter Awa to share from the box of jelly beans the toddler clutched. Placing one in her mother's outstretched hand, Awa eyed me cautiously before handing over a small orange candy, apparently unconvinced by Mouna's claim that I was an "auntie" who deserved a portion of her snack. Settling in next to me on her burnt-orange leather sofa, Mouna explained that she alternated between Wolof and French when speaking to Awa. That way, she reasoned, her daughter would understand everything when they go back to Dakar and would also be ready to start *la maternelle* (French public pre-school) next year when she turned three. Mouna's brother, Ismael, had given me her number in Dakar a few weeks prior, assuring me that his sister could help me with my fieldwork in middle-class Senegalese households in Paris. She only had the one daughter, Mouna said with a smile, but agreed to tell me what she knew about raising a child in the French capital.

After Awa started school, Mouna mused, it would be more important to give her daughter a "Senegalese education" at home. Awa would inevitably receive a "French education" out there, Mouna explained with a wave to the street that led across the Boulevard périphérique and into Paris. But it was only "in here," she said, indicating the confines of their two-bedroom apartment, that she could teach her daughter how to eat around the communal dish, to systematically share food, to be attentive to adults' needs, and do chores for older people. Her efforts to transmit behaviors that relatives in Senegal would expect from a child who was *yaru* (respectful) would take place in the privacy of her home. Outside in Paris, Mouna confessed, she often avoids speaking Wolof, even to Awa. If identified as Senegalese, she explained, other Africans might ask her "to join their *natt* [rotating-credit association]."

Language practices are bound up with economic relations. Everyday talk can be used to organize material exchange or to avoid the circulation of resources. Prodded until they share, children in families from Senegal come to expect that, when eating, others can request their portion. But acts of sharing snacks are not always met with praise. Older children of Senegalese migrants also learn to anticipate adult admonishment to "avoid the wrong crowd" in France. While their parents highlight the importance of showing "solidarity" to relatives, these same adults sometimes avoid contexts where other Africans in France might mobilize this virtue to request funds, acutely aware of the need for *selective* solidarity.

Analyzing interactions in middle-class Senegalese households in Paris and Dakar, this book traces links between the language that mediates everyday acts of material exchange, like food sharing and gift giving, and moral discourses that shape redistribution beyond the household. Foregrounding children's role in transnational relations, it urges us to rethink questions of agency in economic practice, revealing the ways diasporic kinship strategies unevenly enable transnational kin to weather successive economic crises. How do children grapple with the multiple (and sometimes contradictory) moral expectations they encounter in France and in their transnational families? What can their practical struggles tell us about the ways middle-class decline in Europe is impacting kinship connections in the African diaspora?

This ethnography of Senegalese transnational families shows how escalating global inequalities reshape the ways relatives negotiate normative expectations regarding material circulation, which I call "economic moralities" (Yount-André 2017; Yount and Leins nd; cf. Maurer 2009).[2] Inverting economic anthropology's classic concept of "moral economy" (Thompson 1971; Scott 1976), this book focuses on economic moralities (plural) to emphasize the multiplicity of moral pressures that shape economic relations. Approaching material circulation and the speech that mediates it as integrated processes of "language materiality" (Cavanaugh and Shankar 2017), this book is founded on linguistic analysis of everyday talk in Senegalese households and ethnographic observation of acts of material exchanges among kin (food sharing, gift giving, monetary support) in Paris and Dakar.

I argue that the French-born children of Senegalese, acutely aware of the discrimination they face in France, forge affective and economic connections abroad that are key to reproducing transnational kinship. Focusing on children's everyday exchanges, this book demonstrates how the threat of exclusion saturates household interactions, coloring talk of resource redistribution and the economic relations in which families engage. Analyzing how speakers characterize acts of exchange and link them to specific relationships or "types" of people, I show how families navigate questions of belonging in everyday talk, evaluating economic practices in ways that rank people relative to their rights to resources in kinship networks and state systems alike.

The book focuses on the families of middle-class Senegalese migrants in Paris: a shrinking group of African urbanites who were able to leverage French educations into transnational social mobility. The Senegalese consulate estimates that there are around two hundred thousand Senegalese residing in France, but the number jumps to "1.1 million if you include those with dual nationality" (Consulate General of Senegal in France, cited in *Le Monde* 2024) and would be higher still if undocumented immigrants were counted. Of these, some ten thousand Senegalese receive visas annually to study in France. Representing only 0.06 percent of the Senegalese population, this path is available only to a small francophone minority (Ndiaye 2020, 147). There is no way to know the exact number of (middle-class) Senegalese in France, however, as French law bans the collection of data on individuals' race, ethnicity, or religion, in alignment with its "colorblind" approach to immigration (Simon 2008).

Once considered exemplars of integration in France, African intellectuals in Paris increasingly find that their diplomas can no longer protect them from stigmatization. For many, the growing success of the far-right Rassemblement national[3] party represents a public measure of the discrimination their children face when applying to university or searching for jobs. As racial and religious minorities, these families are particularly vulnerable to *déclassement*—that is, downward social mobility or "backsliding" in class terms—which plagues France's middle class (Chauvel 2006; Minni and Okba 2014). The difficulties migrant parents face in transmitting class status to their

French-born children lays bare the fact that, for visible minorities, "integration" is not a state one might achieve once and for all but, rather, a process
that can be undone as the stakes of belonging raise.


## A Question of Education: Middle-Class Migrants
## and Invisible Lines of Integration

Like many middle-class Senegalese in Paris, Mouna Diallo described feeling
as though she had arrived in France "already integrated." Raised in middle-
class households in Dakar,[4] the adults in my study had arrived in Paris with
French language skills and diplomas that allowed them to migrate through
formal channels and find jobs roughly commensurate with their qualifications: teaching in French public schools or working as salaried employees in
accounting firms or insurance companies.[5] Most of the adults, and all their
children, had French citizenship. In many ways, they blended into the masses
of multicultural Paris. Class privilege and cultural capital achieved back in
Dakar allowed them to be perceived as "integrated" and, thus, as I will argue in Chapter 1, invisible as "immigrants."

Their children, however, were French minorities. They faced discrimination at school and in finding employment (or even unpaid internships) that
their parents had never encountered growing up in Dakar and from which
even middle-class parents could not protect them. Francophone, educated
Senegalese in Paris tried to help their children *demonstrate* their integration
in France, aligning even mundane behaviors with the expectations of French
middle classes. Some of these practices, like the effort and resources parents
invested in their children's educations, were choices widely valued in French
society and a defining characteristic of middle classes internationally. But
belonging in France also entailed more subtle, embodied practices to distinguish middle-class Africans from working-class and undocumented immigrants in Paris.

My interlocutors summarized these class distinctions (cf. Bourdieu 1979)
as a question of "*éducation*," a term that refers, in French, to both formal
schooling and the ineffable lessons that make up one's upbringing. Distinctions that make-or-break belonging may be nearly imperceptible, requiring
careful attention to the ways the minutiae of self-presentation shape stigma
in France. A graduate student at the Sorbonne, for example, described realizing, soon after arriving from Dakar, that when he wore anything besides

button-down dress shirts, people mistook him for a janitor and spoke to him "like [he] was there to sweep up." Mouna became sensitive to the scent of *cuuraay* incense on her clothes when she noticed that, in Paris, this spicy sweet smell wafts through the streets near large public housing complexes, clinging to the clothing of children who trail behind women dressed in African-print fabrics. The scent of incense, which, in Dakar, was associated with the feminine arts of welcoming guests and charming one's husband, could be an invisible sign of foreignness in France.

The invisible lines that middle-class Senegalese felt called to draw (cf. "boundary work" in Lamont and Molnár 2002; Mercer 2020) in order to meet French expectations of "integration" shaped the way they spoke and how they used their money. I realized, months later, for example, that Mouna's avoidance of speaking French in her neighborhood had little to do with rotating credit associations (natts) themselves. In fact, Mouna was part of a small natt in France with her in-laws. Each month, she and other relatives sent a bank transfer to her husband's aunt, who then sent the lump sum to whichever participant was set to receive the pot of money that month. Mouna liked that her obligation to the other members pushed her to set aside money each month, allowing her to save without violating Islam's ban on earning interest.

With the women in her neighborhood, however, Mouna was certain that a natt would not be a simple affair. With these ladies—the ones she always heard talking loudly in Wolof, babies strapped to their backs—she would end up *spending* money in order to save, obliged to host the group at her home when it was her turn to receive the funds. "They would want to meet in person," Mouna sighed, imagining. At the outset, they would all promise that the meetings were for "*waxtaan rekk*," only to chat. But sooner or later, someone would serve her guests some hibiscus *bissap* juice. The next host would serve drinks and *fataaya* pastries, beginning a game of one-upmanship that would finish "How? With *méchoui*?" Mouna laughed, imagining the final host proudly presenting her guests the roasted sheep served at the annual *Tabaski* (Eid al-Adha) celebration in Senegal.

It was not their fault, Mouna allowed; it was a question of "éducation." Mouna's background clearly diverged from those of the other Africans in her neighborhood. They were the sort of immigrants her sister Nafi described as having moved directly from "the bush to the *banlieue*." Likening the villages from which (she assumed) they hailed to "the bush," Africa's remote hinterlands, Nafi's description underscored differences between rural Senegal and Dakar, the capital city where she and Mouna had grown up. Drawing a parallel between those who inhabit the Senegalese "bush" and the French banlieue—suburban areas stigmatized as ethnic enclaves—Nafi's expression neatly summarized differences she saw as dividing France's immigrant populations.

Technically, Mouna also lived in the suburbs of Paris. But Malakoff was residential, not a *cité* of towering public housing complexes, architecture that marks banlieues known for crime. Her suburb had the dignity of being recognized by the name of the commune, not identified by its postal code or by the commuter train line (RER) that connected it to Paris. But for her sister to categorize someone as a "bush-to-banlieue" type, they did not have to live in a public housing tower. Subtle details could make one appear maladapted to life in Paris. "I feel sorry for them," Nafi concluded after describing an older Malian man she had seen in the metro, cleaning his teeth with a chewing stick (*soccu*). He should have been a respected elder in his village, but instead was subject to the ire of metro passengers each time he spat on the floor. It was no surprise, Nafi noted, that people like this old man would want to live "among themselves" (*entre eux*) in Paris. Her remark was understanding but, for immigrants in France, the comfort of community comes at a cost. Criticized in public discourses as "*communautarisme*," immigrants living "among themselves" is treated as a public issue in France, thought to impede "integration" and potentially promote the spread of radical Islam.

From primary school on, Nafi and Mouna had attended French schools in Dakar, watched French television channels, and had worn French clothing that aunts and uncles brought back in their suitcases. This middle-class "éducation" in Senegal provided them with social skills for navigating French life. Mouna may have shared a postal code in France and a mother-tongue of Wolof with the Senegalese women in her neighborhood but, in many ways, they were from different worlds. And yet, her class status was no guarantee she could transmit economic stability to her children. Status could even be a liability, if other Senegalese got the sense that she was well off but refused to redistribute her wealth.

## Status as a Double-Edged Sword:
## Moral Expectations of Middle-Class Migrants

Mouna had more formal education than the majority of French and Senegalese citizens alike,[6] but she often found it difficult to send as much money back to her mother in Dakar as migrants who worked as nannies or trash collectors did. Like many educated young people in France, Mouna and her husband cobbled together a living on one-year contracts, in the hopes of one day securing a permanent position. Both worked part-time while finishing master's degrees, her aim being to work in insurance while he was finishing an MBA at a French business school, in collaboration with universities in the United States and China. To take advantage of the economic stability their diplomas could offer, Mouna and her husband had to invest in their lives in France: wearing, eating, and otherwise consuming in ways their middle-class employers, colleagues, and children's teachers would find appropriate.

Demonstrating integration means aligning with the consumption practices of France's middle classes. For Mouna, this entailed things like buying a *"kangourou"* baby carrier to wear when she went out. Although, at home, she found it more practical to strap Awa to her back (like her mother had in Senegal), because it freed her arms for housework. Parents of older children, especially, found middle-class aspirations to be costly. Class trips to the mountains during school holidays and tutoring in English or math were important ways to assure their children's success and avoid association with stereotypes of delinquent "second-generation" immigrant youth. These costs both reduced the amount of money they could send to Senegal each month and simultaneously created an image of privilege in the eyes of other Senegalese in France, for whom privilege implies a moral obligation to *redistribute* wealth.

Whatever her troubles with precarious employment, to the other Africans in her neighborhood, Mouna seemed rich. Her smooth French accent and professional attire sufficed to suggest a status asymmetry that could legitimate requests for money. Outside the deliberately egalitarian structure of the rotating credit association, class inequalities could organize social relations among members of the neighborhood natt. Mouna would represent a well-off friend they might call on for help, a "patron" in the terms of ethnographers who analyzed clientelist (patron/client) relations that organize family and business relations across sub-Saharan Africa (see Ferguson 2013).

Speaking French outside her home could sometimes allow Mouna and other middle-class Senegalese to diplomatically sidestep solicitations for money. She did at times speak Wolof in public, of course, when she chose. But Paris is dense with Wolof speakers, and she could not stop to chat with everyone. Parisians rarely strike up conversations with strangers. Educated Dakarois in the French capital followed suit. Ada, a man who had moved from

Dakar a decade before Mouna, cringed as he described to me moments when other Africans in Paris—strangers, he specified—addressed him saying, *"mon frère,"* a sure sign that they were hoping to sell you something or ask for money.

As awkward as it was to evade strangers' requests, navigating family and friends' expectations of redistribution was far more complicated. Decades of economic crisis have left many households in Senegal dependent on migrants' remittances to get by. The amount of money sent annually by Senegalese living abroad is estimated to *surpass the total sum of development aid* that international donors provide the country (OECD 2017).[7] And, unlike development aid, which filters through government bureaucracy, paying administrative costs in the state and NGOs (and is often pilfered away as it moves through red tape), remittances are sent directly to households and used to pay for families' basic needs.

Beyond monthly money transfers, migrants cover holiday expenses (like buying a sheep for Tabaski) and pay children's school fees. They assist with the costs of weddings, baby naming ceremonies, funerals, and unforeseen hospital bills. To explain why they give, the Senegalese I knew in Paris wove together stories of relatives' obvious need and moral narratives that explained why it was up to them to provide. They framed these financial commitments in terms of the asymmetric but complementary relations that organize kinship in Senegal, or relative to values like *"solidarité."*

Relatives' requests can, however, easily outstrip migrants' earnings. On trips back to Dakar, migrants' physical presence opens them up to a surge of new requests for support, from beggars who line the streets to distant relatives who emerge asking for funds. Refusing to give, or visibly evading requests, could call into question a migrant's moral character in the eyes of family members, who must themselves navigate similar requests every day in Dakar (Moya 2017). In Senegal, people pay attention to things like whether a person is working or unemployed when evaluating one's contribution (or lack thereof) to a household budget. On trips to Dakar, the gifts migrants distribute are surveilled with particular intensity, taken as evidence of their moral fiber and love for relatives (Coe 2013; Cole 2016).

People in Senegal can only guess about migrants' financial means, based on the money they see migrants circulate, the gifts they lavish on kin, and whether they are building a home in Senegal. Senegalese in Paris were sensitive, in turn, to the ways seemingly insignificant details about their lives could be (mistakenly) interpreted as signs of wealth. They carefully managed the circulation of information regarding their jobs, vacations, and trips back to Dakar. Word could spread quickly, Dakar a mere WhatsApp message away.

Just as "integration" had to be constantly embodied in France, in Senegal, migrants had to consistently demonstrate their generosity and continued commitment to relatives. If you so much as "pour a glass of water," Mouna once complained, "they'll be watching to see if you put the bottle down before offering them some. It doesn't even matter if they were thirsty!" Family members in Senegal observe migrants' banal behaviors, searching for signs of their ongoing commitment to those in Dakar.

It was not by chance that Mouna was careful to teach her daughter to share food. Children in Dakar are taught to systematically share whatever they are eating with other children present (and sometimes adults too). Older children proudly divvy up snacks, distributing to younger relatives evidence that they were "big." With uncanny regularity, Senegalese adults use food sharing as an idiom to illustrate how they believe the redistribution of resources ought to take place. In stories, the act of sharing food provides evidence of the largesse of a benevolent benefactor, able and willing to provide for many dependents, whereas the refusal to share reveals the shameless vice of one who profits from others and refuses to give. Moral narratives endow acts of food sharing with symbolic meaning, rendering the everyday act of eating a gauge of moral fiber and social status, indicative of who you care for and who takes care of you.

At her parents' home in Dakar, Mouna's nieces and nephews had developed the reflex to distribute portions of their snacks before they could even talk. If they toddled into a group while holding food, they found themselves encircled by outstretched hands. At the center of a chorus of appeals to "give me some" (*may ma*), small children learn not only how to share but also to avoid eating in front of others if there is not enough to go around. With her relatives in Paris busy with full-time jobs and long commutes, Mouna could not rely on a crowd of cousins to teach her daughter how to dole out portions of her snack. So, she herself prodded the little girl to share, recruiting me to the role of "auntie," so that Awa might learn to expect that, when eating, others have a right to request their part.

Through judicious choices regarding who they associated with and how they spoke, middle-class Senegalese in Paris limited the requests they encountered for monetary aid. But every adult migrant I knew also regularly sent money back to Senegal and took it for granted that they had a responsibility to support relatives. Whether their children felt a similar sense of obligation was another story, one told in the chapters of this book.

## Tubabs and Immigrants:
## The Economic Moralities of Belonging

All over the world, middle-class families like Mouna's have had to alter their expectations about how people "ought" to earn, spend, and redistribute resources as white-collar jobs have become harder to come by and permanent contracts replaced by short-term positions and long-term precarity (Gudmundson 2019; Chauvel 2006, 2023). In both Paris and Dakar, the idea that moral notions regarding the redistribution of resources in Africa diverge from those in Europe seemed obvious to the people I spoke with. In both places, speakers attributed these divergent expectations to "cultural differences," whether national, between France and Senegal, or continental, between Europe and Africa. They spoke about these values as if they were embodied principles that people carried with them, even when they migrated to (or colonized) new lands.

Explanations of economic moralities that focus on place highlight certain similarities thought to unite "French" or "Senegalese" people in certain ways. This framing erases, however, a diversity of ideas about how one "ought" to use money, which all coexist within a single geographic space or "culture." Generational struggles over shared resources underpin tensions between juniors and elders in Africa (Bloch and Parry 1989), as they also foment recent protests in France over pension reforms. Morally charged ideas about how one earns and uses money are central to class distinctions often glossed as "taste" (Bourdieu 1979). But culture-based explanations (Africa versus Europe, Senegal versus France) obscure the ways that economic moralities vary with generation and class, giving rise to understandings of people's ethical and economic practices as organized by ethnicity or race.

Racial tropes supporting the notion that Europeans and Africans have fundamentally different relationships to money circulate in Dakar and Paris alike. In Senegal, these stories center around the figure of the selfish tubab—Europeans or white people—whose individualism allows them to get rich at others' expense. Meanwhile, in France, images of irrational (or even fraudulent) African immigrants who waste money on lavish holidays back home commonly circulate in French music and media.[8] Stereotypes, these essentialized portraits take certain elements of some people's behavior in abstraction, highlighting them with a label that suggests that these qualities are common among all who fall into the category of "tubab" or "immigrant."

Like any social type that people use to make sense of their world, labels like "tubab" and "immigrant" serve to "fix" the variability of people's behaviors into static categories, recognizable to certain people. These essentializations not (only) serve to categorize observed behaviors, they also guide assumptions about how one would behave in other situations. Shaping how we perceive and treat others, social types like "tubab" and "immigrant" carry out social work. They influence the sorts of jobs we imagine people to be capable of doing, ideas about whether they will pay back a loan, and if and how we are willing to let our own finances intermingle with theirs. In short, these stereotypes are tangled up with moral ideas about economic practices, which shape people's rights to resources and the material responsibilities that belonging entails (see Zuckerman 2020 on "moral-economic types").

The categories "tubab" and "immigrant" both index foreignness, but to different effects. Whatever its negative connotations, the label "tubab" is also associated with wealth, a likelihood that one has had formal schooling and possesses professional skills. One cannot be sure that a tubab will make for a generous kinsman, but these (presumed) characteristics render them desirable job candidates and business partners. Being perceived as an "immigrant" in France, however, can be a liability for one's professional prospects. African immigrants are associated with unskilled jobs, as housekeepers or security guards. Those educated Senegalese who do manage to find salaried employment in professions associated with the French middle classes are often not considered immigrants at all but described, instead, as French "of Senegalese origins."

Similarly, in Senegal, when I learned to offer my interlocutors small gifts upon arriving in Dakar (*sarice*), I was met with the pleased exclamation "*Lèegi, Senegalaise nga!*" (you're Senegalese now). Learning to redistribute resources according to practices valued in Senegal transformed me (at that moment, at least) from a tubab to an honorary Senegalese. Although people change over time and adapt to their surroundings, categories like "tubab" and "immigrant" remain fixed. These social types do not merely reflect reality, they create it, guiding our interactions with others and the roles and relationships we can imagine taking up vis-à-vis them (cf. Sweet 2023).

One's ethical priorities and economic practices not only change over the course of one's lifetime, they shift with the situation at hand. Mouna valued her family's rotating credit association but had no interest in participating in a natt with women in her neighborhood. Her shifting position underscores a central aspect of morality in our lived experience: it hinges on context. Economic moralities are enacted in the bustle of ongoing interaction. Central to the "ordinary ethics" (Lambek 2010) of everyday life, moral priorities about the circulation of material resources inevitably impinge, from time to time. Their achievement is circumscribed by the material conditions of people's lives, their time constraints, and their finite resources.

## Types, Values, and Resource Flows: The Moral Meta-Language of Exchange

People navigate moral expectations about resource redistribution, in large part, through language. The words we use to label people, events, and practices provide us with a script for how an interaction might unfold, often including an anticipated time, place, cast of characters, and set of actions. Whether we conceive of an exchange as a "gift" or a "loan" structures our expectations—and moral evaluations—of future events, shaping the relationship between the people involved. To describe a group as a "natt" is to prescribe a series of monetary exchanges among members at predetermined intervals. It establishes social roles (natt organizer and participants, host for the day and guests) and sets the terms of their economic relations relative to the moral obligation to remain in the group until each person has received the lump sum once. To understand what a natt is requires some awareness of how it functions. Mouna's familiarity with a natt's functioning allowed her furthermore to anticipate the extra costs of hosting and the possibility that participation could give rise to requests for monetary support outside of natt relations.

Labels like gift, loan, natt, or even "bank transfer" serve to categorize acts of material exchange in ways that presume and entail certain moral and material relations among people. These *types* divide ongoing interaction up into discreet events, helping us make sense of what is going on by likening the interaction at hand to other events with which we are familiar. People creatively make and remake types in their daily lives, engaging in processes of *typification* by adapting extant types, recontextualizing them, and creating them anew. Before Nafi used the term, I had never heard of "bush-to-banlieue"-type immigrants. But, in French, it required little explanation, combining two well-known words for (potentially dangerous) places outside of cities.

The social type Nafi invented drew on an axis of differentiation (Gal and Irvine 2019) commonly used to distinguish "immigrants" from "integrated" foreigners, who are able to melt into the French masses. This line of contrast maps onto broadly recognizable types of "good" versus "bad" immigrants, cemented in political discourses like former French President Nicholas Sarkozy's claims that France must facilitate *"immigration choisie"* (chosen immigration) and squelch *"immigration subie"* (inflicted immigration). French politicians never specified exactly what constitutes immigration "inflicted" upon France, but the specters of parasitic immigrants who scam the system haunt representations of racial and religious minorities.

Just as the terms we use to distinguish between various types of exchange work to structure material circulation, person types serve to position biological individuals in hierarchies that structure their access to resources. Nafi's description of "bush-to-banlieue"-type people positioned her relative to other Africans in France. Her description of others who struggle to fit in underscored her own ease at integrating, having never lived in the bush or the banlieue, given that she had moved from one capital city to another. Whether fleeting or durable, informal or institutionalized, social types are inevitably political. They mediate power relations by locating people, practices, and places in hierarchies of value. The ways people engage with processes of typification is structured by their own stakes in a situation. The work of comparing, evaluating, and assessing is organized according to how one stands to gain or lose from association with a given category.

This book takes a semiotic (sign-focused) approach to understanding the communicative practices through which people attempt to influence the circulation of material resources. Borrowing from Charles Sanders Peirce (1955, 99), I define a sign as anything in the material world that stands for something to someone, in relation to a specific idea or perspective. The labels we use to make sense of our world function as signs that give us clues about how to behave and how to construe other people's actions. But typification, explored below, is only one of many processes through which language serves to slice up our social worlds into discernable "chunks." Mouna consciously altered her language practices to distance herself from other Wolof speakers in Paris, shaping the economic expectations she encountered. Her French accent, cultivated through years of schooling, positioned her in ways that shaped her professional opportunities and the economic expectations she encountered. To her African neighbors, Mouna's accent indexed wealth, while it simultaneously signaled "integration" and middle-classness in French society more broadly.

One key difference between the work of typification that Nafi engaged in (with her "bush-to-banlieue" type) and the ways that Mouna's accent marked divisions among Africans in Paris is that Nafi was using language to characterize other semiotic processes. Linguistic anthropologist Michael Silverstein (1993) argued that this typifying level of language serves to "regiment" how the context surrounding a speech event is interpreted, guiding participants' attention and uptake of signs. Nafi's evaluation guided listeners' interpretations of signs like the Malian's stick-toothbrush, linking it to a specific person type that she characterized as out of place in Paris. Baked into the category she proposed was a moral evaluation of the sort of person she described, which marked her own orientation toward values broadly recognizable in French society. Taking for granted that immigrants ought to adapt their practices to succeed in France, she aligned herself with French values of immigrant integration.

Economic moralities depend on context. Social actors shape that context through language, orienting interpretations of communicative acts as they unfold. Typification is a reflexive practice that takes place in talk about talk or talk about other semiotic acts. Because "pragmatics" is the study of the relationship between language and context, Silverstein (1993) called language's typifying level "*meta*pragmatics." Metapragmatic categories rely on shared sets of beliefs and values that orient the ways we construe language and other sign systems. The metapragmatic categories speakers use provide clues about the assumptions they draw upon to make sense of a given social interaction. With these "contextualization cues" (Gumperz 1992) speakers work to regiment others' uptake of signs, to influence the outcome of the interaction, and shape the ways that material resources change hands. Acts of dividing the world up into discreet practices, types of people, and events are always understood relative to partial, positioned ideas about the world and how social interactions (ought to) work.

Unlike Nafi's (metapragmatic) act of typification, which guided listeners' interpretations of the behaviors she described, Mouna's accent in French sounds "educated" relative to other, contrasting ways of speaking. Like many speech patterns, accents are socially meaningful signs only in relation to what linguistic anthropologists call "language ideologies," which link ways of speaking to things like education, wealth, and belonging. Language ideologies are "morally and politically loaded representations of the structure and use of languages in a social world" (Woolard 2020, 1). Apparently innocuous statements about the ways people speak are never only about language (Gal and Irvine 2019). Embedded in ideas about language are presuppositions about types of people, their relationships, and roles, which undergird social inequalities.

The language ideologies that allow us to grasp the social significance of different ways of speaking simultaneously link language to a variety of other signs: how one dresses or eats, one's job, and one's family life. When portraying an African mother in comedy sketches on French television, for example, actor Omar Sy spoke loudly, in a thick accent, wearing an oversized housedress and leopard-print scarf.[9] Sy's parody populated his French audience's imaginations with a token example of a type of African woman in France who spent her days at home, caring for her family (and collecting welfare benefits). Identified by her reproductive roles rather than any productive contribution to the economy, French audiences did not require explicit information to grasp that it was a caricature of an uneducated immigrant who would never completely integrate.

Mouna's speaking practices took on value relative to critical evaluations of African mothers embedded in language ideologies that distinguish her accent in French from the accent Sy parodied. Language practices have material effects, shaping the opportunities (and prejudices) one encounters in a job search and day-to-day life. Webb Keane argues that practices that cue "the kind of event now taking place, and the kinds of participants entering into it," bring with them "moral evaluation and materials for political contestation" (2008, 33). Slicing the world into discreet types of people, practices, and events, these reflexive characterizations position individuals and groups relative to one another in social hierarchies founded on supposed moral distinctions (Gal and Irvine 2019). Through this "moral metalanguage" (Keane 2008), speakers position themselves relative to diverse value systems, in ways that have material and financial effects.

If Mouna is better off than African mothers like those Sy parodied, this makes sense relative to moral discourses that claim "integration" is vital to immigrants' material success. Presuppositions about who would make a good employee and who might take unfair advantage of benefits shape the flow of resources distributed by employers and state agents alike. Obscuring differences of class and education that inform immigrants' capacity to "integrate," these economic moralities frame deservingness in terms of individuals' ability to align with (middle-class) French values.

## Talk That Moves Money:
## Economic Moralities and Language Materiality

This book is about the ways moral language moves money and other material resources. Specifically, it examines how value-laden discourses structure the ways people spend and share their money, how they teach their children to align with certain values, and how this structures the circulation of resources on a transnational scale. Tracing the ways household exchanges of talk and food shape moral discourses that organize resource redistribution, I use the tools of linguistic anthropology to address questions about morality and economics that have been at the heart of anthropology since the start of the discipline (Mauss 2002 [1950]). Early anthropologists examining vast networks of nonmonetary exchange argued that economic practices must be understood as socially "embedded"—that is, organized by social relations and institutions (Polanyi 1944). To make sense of embedded economic practices, scholars worked to understand how morals drive exchange. For instance, in his seminal study of the gift, Marcel Mauss pointed out that apparently altruistic acts of giving are motivated by a tripartite obligation to give, receive, and reciprocate gifts. He famously argued that this moral obligation provides a sort of social glue, connecting people across time and space.

This interest in the morals that underpin economics led anthropologists to embrace the concept of a "moral economy." Examining (respectively) the demands of English working classes in the eighteenth century and of peasants in Southeast Asia, Thompson and Scott both treated the moral economy as "traditional rights and customs" (Thompson 1971, 78) that were called into question by the encroaching market economy. Contrasting the moral economy of peasants with the amoral or immoral functioning of capitalism, the moral/market dichotomy provided a vantage from which scholars could critique the ways that poor and colonized peoples were dispossessed of resources in a shift toward a "modern," capitalist system. But these categories also sparked criticism from scholars who pointed out that so-called moral and market economies overlap and intertwine, their boundaries blurry and fluid (Gibson-Graham 1996, Robbins 2008, Tsing 2013).

The perceived opposition between moral and market economies came with many potential pitfalls. Bloch and Parry summarize that this dichotomy encourages a "tendency to postulate a fundamental division between non-monetary and monetary economies (or even *societies*)," an opposition that gets elided with "other dichotomies—'traditional' and 'modern', precapitalist and capitalist, gift economies and commodity economies" (1989, 7). Embedded in categories that purport to merely describe different economic systems are value-laden assumptions that unequally position different "types" of people in moral-economic hierarchies. Tangled up with notions of "modernity" and "development," these moral narratives have a dangerous capacity to explain away global inequalities, framing economic development as iconic of a group's nature, rather than indexical of the exploitative colonial relations through which they were inducted into global capitalism.

Feminist scholars have pointed out how the moral/market divide also carries out the social work of justifying and reproducing gender inequalities (Ong 1987; Rosaldo 1980; Strathern 1988; Weiner 1992). Here, it is the (feminine) *household economy* that is framed as moral, in opposition to the self-interested market relations of the (masculine) public sphere. Framing gendered care work as a labor of love, the moral versus market division works, in this case, to reinforce the notion that (women's) everyday tasks of cooking, cleaning, and caring for one's family exist beyond the bounds of the monetary economy and thus require little or no remuneration. Feminist scholars convincingly argued that economically "unproductive" forms of care work and kin work (Di Leonardo 1987) represent labor that is critical to the market economy, reproducing the workers and consumers who make up the economic system.

But which system are they reproducing? The future of the economy depends on how the next generation takes up economic practices. But we know almost nothing about the ways children come to take part in economic relations. Through the public school system, states work to produce tax-paying, gainfully employed citizens. Parents invest in their children's educations, speculating on which skills will pave their way to fulfilling and lucrative careers. These socializing processes have significant economic stakes. They are the subject of political debates and household deliberations, but they are rarely discussed in economic terms. Instead, they are largely couched in the language of "national" or "family values."

Pierre Bourdieu (1977, 1979) famously theorized that class distinctions are reproduced through the intergenerational "transmission" of unconscious dispositions he called habitus, which subtly reveal one's economic means and social capital. He made clear that caregivers' own habitus structures the skills they can transmit to their children, reproducing a class-based division of labor. But less clear in Bourdieu's account are the actual processes through which children embody capital. He described the transmission of habitus as a top-down process of acquisition, but scholars of childhood have questioned this assumption. Detailed analysis of children's interactions revealed socialization to be an interactional process, emergent and improvised, in which children play an active role (Goodwin 1990; James and Prout, 1990; James & James 2008; Montgomery 2008; Schwartzman 1976, 2012).

Linguistic anthropologists Elinor Ochs and Bambi Schieffelin (2012) argued that not even language is simply "acquired." Instead, people develop language skills though culturally structured exchanges between more- and less-experienced speakers, in which children and adults co-construct their social worlds (Kulick and Schieffelin 2004; Duranti, Ochs, and Schieffelin 2012). As they learn to speak, children gain the communicative ability to take up—and resist—social roles available to them, according to age, gender, race, and class (Rosa 2019). Although scholars have noted that children take active part in the reproduction of society, reconfiguring social relations as they embody them (Cole 2011), studies have yet to explicitly examine the ways that children shape economic systems.

## Children as Transnational Economic Actors

This book joins a growing body of research that explicitly approaches children as economic actors, foregrounding their role in transnational processes of class- and kinship-making. Elise Berman (2019) has argued that children in the Marshall Islands are economic actors, "not in spite of, but rather precisely because of, their childishness" (Berman 2019, 7). Perceived as immature, children are at liberty to transport resources, like food, in ways deemed inappropriate for adults, playing an important role in inter-household exchange. Rather than "pre-economic" adults-in-training, children's social position as non-adults allows them to shape economic relations in particular ways.

In transnational families, children represent critical nodes in socioeconomic networks linking relatives at home and abroad as motivators of migration and as migrants themselves (Coe et al. 2011). Children who were left behind by migrant parents or born abroad and sent back to be raised by relatives in Africa drive migrants' remittances (Bledsoe and Sow 2011). These long-term fostering arrangements link household budgets across continents in the name of feeding and providing for children, reinforcing affective and economic relations between migrants, their children, and their children's caretakers (Grysole 2018).

While children's economic role linking migrants to their country of origin has become clear, we know almost nothing about the economic role that immigrants' children growing up abroad might play in their transnational families. Scholarship on "second-generation" children has largely focused on integration and stigma, examining barriers that block youths' full belonging in their country of birth. Attending to the transnational practices of children who have, themselves, never migrated offers a new vision of economic practice in migration. It forces us to look beyond the idea that remittances are driven by adult migrants' sense of "debt" to those back home to ask, instead, how people of different ages experience and engage with socioeconomic relations that mediate transnational kinship.

I take seriously the impact that even brief and irregular trips to Senegal have on the children of migrants, studying the ways that these interactions live on in families' tales. Whether the tale emerges out of boisterous reminiscing around a dish of *ceebu jën* (rice and fish) on a videocall with relatives abroad or is reserved for a quiet intimate moment of family time, I show how children experience and make sense of their interactions with transnational relatives and the ways that this affects their perceptions of how resources "ought" to circulate. Families' everyday lives are shot through with economic stakes. Far from being shielded or excluded from their families' economic calculations and the material give-and-take of kinship, children's worlds are organized according to economic calculations.

## Inverting the Moral Economy: The Economic Effects of Ordinary Ethics

If we accept this book's premise that the material exchanges that make up children's and families' everyday lives are fundamentally economic, we are forced to reconsider the relationship between so-called "microeconomic" and "macroeconomic" processes. The household appears at the center of the global economy, fleeting and forgettable moments of family life providing the foundation for larger-scale resource flows, like migrants' remittances that make up 10.5 percent of Senegal's gross domestic product (World Bank 2023). As we watch the boundaries between the micro and the macro blur in moral-economic terms, a series of other dichotomies melt away alongside it: household versus market, traditional versus modern. Children and adults appear as economic actors, each in their own right. Age does not distinguish *whether* they take part in the economy, but how. It is one difference among many that organizes interdependencies between social actors.

This requires us to fundamentally reconsider the ways we think and talk about moral-economic processes. Studying the economic in children's lives invites an analysis across scales, foregrounding the ways that families' inter-actions are constitutive of processes that shape "cultures of circulation" (Lee and LiPuma 2002) on a transnational scale, through the sedimented mark they leave on people's habitual practices and expectations. The term eco-nomic moralities offers a single analytic that spans contexts and scales, al-lowing us to examine side by side normative expectations that organize family life, class relations, and national belonging. The term applies as much to the moral expectations of French middle-classness—measured by how one earns, spends, and saves—as it does to the material obligations that me-diate kinship. Attending to the ways social actors navigate economic mo-ralities in their daily lives, I reveal how they grapple with shifting notions of belonging and rights to resources, in kinship networks and state systems alike.

Rather than examining the morals embedded in economic relations, I focus on the ways economic processes are achieved through everyday ne-gotiations of morality. The language that mediates children's micro-level interactions—the ways they give, take, and share food or possessions—is shaped by macro-level concerns, like ongoing racialization and economic de-cline. Families' reactions to the stakes and strains of their daily lives in France impact, in turn, the ways they weave kinship relations, structuring migration trajectories and class relations on a transnational scale.

Expectations about resource redistribution vary with context and scale, depending on whether one is talking about state funds, a child's snack, or a meal at a baby-naming ceremony. Social actors shift between moral-economic scales in their everyday interactions with the same ease that Dakarois dis-play when they switch between French and Wolof in a single sentence. These scalar projects (Carr and Lempert 2016) have material consequences, recon-figuring alignments between speakers and the institutions of state and family, drawing and redrawing group boundaries and with them questions of who has what rights to shared resources.

Anthropologists have often observed that *all* economies are moral econ-omies, highlighting the moral logics that underpin even the most neoliberal capitalist systems (Muehlebach 2012; Whyte and Wiegratz 2016; Browne and Milgram 2009). As social actors move between contexts and groups, they must navigate between diverse moral priorities, which influence how they use their limited resources. How do people determine which moral logic matters in a given context? How does one recognize whether something is a gift or a loan? These are precisely the sorts of questions that attention to the metapragmatic language of economic moralities is honed to answer.

Matters of routine, economic moralities are often signaled through nearly imperceptible cues, rather than explicit labels. But practices that seem obvious to adults require more explanation for children, especially for migrants' children who have limited experience in their parents' countries of birth. None of the children in the middle-class families I knew in Paris spoke Wolof fluently. Its repertoire of terms for gifts and other events when one might expect to receive resources (or be obliged to give) escaped them, with all the cultural information encoded therein. Moral expectations that appeared natural to their parents and other relatives raised in Dakar often seemed strange to these French-born children. Many struggled to reconcile their parents' behaviors in Dakar, doling out cash to every distant relative who wandered by to wish them well, with their thrifty habits in Paris, where clothing brands and technological devices common among children's classmates were treated as prohibitively expensive.

Economic moralities are not "acquired" through a straightforward process of "transmission," but emerge from the (sometimes fraught) give and take of children and caregivers' everyday interactions. Caregivers' efforts to guide their children's moral-economic behaviors reveal adults' own anxieties about the future and what they see as the material stakes of aligning with specific moralities. Children's behavior reflects on their parents, and truancy could upend careful attempts to fit into France's middle class. Parents' attempts to guess which paths might have value in the future are tangled up with everyday concerns about whether their children are behaving appropriately, such that their teachers and other adults might give them a fair chance at future opportunities.

Adults' own future welfare depends on how the next generation conceives of and enacts economic moralities. In Senegal, intergenerational reciprocity is most often achieved within families, mediated by notions of social adulthood as defined by one's capacity to provide for children and former caregivers. In France, these intergenerational relations are organized on a national scale, via pensions disbursed by the state's social security system. But this system, founded on notions of citizens' rights, is being reconfigured by neoliberal reforms that chip away at the protections of European welfare systems, making middle-class status increasingly difficult to maintain in France, particularly for racial and religious minorities. Migrant parents' struggles to transmit middle-class status to their children reveal how normative expectations of kinship in Africa are bound up with the class-based moralities that mediate immigrant integration in Europe.

A focus on middle-class children brings to the fore the increasing uncertainty of class mobility for a previously privileged segment of the Senegalese diaspora. It also sheds light on the ways that kinship practices that helped their parents migrate to escape diploma inflation and economic austerity in Senegal since the 1970s may help contemporary youth forge new migration trajectories to avoid falling prey to these same processes now unfolding in France. Theorizing the diverse moral expectations that underpin transnational socioeconomic relations, this book demonstrates how the material expectations of kinship in Africa are bound up with values of immigrant "integration" in Europe.

## Locating Transnational Middle Classes

This book is based on an ethnographic study in Senegalese households in Paris and Dakar. It is rooted in my research in Senegal since 2005, when, as an undergraduate studying abroad in Dakar, I learned to identify the homes of migrants' relatives: spacious multi-story houses, often in perpetual construction. Their many stories, built gradually over time, stood as testaments to years of remittances from abroad, a promise of migrants' eventual return. Elderly heads of households housed their grandchildren and great-grandchildren, nieces and nephews, friends, and friends' children who had come to Dakar to study or work. But their own adult children were often absent, some living in France, others in the United States, Spain, or Italy.

Families I knew from middle-class neighborhoods in Dakar (like Mermoz, Baobab, Sacré Coeur, the SICAPs), put me in touch with their relatives who had studied and subsequently settled in Paris. These introductions allowed me to study a group that is routinely overlooked in research on transnationalism: middle-class migrants whose privileged upbringing in Africa provided them the economic and cultural capital necessary to integrate in France with comparative ease. Rather than focusing on a specific religious group or neighborhood in Paris where African immigrants gathered, I worked with Senegalese who kept their distance from *les quartiers africains*

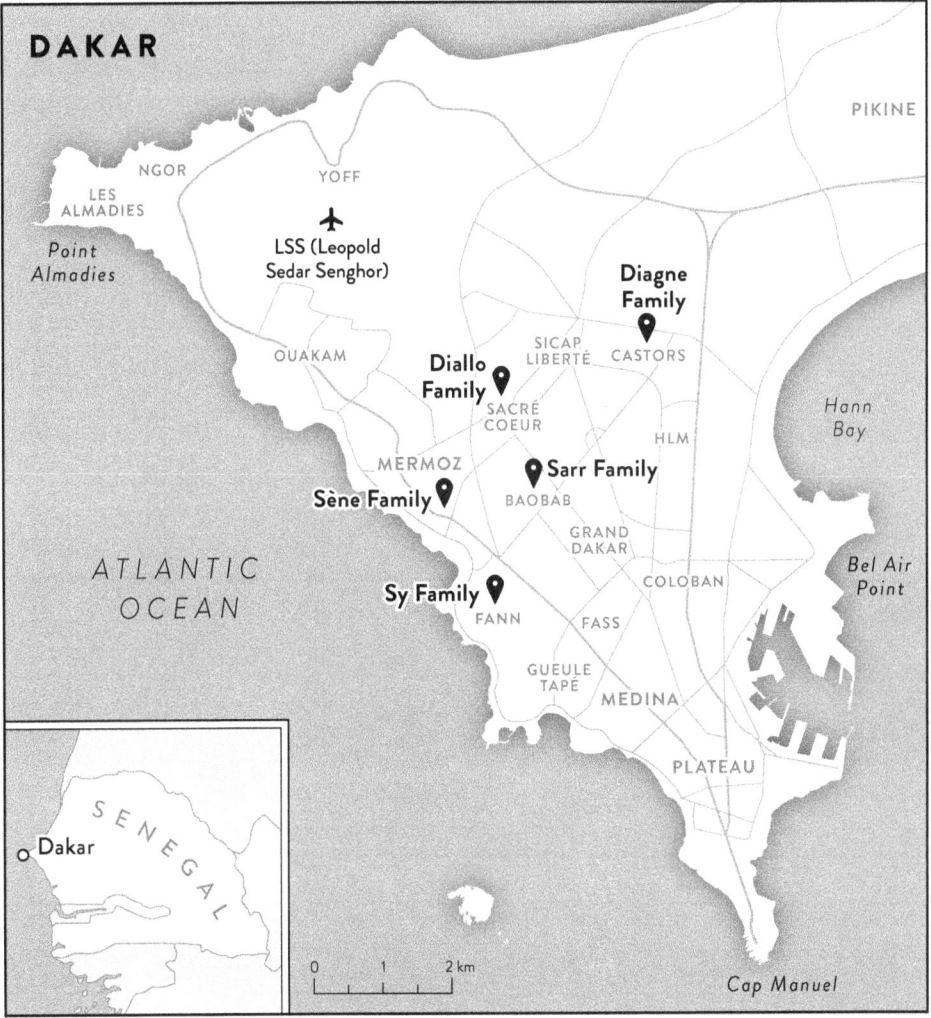

Figure 1. Dakar and its nearby suburbs, noting the neighborhoods of the families in this book. Map by Erin Greb.

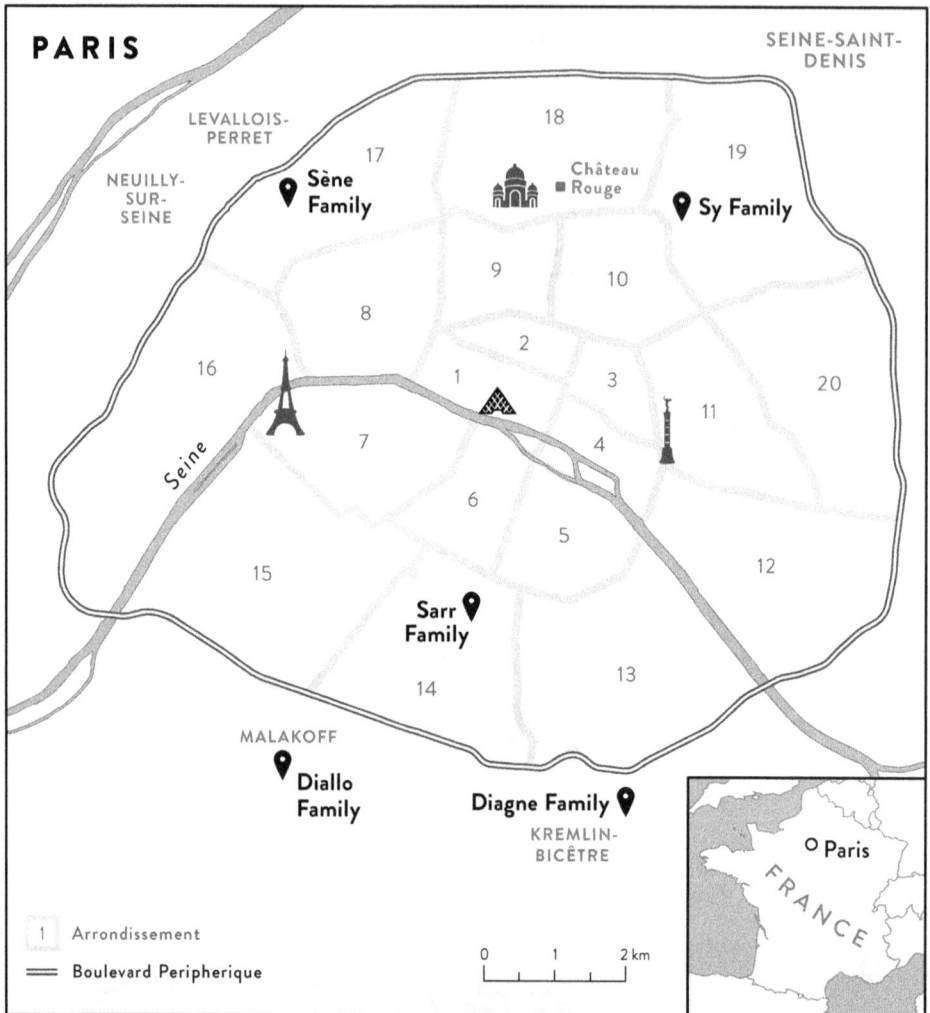

Figure 2. Paris and its nearby suburbs, noting the neighborhoods of the families in this book. Map by Erin Greb.

(African neighborhoods) and had little interest in most Senegalese events and religious gatherings.

Over a year and a half (2014–2015), I rode the metro between arrondissements, visiting Senegalese scattered throughout Paris and its nearby suburbs. I got to know families from diverse class backgrounds and regions of

Senegal, but gradually focused on five households in which the parents had grown up in Dakar and at least one adult held a French diploma. Their apartments in Paris were cozy, with the cramped feel shared by all moderately priced housing in the French capital. Narrow kitchens overflowed for lack of storage space. To reach bathroom sinks you had to squeeze past drying laundry. But, unlike stereotypes of large African families in France, who pile into tiny apartments, the families I studied had only one to three children and lived in apartments large enough for each to have his or her own bedroom or to share with one sibling.

If ethnography is participant observation, what does it mean to "take part" in someone else's family? For me, this meant spending hours at families' apartments after school and on weekends, talking with parents and children, sharing meals, attending school plays, and celebrating holidays with them. In Wolof, the verb *yendu* means to "spend the day" with someone. Among working families in Paris, this practice was relegated to weekends but meant that I could stay for hours, my visits overlapping with those of their neighbors and friends in Paris and relatives from Dakar. For the parents, I was an American who knew her way around Senegal. We situated ourselves relative to neighborhoods in Dakar and the Senegalese people we knew in Paris. Although we spoke mostly in French, I was, importantly, not from France. This meant that they could offer advice on my struggles with immigration services and could voice critical assessments of France in front of me without fear that I take it personally. Because my research brought me to travel regularly between Dakar and Paris, Senegalese adults often recruited me to an informal role of courier. Transporting gifts like perfume and palm oil between family members in France and Senegal, I took part in material exchanges that reproduced transnational kinship.

For children, my knowledge of Wolof and tendency to ask after relatives in Dakar positioned me, first, as friends of their parents. Their parents urged them to address me using kinship terms, calling me *tata* (auntie). Gradually, I took on other roles vis-à-vis the children—Facebook friend, English tutor, and occasional caregiver who picked them up from school. I audio-recorded "Facebook tour" interviews, in which I asked children to take me through their Facebook page, describing the interactions they had with relatives abroad. In Chapter 5, I analyze these relative to children's drawings of their "family trees." The bulk of my data came from audio recordings: child-led recordings (Hunleth 2011), semi-structured interviews, and hours of naturally occurring conversations in Senegalese households. I developed fine-grained transcripts (see the appendices) of families' stories of material exchanges, in which they collaborated to make sense of past events or competed to get their version of the story heard.

## Outline of the Book

Each chapter of this book is organized around stories of material exchange recounted in Senegalese households in Paris and Dakar. Each approaches the question of how talk moves money from a different angle, tracing connections between the moral language of family life and discourses more readily perceived as economic, concerning migrants' remittances or welfare state resources. Through storytelling, speakers make sense of their experiences, (re) interpreting them relative to others' perspectives (Ochs and Capps 2001). I approach these instances of collective meaning-making as moral acts, in themselves, through which speakers and listeners process past events in ways that shape their reactions in the future.

Chapter 1 begins by examining the semiotic processes through which the families of university-educated Senegalese work to position themselves as middle class in both Paris and Dakar, drawing axes of differentiation to distance themselves from stereotypes in Senegal of rich but selfish migrants who spoil their children and from tropes of working-class immigrants in France thought unable to integrate. It provides a deeper look into the political, economic, and historical contexts that mediate Senegalese migrants' struggles to transmit middle-class status to their children.

In the space of a single conversation, Senegalese family members shift between critique of the lack of "solidarity" they find in Paris and expressions of alignment with French state discourses that divide minorities into "integrated" foreigners (deserving of state resources) and potentially problematic "immigrants." Chapter 2 theorizes the material entailments of shifting between moral logics in unfolding interactions to reveal how speakers use language to move between scales of redistribution, negotiating belonging in French society and their transnational families. Here, I develop my semiotic approach to analyzing economic moralities to illustrate the heuristic value of inverting the focus of studies of "moral economy."

Transnational families' efforts to maintain middle-class status in both home and host countries place unique pressures on French-born children, for whom being a "good" child implies conscious management of social connections while simultaneously embodying forms of generosity valued among Senegalese kin. Chapter 3 explores how children grapple with normative expectations that underpin food sharing, to illustrate how youth try to position themselves as equal to other children in France while struggling to make sense of their palpable privilege in Senegal. It focuses on the ways speakers use spatial deictics—words like "here" and "there," whose meanings depend on context—to set the key of social interactions. Providing cues as to what sorts of economic moralities might hold sway, these terms link moral logics to national spaces and verbally divide up the physical spaces surrounding these families' apartments in Paris and the people who inhabit them.

Chapter 4 shifts focus to families' trips to Senegal, analyzing the ways economic moralities emerge in acts of storytelling, through which families negotiate normative expectations. I consider how youth growing up in France become aware of and embody—or resist embodying—status positions in systems of rank-based redistribution in Senegal through examination of children's impressions of expectations for gifts and monetary support their families encounter on trips to Dakar. Examining language practices, like singing another's praises, through which migrants' relatives in Senegal might position themselves as low-ranked relative to their kin in Europe (and, thus, deserving of resources), I examine how youth from France develop tactics of their own to dodge requests and enact strategies of selective solidarity with kin back in Senegal.

Chapter 5 traces the ways that talk can materialize into flights to Dakar and monetary gifts, examining exchanges on social media between children in France and their relatives in Senegal and its diaspora. Focusing specifically on an innovative form of "cross-cousin" relationship in the Senegalese diaspora, it illustrates how adults create cultural scaffolding around children who speak little Wolof and are often unaware of the kinship terms for the relationships in which they are implicated. Metapragmatic discourses through which kinship relations (like cousin marriage) are endowed with different indexical meanings over time and, across space, shape the ways relatives transform kinship practices in migration. I demonstrate how Senegalese selectively reinforce socioeconomic connections with certain family members, strategically weaving transnational connections in ways that shape migration trajectories and class relations within families.

The Conclusion proposes a reframing of our understandings of how language shapes political economic practices and which social actors might be the authors of these processes. Drawing together the book's central arguments addressing the impact of European middle-class decline on transnational kinship relations, it shows how the struggles of middle-class families to maintain their status in Europe encourage children to embrace transnationalism, looking onward toward Canada and China, or back to Africa. Together, these chapters trace the relationship between the moral language of family life and practices more readily perceived as economic, like migrants' remittances, class-based consumption, and resources distributed by the welfare state. Families' everyday talk is not only embedded in the political and economic contexts from which it emerges, but simultaneously produces and transforms those material conditions, filled with subtle cues about who deserves access to scarce resources. Examining the material effects of semiotic processes through which proximity and distance are achieved through language, this book theorizes how language mediates the structural conditions of mobility.

## CHAPTER 1

# Integrating into a Disintegrating French Middle Class

"Not this year, there was no time!" Hélène Sène shook her head, imagining the Herculean feat that taking her daughters to Senegal would have been that summer. They hadn't had the luxury of taking off a full month in August, she explained, because they had to get back early to prepare the girls to start at their new schools. "Mathie started middle school this year," Hélène explained. "We wanted her to be at a good school [*un collège bien côté*], to make sure she stays on the right path." A knowing nod in my direction punctuated Hélène's response to my queries about why they had decided to transfer the girls out of the French public school system.

Parents in France see the start of middle school as a decisive moment in their children's education, a time when the risk of problems—fights at school, hanging out with the wrong crowd, unwanted attention from the opposite sex—seems to suddenly grow. In Paris, this is a moment when many parents choose to move out of the city or to transfer their children to private schools (Felouzis and Perroton 2005; Beaud 2011). By middle school, the "social diversity" (*mixité sociale*) that parents and teachers saw as desirable in primary school transforms into a visible absence of white children in many urban public schools. Hélène's daughters, meanwhile, each found herself to be the sole Black student in her class at their new private Catholic schools.

As members of Senegal's small Christian minority (4 percent), the Sène family enrolled their daughters in a parochial school a ten-minute walk from their apartment in the 17th arrondissement. The school choice oriented the entire family's activities southward, toward the wealthy area surrounding the Pereire metro stop, where gourmet pastry shops and a bilingual Montessori preschool lined wide boulevards. It distanced them from the *périphérique* highway to the north and the Muslim immigrants who lived in that direction. The new schools reconfigured the family's physical path through the city, shaping the areas they spent time in, their children's friends, the families they knew, and their activities. Their entourage expanded to include friends Mathie made while acting in her school play, whose families lived in the wealthy suburbs to the west of Paris (Levallois Perret, Neuilly-sur-Seine), children who crossed the périphérique on their way to school each day in their parents' BMWs and Mercedes.

The Sènes did not have a car. The family of four lived in a two-bedroom apartment in northwest Paris, at the edge of the city where the elegant stone facades and wrought iron balconies of Haussmannian buildings gave way to a narrow strip of public housing. Unlike the graying cement high-rise HLMs (government subsidized housing) scattered throughout the 18th, 19th, and 20th arrondissements to the east, however, theirs was a handsome seven-story brick building with a grassy courtyard out front. It took months of regularly visiting the Sènes before I even realized their building was an HLM. Hélène told me that they had been fortunate to find their apartment on the sixth floor, filled with natural light. Indeed, finding affordable housing in the 17th had been a stroke of luck.

Their neighborhood was sandwiched between the 16th arrondissement, synonymous in Paris with opulent wealth, and the 18th, home to the city's oldest African neighborhood (Château Rouge). Hélène could easily find the dried fish (*géji*) and sea snail (*yètt*) that give ceebu *jën* its flavor at an "Exotic Foods" shop nearby. Meanwhile, the family went to the library and public swimming pool in the wealthy (white) area near their home. The Sènes' proximity to expensive areas in the 17th helped them keep physical and symbolic distance from minorities accused of "keeping to themselves" or "communitarianism." In their neighborhood, immigrants became noticeable only in the trams and buses that run along the périphérique highway, packed with passengers as likely to be speaking Wolof or Arabic as they were French. The metro, which runs farther south, is calm and half-empty in the 17th, as it approaches Paris's wealthy western suburbs.

The girls' Catholic school helped the Sènes achieve markers of integration into the French middle classes, offering a buffer of protection (in some contexts) from prejudice against Muslim immigrants in France. But this did not insulate the family from racial stigma. Years later, after both girls were at university, they reminisced about classmates who had avoided speaking

Figure 3. The 17th arrondissement near the Sènes' apartment. Photo: Yount 2015.

to them. "They thought we weren't good enough for that school," Hélène concluded. When the popularity of France's far-right nationalist party, the Front national (now Rassemblement national) began to grow during my fieldwork in 2015, Hélène had been somber but unsurprised. She could feel the growing prejudice, she said, in little things, like the way her employer spoke to her about laws regarding holiday leave "here in France," even though she had spent her entire working life in Paris.

By changing schools, the Sène family made a strategic investment in education, aimed at transmitting middle-class status[1] in France to their children, a process that has become substantially more difficult (particularly for racial and religious minorities) over the past twenty years. The value of diplomas in France has plummeted over the course of a generation. Thirty years ago, a high school degree was enough to gain secure employment in a middle-class profession with a permanent contract (CDI, *le contrat à durée indéterminée*—see Chauvel 2006). Today, a university degree is a prerequisite for nearly all white-collar jobs, but investment in higher education is no longer a guarantee of economic stability the way it was in generations past.

The postwar expansion of France's higher education system filled the job market with highly skilled professionals, just as "*les trente glorieuses*" (thirty years of postwar economic growth) were drawing to a close, giving way to economic stagnation in the 1980s. Education became a substantially less reliable path to economic stability in France, and the country saw an overall devaluation of high school and university degrees (Peugny 2009, Beaud 2011, Dubet and Duru-Bellat 2006; Bigot 2009). Meanwhile, neoliberal reforms favoring freelance work and short-term contracts (CDD, *le contrat à durée déterminée*) have made the security of permanent contracts increasingly scarce. The "end of the CDI (permanent contract)," as news outlets have called it (Vujasinovic 2017), has meant a loss of security for great swaths of the French middle classes. CDI contracts promise lifetime employment, with paid vacations and a pension. But beyond the contractual rights they offer workers, CDIs also act as second-order signs of security, providing proof of one's ability to pay rent or to reimburse a mortgage. For those without a European passport, CDIs offer a path from a student visa to permanent residency.

News articles on the (decline of the) French middle classes depict the group as predominantly white, but middle class decline disproportionately impacts West and North African immigrants and their children (Chauvel 2006; Jones 2013; Hargreaves 2007; Minni and Okba 2014). Educated immigrants are 50 percent more likely to occupy a position below their qualifications than equally qualified French citizens (Picut 2014). Credentials from many schools and universities in Africa are not recognized in France, forcing new arrivals (who can afford it) to redo accreditations or accept a job below their qualifications and the *déclassement* (abroad, but not back home) that comes with low-skilled positions. Boris Nieswand calls this the "status paradox in migration" (2011), noting that migrants gain status in their countries of origin by virtue of accepting a (sometimes substantial) loss of status in the receiving country, often for the duration of their lives abroad. For immigrants all over the world, migration entails a loss of class-status over an individual's lifetime, often with the hope of improving the lives of one's children and relatives, to achieve *intergenerational* social mobility (Grysole and Bonnet 2020).

It is precisely this potential for intergenerational social mobility, however, that is called into question by middle-class decline. The threat of intergenerational déclassement has become increasingly palpable in France over the last decade, detailed in news articles predicting that today's youth will be the first generation to "have less" than their parents—that is, experience a lower quality of life than previous generations (Le Monde 2009). Maintaining middle-class status over time is notoriously difficult. Barbara Ehrenreich (1989) argued that the intergenerational transmission of middle-classness is less obvious than that of wealth or poverty, and a "fear of falling" is thus intrinsic to this class position. But at moments when "falling" becomes the norm, experienced by the (white) middle-class majority, it can appear inevitable to immigrants and their children, who face discrimination at school and in key processes of class-making like searching for internships, jobs, or a decent apartment (Yount-André 2020a, 2020b).

The act of achieving and maintaining middle-class status is a fundamentally racialized process. Discrimination against racial and religious minorities in French housing and job markets has been widely documented and is reported to be on the rise (Lê et al. 2022; Barou 2014; Beaud and Pialoux 2006; Simon 2008; Simon and Madoui 2011). It was the topic of hidden-camera TV shows that my Senegalese interlocutors had seen and referred to when describing their own difficulties finding a stable job or buying an apartment in Paris. A study by Adida and colleagues (2010) revealed particularly concretely the obstacles that Muslim Senegalese face in finding employment in France, with an experiment that showed job applications from Senegalese candidates with a Catholic first name were more likely to receive a positive response than the *exact same application* with a Muslim first name.

As Blacks and (mostly) Muslims, educated Senegalese in France today are disproportionately vulnerable to the downward mobility that plagues the country's middle classes. But, only decades ago, they held a relatively privileged position, treated, not as "immigrants," but as "African intellectuals," who had successfully integrated into French society ("assimilated" in colonial terms—see Wilder 2005). French skills no longer distinguish educated Senegalese from Paris's "immigrant masses" and diplomas no longer assure stable employment (in France or Senegal). For middle-class migrants, the end of permanent contracts in France is a process that fundamentally destabilizes their bids at belonging and efforts to protect their children from prejudice. Impacting their earning potential, French middle-class decline simultaneously shapes migrants' ability to invest in their class status—or any future—back in Senegal.

This chapter is organized around a puzzle: If maintaining middle-class status is notoriously difficult and getting harder throughout Europe, why (and how) do Senegalese migrants try to achieve middle-classness in *two* countries? To answer this question, I examine the semiotics of belonging. In Paris, embodying signs of middle-classness allows educated Senegalese to avoid stigma and distinguish themselves from poor immigrants who struggle to integrate. In Dakar, positioning themselves as middle class (but not rich) is essential to limiting relatives' expectations of gifts and money, while distancing themselves from stereotypes of rich people too selfish to redistribute.

French middle-class decline (déclassement) is a racialized process that disproportionately impacts visible minorities and is bound up with the ongoing racialization of Muslims (Fernando 2014). By tracing the gradual undoing of the "integration" of an educated minority of Senegalese, I show how the racialized effects of déclassement radiate outward, shaping the transnational kinship relations and the circulation of resources across these affective circuits (Cole and Groes 2016).

Middle-class decline is a process that is difficult to point to yet palpable in the everyday lives of children and their families. In this chapter, I show how, by comparing the experiences of two eleven-year-olds: Miriama Diagne and Malik Sy. In each child's family, the parents grew up in Dakar and migrated to Paris as students. But twenty years separated the arrival of Miriama's father and Malik's parents—two decades during which the economic stability that a French university degree could offer diminished drastically. Miriama and Malik are the subjects of Chapters 5 and 3, respectively. Here, I compare their relationships with relatives in Senegal to demonstrate how middle-class decline in France is reshaping the ways Senegalese migrants and their children invest in and imagine Africa.

## Transnational Middle Classes: Negotiating Status in Multiple National Contexts

The concept of being "middle class" has gained international recognition in recent decades, orienting the material ambitions and family lives of people across the globe (Heiman, Freeman, and Liechty 2012). In French, the expression, "les classes moyennes" (plural) has gradually replaced "la bourgeoisie" in media and scholarship (Bidou-Zachariasen 2004). The appeal of being "middle class" has coalesced in France as access to the category itself has foreclosed for many. In West Africa, the term has similarly gained ground recently in scholarship and among educated urbanites (Lentz 2016, 2020; Yount-André 2020a). Yet, "middle class" remains a social category that is notoriously difficult to define, and whose meaning varies immensely across contexts and cultures. For my interlocutors, these competing ideas matter, because belonging in their home and host countries, both, depends on the ways they navigate between overlapping and dissonant expectations of middle-classness.

A spate of research on African middle classes has emerged in the past decade (Darbon and Toulabor 2011; Kroeker, O'Kane, and Scharrer 2018; Kroeker 2018; Lentz 2016; Melber 2016; Nallet 2012; Mercer 2014; Mercer and Lemanski 2020; Ncube and Lufumpa 2015; Pauli 2022; Southall 2016; Spronk 2012). Unlike the middle classes of their former European colonizers, which were created and sustained through welfare-state interventions (Boltanski 1987; Kocka 1981), middle-class Africans today have maintained (or achieved) social mobility in neoliberal capitalism, weathering the booms and busts of global markets after forty years of state austerity measures. The civil servant (intellectual) has faded as symbol of success in Senegal (Hannaford 2017) and elsewhere in Africa (see Cole 2011), but this functionary middle class lent its privileges to the creation of today's middle classes, whose status hinges on a combination of (often international) educations, salaried employment and side hustles, work experience abroad, and transnational networks.

Building on recent scholarship on African middle classes, as well as studies of transnational migration and social mobility (Grysole and Bonnet 2020; Coe and Pauli 2020), I use the analytic "middle class" to draw attention to families' efforts to avoid intergenerational déclassement on a transnational stage. However different (and fatefully intertwined) the histories and political economic structures of (the "middle") classes in Europe and Africa may be, juxtaposing families' efforts at class-making in both places draws attention to the transnational consequences of French middle-class decline. Approaching educated Senegalese in Paris as "middle-class migrants,"[2] I examine déclassement not (only) as a symptom of migration, but as a systemic issue faced by middle-class majorities in Europe (and internationally), which disproportionately impacts racial and religious migrants and their children. Examining parents' struggles to transmit economic stability to their children, I take my cue from Marxist analyses of class, focused on the retrenchment of inequalities in global capitalism. But, rather than functioning (only) as a reserve army of labor, middle-class Senegalese draw our attention to the ways migrants can also embody forms of capital valued on a transnational scale. My sign-focused approach attends to acts of "boundary-work" (Lamont 1992; Barth 1998 [1969]) that transnational families use to mark their "distinction" (Bourdieu 1979) from both lower and upper classes in their home and host countries. Placing children at the center of this study of global economic transformations, I take inspiration from substantivist feminist approaches in economic anthropology that highlight the ways capitalist production depends on (unpaid) intergenerational care-work, efforts at class-making, and processes of family-making (Ong 1987; Rosaldo 1980; Strathern 1988; Weiner 1992; Bear et al. 2015).

An amorphous group, middle classes are thought to be broadly similar in terms of profession, income, and education level, and are often imagined to be united by some sort of middle-class "values"—that is, shared notions of appropriateness regarding how one earns, spends, and saves money (things I have been calling economic moralities). Moral-economic positions that mediate class-belonging not only structure economic decisions on how to spend and save, they also shape intimate relations: ideas about who "counts" as family, which relatives might cohabitate, and who is thought to deserve monetary support. Class-making is part and parcel of processes of kinship-making everywhere, but the type of family that is thought to illustrate middle classness varies from place to place.

The nuclear family is emblematic of European and North American middle classes. French sociologist Pierre Bourdieu observed in the 1970s that aspiring members of France's middle classes went so far as to break social ties with members of their extended family who "create obstacles to individual mobility," asserting in blunt terms that "one has neither the means nor the taste to maintain relations with other members of the family who have not known how to 'sort themselves out'" (1974, 246). In Senegal, however, one's ability and willingness to support extended kin defines middle-classness. On average, families in middle-class areas in Dakar feed and house *more people* than those in poorer areas (Antoine et al. 2004, 12). Middle-class Dakarois regularly host the children of rural relatives who come to the capital to study. When cousins fall on hard times, they find ways to free a bedroom, moving inhabitants to new sleeping spaces so that they might lodge relatives in need and their families, sometimes for many months. There, a refusal to support one's relatives suggests that a person is either struggling to get by or selfish and unwilling to share.

While recent scholarship on African middle classes appears to have settled decades of debate regarding whether "class" is even an analytic that may be usefully applied in African societies (see Lentz 2020; Copans 2020), the continent remains a complicated place for theorizing middle-classness. Throughout Africa, status has historically been conceived in binary terms:

between patrons and clients, "noble" (uncasted) people and their (casted) dependents, men and women, elders and juniors. Additionally, African cities have never seen a middle-class majority. The small, privileged group of Africans described today as "middle class" have historically been analyzed as "elites" (Lentz 2016). Certain signs of middle-class status common elsewhere in the world, like living with one's nuclear family or reliably possessing a disposable income, are complicated in Africa by expansive notions of kinship, which place significant pressures on relatives who are (even marginally) better-off to house and support kin in need.

Africa's diaspora plays a key role in the creation and maintenance of middle classes on the continent (Darbon and Toulabor 2011; Courtin and Darbon 2012), but we know almost nothing about how the specificities of middle-classness in Africa articulate with the middle-class moralities migrants encounter in diasporic settings, like France. Studies of transnationalism have overwhelmingly focused on migrants who aspire to middle-classness in their country of origin but live as lower-class immigrants abroad (Glick Schiller 2004; Nieswand 2011; Kane 2011; Schielke 2012; Coe 2020). For undocumented and labor migrants like Ousmane Kane's (2011) Senegalese interlocutors in New York, the "homeland is the arena" for all their status-ambitions.

I use the term "*diasporic middle classes*" (cf. Courtin and Darbon 2012) to refer to migrants who focus their class-ambitions on their country of origin, distinguishing this orientation from those I call "*transnational middle classes*," like the educated Senegalese at the center of this book, who aim to achieve markers of middle-classness that were legible in both Paris and Dakar.

For university-educated Senegalese, the choice to invest exclusively in their country of origin would be to forfeit the financial security their diplomas can provide. Striving for status in Paris limits migrants' ability to act as dutiful kinsmen by sending money back home. Their investments in France are not evidence of their rejection of responsibilities in Senegal, however. The middle-class Senegalese I knew in Paris remitted regularly and took their children back to Senegal as often as their budgets allowed. Instead, investing in their lives in France had allowed these educated migrants access to salaried positions and the means send money back to provide for those who raised them and collaborated to finance their studies. The experiences of a shrinking group of transnational middle-class Senegalese who have been able to leverage formal education into international social mobility tell a story of class-making (and unmaking) at a global scale, revealing how the decline of Europe's middle classes radiates outward to reconfigure the lives and liveli-hoods of families in Africa.

## Indexing Integration:
## The Semiotics of Interconnected Belongings

Like Mathie Sène, whose story began this chapter, eleven-year-olds Miriama Diagne and Malik Sy had both just started middle school at the time of my fieldwork. But, unlike the Sène girls, Miriama and Malik both attended pub-lic schools. Miriama lived in the residential suburb Kremlin-Bîcetre, to the south of Paris. After school, she took singing classes and solfège (music read-ing) lessons at the community center for the arts. Malik's middle school was near his home in the 19th arrondissement, an area known for being home to many immigrant families. After school, he played in the courtyard of his building or went to soccer practice at the neighborhood gym with friends, most of whose parents had moved to France from Morocco, Algeria, or Mali.

Each child had a parent who taught at a French public high school, but Malik's family was struggling to achieve the middle-class stability that Mir-iama and her parents enjoyed. Kadar, Miriama's father, had lived in Paris since he did his bachelor's (la license) there in the late 1970s. He held a per-manent contract at a high school walking distance from his home. Malik's parents arrived later, in the 1990s. Since earning her master's degree, his mother, Rama, had been taking a commuter train (RER) each day to teach in an ill-reputed suburb, on annual contracts with no promise of long-term security. Although most public-school teachers in France are civil servants with the most secure form of permanent contract, in districts where it is dif-ficult to retain staff, annual contracts have become common. Over the twenty years that separated the arrival of Miriama's father and Malik's mother in France, the opportunities a university degree could offer had faded substan-tially. Educated Senegalese who moved to France in the 1990s and 2000s are likely to hold positions perceived as middle-class in terms of social status (freelance consultants or teachers on annual contracts), but which lack the security of a long-term contract. These jobs enabled them to distinguish themselves as educated professionals whose daily commutes and business at-tire resembled those of the middle classes, but their lives were characterized by intermittent precarity.

The security that higher education provided Miriama's father, by way of a CDI, had facilitated the family's move to their residential suburb. Their neighborhood was safer and better connected to Paris than France's notorious *cités*, suburbs filled with towering complexes built in the 1970s to house the families of immigrant workers (Tetreault 2008). In their residential neighborhood, Miriama's parents felt comfortable letting her move independently between school, home, and her friends' houses. For Malik's family, the instability of Rama's annual contracts made it difficult to find an apartment better than the two-bedroom they inhabited on the seventh floor of a public housing tower in an "immigrant neighborhood." In the 19th, Rama worried, people *expected* to see minority children who were "up to no good." For a young Black boy, the chances of being in the wrong place at the wrong time were high.

Malik's mother worked carefully to distinguish her family from their working-class neighbors in the eyes of her children's teachers and French society. She was careful to respond to teachers' notes promptly, in impeccable French. If her children struggled in school, she did not want their teachers to think that their parents were illiterate and could not provide them academic support. She avoided wearing wax-print African fabrics in public, preferring, she explained, to wear jeans or a "normal" pair of pants when she left the house. Rama sensed that it was in these everyday interactions that the limits of belonging are traced, dividing good, "integrated" foreigners from (potentially problematic) "immigrants." The French-born children of Muslim immigrants have been at the center of some of France's most heated and public battle over integration. Notably, the fifteen-years-long "headscarf debate," which culminated in the 2004 legal ban of conspicuous signs of religion in public schools, was sparked by expulsions of Muslim French girls for refusing to remove their head coverings in class. After the law passed, schools have remained sites where French secularism is debated and enforced.

France's official approach to immigration is based on a contractual notion of citizenship, which treats integration as an immigrant's civic duty and legal obligation. The Office of Immigration and Integration (OFII), which grants residence permits, requires immigrants from outside the EU to sign a "Reception and Integration Contract" declaring their intent to "integrate into French society and to accept the fundamental values of the Republic" (Yount-André 2017). But the specifics of what this obligation entails are imprecise. Most behaviors treated as antithetical to integration (like communautarisme) are not illegal. Yet, enshrined in government discourse, value-laden judgements of immigrant "integration" function as a powerful semiotic framework through which immigrants' and their children's everyday practices are judged.

France's so-called "colorblind" approach to immigration is based on the idea that anyone, regardless of religion or ethnic origin, may "become French" by demonstrating the will to integrate into French society (Lamont 2004, 148; Raissiguier 2010). Integration, in these discourses, is often measured in terms of secularism. Fernando explains, "to be an integrated, secular citizen means abstracting one's Muslimness and rendering it invisible in the public sphere" (2014, 36). In everyday language, Senegalese in France who prove sufficiently "integrated" (secular and middle class) are not called "immigrants" at all but, rather, "French of Senegalese origins." The legal distinction between naturalized French citizens and immigrants, in practice, becomes a class- and education-based division between minorities who have the means to manage their practices according to French expectations and those who do not and thus remain "immigrant" others. Integration, like middle-class status, is not a position one can achieve once and for all but requires ongoing efforts to orient one's everyday practices such that they point to (ever-changing) expectations of belonging in France.

Signs that "point" to their objects are called *indexes*, in Peirce's triadic theory of signs. Unlike icons, which bear a physical resemblance to their object (like a map), or symbols (like words), which are related to their object by convention or law, the relationship between indexes and their objects is one of contiguity or co-occurrence. Indexing or "pointing" to belonging is often a blurry process, one that often unfolds in a world of *non-dits* (things left unsaid), signaled by subtle cues (see also Zuckerman 2022 on "evaluative gaps"). Nowhere is it written that the smell of cuuraay incense can make a person seem "traditional." Some might disagree. Yet, the scent is often found in contexts (near HLM public housing, in "immigrant neighborhoods") in which other co-present signs (West African languages and accents, clothing in wax-print fabrics, street vendors selling grilled corn on the cob) could be construed as evidence of a group's lack of integration. Similarly, banal details of children's lives—the ways they eat (Yount-André 2018b), the track suit Malik wears to soccer practice, or Miriama's solfège workbook—may be taken up as signs of belonging or failure to belong.

Sports clothing and music workbooks do not directly point to integration. But, when construed relative to French tropes of class and race, they indirectly index (Ochs 1992) imbricated notions of class and national belonging. One's social practices and self-presentation—how one speaks, eats, dresses—can directly index social meanings (or person types), which index, in turn, particular modes of belonging. Take Malik's track suit, for example. This athletic attire might point to soccer practice. But, in France, polyester track suits made by Adidas and Nike are also associated with the social type *"racaille,"* a pejorative term for lower-class men (and sometimes women), often of North or West African descent, who are assumed to be delinquents (Tetreault 2015). French worries about racaille are entangled with fears that the children of Muslim immigrants fail to integrate into French society. Track suits (worn by visible minorities) can, thus, indirectly index failed belonging. Miriama's solfège music-reading classes, in contrast, index the cultural capital of classical music training. The only Black child in her class, Miriama's after-school activity was associated with France's white, middle, and upper classes. As such, her solfège workbook and presence in the class work to indirectly index her belonging in middle-class (white) French society.

Miriama and her family's path to integration was facilitated by inequalities of gender and generation in France. Her father had arrived in France at a moment when the economic opportunities available to Senegalese (men) through education were historically high. This allowed him to bring up his daughter in a majority-white residential suburb, where the after-school activities available catered to non-immigrant French children. Furthermore, gendered preferences that shaped children's choices of after-school activity facilitated Miriama's (but not Malik's) belonging in France. Boys made up only a small minority of participants in Miriama's middle-class music lessons. Whereas soccer, in France, which is perceived to be a typically masculine activity, is also associated with France's lower classes (Packer 2019; Héas et al. 2004). Embedded in French notions of integration are ideologies that work to situate French-born children relative to an axis of contrast dividing well-"integrated" foreign residents from (potentially problematic) "immigrants," such that their most everyday practices may be taken up as signs of belonging.

Indexes are inherently indeterminate, their uptake mediated by the ever-changing political-economic context. Terrorist attacks during my fieldwork in Paris in 2015, for example, inspired reevaluations of what constitutes secularism in France. Following the shooting at the *Charlie Hebdo* magazine in January, a Muslim middle-school girl was sent home from school for wearing a black ankle-length skirt that her teachers deemed insufficiently secular (Beyer 2015). The following autumn, the French Ministry of Education instated educational reforms that required teachers and parents to attend informational sessions on the expectations of secularism (Piquemal 2015).

Whether something in the material world—like a long skirt—is taken as a sign (of integration or otherwise) depends on context: the political climate surrounding Islam and immigration in France at that moment and a variety of other co-occurring signs. For racial and religious minorities in Paris, whether their actions are subject to suspicion and prejudice depends on things like where they are in the city, what they are doing, how they are dressed, and who they are with. Taken together, a series of nearly imperceptible objects in the material world become part of a constellation of signs that factor into everyday appraisals of racial minorities' belonging in France.

### The Transnational Middle-Class Dilemma

If aligning with French middle-class values was a critical means by which educated Senegalese indexed their integration in France, belonging in transnational families also depends on their capacity to position themselves somewhere between the rich and the poor in Senegal. For people in Dakar, the possibility that migrants "forget" their relatives back home is an ever-present threat. In Senegal, narratives abound about selfish rich people who refuse to redistribute, neglecting those who helped them get where they are. To demonstrate their moral fiber and ongoing commitment to those in Senegal, migrants must distance themselves from tropes of affluent, unethical Africans. Simultaneously positioning oneself as middle-class in Paris and Dakar thus required opposed forms of social distinction. In France, educated Senegalese must distance themselves from pejoratives stereotypes of *poor* immigrants, unable (or worse, unwilling) to integrate. Whereas, among Senegalese, to temper expectations of money and gifts, they had to make plain that—although they might live in Europe—they were not rich.

The parents in my study grew up in (upper-)middle-class areas in Dakar, neighborhoods like Mermoz, Sacré Coeur, Baobab, and other SICAPs. Their families' connections to successful migrants abroad were evident in the architecture of their homes, which had visibly expanded over the years as remittances financed the construction of new wings and upper levels to house adult children and their families. For adult migrants, the expectations to redistribute that they encountered in Dakar were a natural part of their families' social status. For their French-born children, it was jarring to realize that, on trips to Dakar, they were perceived as wealthy. In Paris, they were accustomed to being poorer than their classmates. Migrants' children often struggled to convince their parents to buy the clothing, phones, and tablets that were popular among their friends. They spent most school breaks in Paris, while other families traveled. Government-subsidized housing made it possible for families like the Sènes to live in areas that would otherwise be prohibitively expensive. But their modest rent costs meant that even families like Malik's, who lived in a so-called "immigrant neighborhood," were surrounded by households that paid three to four times more to rent private apartments across the street.

For children, it was often disconcerting to witness the sheer quantity of gifts their parents distributed to family members upon arriving in Dakar. Miriama and Malik were not fluent in Wolof, but both had grasped that their parents encountered continual requests for money in the streets of Dakar and at relatives' homes. When adults fished coins from their pocket to give to *talibé* (child beggars who scrounge for change and leftovers on the street), children like Malik could see that the offering was motivated by their families' relative affluence. "Senegal is a poor country," he explained to me, citing Dakar's frequent power outages and water shortages as evidence. This, he reasoned, was why his relatives offered money and meal leftovers to talibés, who struggle to survive.

At relatives' homes, however, wealth disparities were less apparent. Miriama remarked that her family's entire apartment in Paris could nearly fit into her grandmother's spacious living room, furnished with oversized couches that she sunk into, her feet dangling above the ground. Miriama and Malik's relatives had smartphones and flat-screen televisions, some equipped with videogame consoles. They had maids who prepared meals and did the laundry by hand. And yet, when they visited from Paris, it was *their* parents who doled out cash each time a long-lost relative came by to wish them well. Confusion at these offerings sometimes turned to frustration when children learned that they, too, would be expected to leave behind their possessions as gifts for cousins they hardly knew (as we will see with Badara's story in Chapter 4).

Seen as rich in Dakar, but poor in Paris, these children's experiences of Nieswand's "status paradox" were shaped by their parents' deliberate efforts, in both places, to position their families somewhere in between. With bachelor's and master's degrees, these Senegalese parents were among the 16 percent most educated in France (Insee 2016) and the 6.4 percent most educated in Senegal (ANSD 2014). Yet they struggled to position themselves as middle-class in the expensive French capital. These obstacles were compounded by efforts to achieve class status on a transnational scale. No matter how much they earned, the money they sent to Senegal meant that they could never consume like others in their income bracket in France. Their class-making efforts in Senegal, meanwhile, were complicated by investments in France, where a middle-class job means little if not accompanied by consumption practices deemed appropriate to this status. Consumption is critical to class-making in Dakar, as well, particularly for migrants whose physical absence means that their status must be materialized through money spent. Migrants who live in poverty abroad can surpass university-educated migrants in status markers in Africa, if they are able to invest in ambitious construction projects and to lavish gifts on relatives.

This reflects a fundamental dilemma faced by transnational middle-class migrants. Although the economic and cultural capital they possess premigration allows them to occupy a position of relative privilege abroad, they are not necessarily able to send more back in remittances than lower-class migrants, because maintaining this status requires investment in their host country. For instance, the educated Senegalese I knew in Paris all lived in nuclear families, in apartments large enough for children to have their own room or to share with one sibling. This living arrangement aligned with French expectations of middle-class families but precluded certain money-saving techniques common in Senegal's diaspora. Male labor-migrants often leave their spouses and children behind in Senegal, spending most of their adult lives in Europe, where they share cramped bedrooms in overcrowded housing projects (Mbodj-Pouye 2016, 2023). Even if both parents live abroad, many couples send their children back to Africa to live with relatives, where the costs of childcare are negligible and money sent to provide for children simultaneously supports the kin who care for them (Coe 2013; Bledsoe and Sow 2011; Grysole 2018).

Questions of how and on whom one spends money are central to middle-class values in France and Senegal alike. But normative expectations vary with context. Efforts to belong transnationally thus require strategic investments in multiple middle classes and skilled navigation of the economic moralities that mediate class status. These status negotiations have become increasingly complicated over time due to déclassement and a growing gap between middle-class moralities in France and Senegal.

## Integration Undone

Over the past fifty years, a growing political and economic distance between Senegal and its former colonizer has complicated the transnational middle-class ambitions of university-educated Senegalese. Tensions surrounding immigration have escalated throughout Europe, resulting in heightened pressures to demonstrate secularism in France. Concomitantly, in Senegal, Islam has become increasingly associated with lucrative paths to mobility. The trope of the "African intellectual" and the concept's fall into disuse illustrate how diminishing opportunities available through a French education, combined with divergent perceptions of religion in France and Senegal, have made transnational class ambitions increasingly difficult to achieve.

In France, the person-type of the "African intellectual," often used as shorthand for African students abroad, was once conceptually linked to Senegalese, who were among the first African students in Paris, arriving in the 1930s, thanks to a colonial expansion of Senegal's education system, which included scholarships to study in France (Thomas 2007). As African immigrants became increasingly common in Paris after World War II, Senegalese retained a reputation for being particularly modern and educated, compared to immigrants from less urbanized African nations (Wallerstein 1965). Senegal's first president, Léopold Sédar Senghor, epitomized the figure of the African intellectual and the political role they played. After attending the Sorbonne, Senghor went on to lead his newly independent nation, advocating for French to be the national language and the maintenance of close Franco-Senegalese political ties (Wilder 2005).

French colonial efforts to establish a mass education system in West Africa were premised on the notion that French schooling could offer Africans the tools to "evolve," or become "civilized"—that is, to become French (Conklin 1997). This assertion was written into law in 1914, when francophone residents of Dakar and the three other Senegalese cities called the "Four Communes" became eligible for full French citizenship (Wilder 2005, 129). Until independence, in 1960, certain educated residents of the Four Communes were able obtain French nationality without ever having left Africa (Wilder 2005, 109). An *évolué* (literally one who has "evolved") was a term French administrators used to refer to a francophone Senegalese elite who (they saw) as meriting French citizenship and who played a key role of intermediary between French and Senegalese populations (Wilder 2005, 121).

By granting *les évolués* citizenship, the French colonial administration applied an axis of differentiation that had previously distinguished European colonizers from Africans in terms of "civilization," and projected it upon Senegalese populations. This legally divided residents of French West Africa (AOF) into (urban, francophone) French citizens and (lower-class and rural) colonial subjects, reinforcing inequalities between urban and rural Senegal. Meanwhile, in Dakar, this reinforced emergent hierarchies between educated francophones, who had privileged access to the formal economy, and illiterate Wolof-speakers who got by on the informal economy.

When Senghor came to power, the social significance of the figure of the African intellectual was at its height in Paris and Dakar. Like Senghor, the "*intello*" was typically male. Students who returned from abroad to find jobs in Senegal's socialist government became sought after as husbands. In Dakar, marrying a "*salarié*" (salaried employee) return migrant seemed a sure ticket into a new, educated, urban class. The French government, meanwhile, *encouraged* immigration among this educated minority, long after independence, through visas and scholarships issued by the French Ministry of Cooperation. This ministry, which managed decolonization, treated African students as essential to the maintenance of close Franco-African political-economic ties (Chafer 2003; Martin 1995).

Senegal's independent government framed mass education as a democratic tool that could bring modernity to the nation. But, beginning in the 1970s, intellectuals saw their prestige fade, as economic downturn (in both Africa and Europe) severely limited the opportunities a French education could offer (Kane 2011; Riccio 2001). In France and Senegal alike, the role of religion in questions of belonging and middle-class respectability rapidly shifted, in ways that were directly opposed: tensions surrounding Islam and immigration escalated in Europe, while, in Senegal, the transnational networks of Muslim brotherhoods emerged as a path to class status more widely accessible than mobility through formal education.

In 1974, as postwar prosperity drew to a close, governments throughout Western Europe announced the end of labor migration from non-European countries (Castles 1986). Rather than discouraging efforts to immigrate, however, this policy encouraged a quick and lasting shift away from circulatory migration and toward permanent, family-based settlement in France (Gueye 2002; Tall 2002). As male immigrants from France's former colonies brought their wives to settle in Paris's working-class neighborhoods, fears grew that children raised in "ethnic enclaves" would never integrate into

French society (Barou 2014). Muslim families were increasingly stigmatized as a dangerous new class—a threat to national cohesion and security (Sargent and Larchanché-Kim 2006).

Thus began a period of unrelenting public debate on "integration" and "secularism" (Barou 2014; Fernando 2014) in France. Anthropologist Myathi Fernando characterizes these as part of an ongoing process of Muslim racialization in France, through which religious differences between Muslims and "majority" French society have increasingly come to be treated as insurmountable in French society (see also Fassin and Fassin 2006). In Senegal, meanwhile, the economic push to emigrate intensified as legal channels for migration narrowed. Beginning in 1980, Senegal underwent a series of increasingly severe Structural Adjustment Programs that culminated in the 1994 devaluation of the franc CFA by 50 percent. Migration became even more critical to households in Senegal, as remittances doubled in value and finances in Senegal were spread thin (Daffé and Diop 2004).

Civil servants in Senegal were laid off and unemployment increasingly affected university graduates, "undermin[ing] the faith in education among some sectors of the population" (Kane 2011, 224; see also Tall 2002, 552; Perry 1997, 33). Throughout sub-Saharan Africa, the 1970s bore witness to the disintegration of "the modern dream of education" (Cole 2011, 69) as a viable path to economic stability. For educated Senegalese in Paris, the rapid disappearance of opportunities for college graduates back in Senegal encouraged many to envision staying abroad for the foreseeable future, attempting to bring up their children middle-class in France. For would-be emigrants, France's tightening immigration policies encouraged many to set their sights on new migration destinations, especially via Murid trade networks that developed in Italy, Spain, and the United States (Babou 2021; Carter 1997; Maher 2017).

Informal trade networks offered a path to migration (often undocumented), for growing numbers of Africans (Perry 1997; Stoller 2002). Economic liberalization allowed the Murid Muslim brotherhood to transform informal rural trade networks into transcontinental import/export businesses (Riccio 2001). The brotherhood was once associated with illiterate villagers, ridiculed by francophone urbanites in Dakar. But, today, Murids are associated with profitable transnational connections, and even educated urbanites increasingly join their ranks (Hannaford 2017; Kane 2011). With the brotherhood's growing power and legitimacy in Senegal, Islam has gained new visibility and political clout (Buggenhagen 2013, 52). Religious piety has long been associated with status in Senegal (Irvine 1974). The wealth circulated by Murid migrants further links Islam to status achieved through consumerism and cosmopolitanism, rendering public piety increasingly critical to illustrating class status in Senegal.

The divergent meaning of religion for French and Senegalese middle classes developed within the broader breakdown of privileged postcolonial relations between France and its former colonies. Senegalese leaders have increasingly oriented the country politically toward the Muslim world, especially since the presidency of Abdoulaye Wade (2000–2012), the first president to publicly declare himself a Murid disciple. Senegalese in Paris and Dakar voice their disillusionment with France. Students in Paris often admitted to me that France had not been their preferred destination and they saw it as a first step on longer migration and professional trajectories.

In France today, the figure of the African intellectual is a distant memory. Senegalese are no longer perceived as particularly educated or integrated. Yet, men like Miriama's father, Kadar, continued to perform identities of African intellectuals to demonstrate belonging in France. Kadar made frequent reference to his studies in Paris in the 1970s and the two bachelor's degrees (in literature and physics) he had earned. The walls of his apartment were lined with bookshelves overflowing with texts by French and Senegalese authors, a material monument to his education. Older intellectuals, who have spent decades in France, are also known (among Senegalese) for drinking alcohol. Drinking wine, in particular, exemplifies belonging in France. Minorities can simultaneously demonstrate their secularism, appreciation of French culinary heritage (Fischler 1999), and middle-class taste (Demossier 2010), through their "*savoir boire*," or embodied knowledge of "how to drink" (Pettit 2023; Nahoum-Grappe 1991). Kadar relished in drawing my attention to his love for wine, but his alcohol consumption in France was considered morally suspect by many in Senegal, evidence that he had been abroad for so long that he had forgotten Senegalese values.

None of the Muslim women I knew drank, nor did many of the men who had arrived in recent decades. Senegalese like Malik's mother, Rama, demonstrated their secularism by carefully distancing themselves from signs of religion when in public in France. On Muslim holidays, when immigrants in colorful boubous glittered along the platforms of Paris's metro, Rama (like most of my interlocutors) preferred to don her boubou only after arriving at her host's home, unless she could find a friend who could pick her family up by car. When speaking, movement between middle-class moralities in France

Figure 4. Overflowing bookshelves in the apartment of a "Senegalese intellectual." Home of high-school teacher Kadar Diagne, in Kremlin-Bicêtre. Photo: Yount 2014.

and Senegal involved careful code-switching. Words like "Inshallah" and "Al-hamdulillah," which peppered her speech and marked Muslim virtue with Senegalese, disappeared when Rama spoke in public in Paris. The stakes of signaling Islam in a public space like their children's schools or at work were so palpably high that, for most educated Senegalese, this linguistic exercise required no conscious thought. Wine consumption may have given Kadar an efficient means to mark integration in a France but, having left Senegal at a time when public piety played a less significant role in class moralities, he struggled to align with contemporary expectations of Muslim middle classes on visits to Senegal (Yount-André 2020a).

## Middle-Class Decline and Family Trips to Dakar

Like évolués before them, the privileged status of "integrated" immigrants is justified by a belief in the transformative power of education. But, in postcolonial France, the stakes of belonging have shifted. All immigrants—not just the privileged few who were able to access French education pre-migration—are expected to integrate. Failure to do so exposes racial and religious minorities to prejudice that shapes the jobs they get, the neighborhoods they live in, and the schools where they can enroll their children. But déclassement influences migrants' investments in Senegal in somewhat counterintuitive ways. The relative security that higher education had assured Miriama's father, juxtaposed with the precarity that Malik's mother faced, reveals the effects of French middle-class decline on the everyday lives of transnational families.

Malik's mother, Rama, struggled to achieve markers of middle-classness in France, despite holding degrees higher than Miriama's father did. She dreamed of moving out of their HLM, getting a permanent teaching job, and owning a home. But the material conditions necessary to make these things possible were slow to coalesce. She often wondered about possible opportunities in Senegal, especially since her brother had left France two years prior, to start a business in Dakar.

Miriama's father, Kadar, in contrast, struggled to imagine eventually returning to Senegal. At sixty years old, he would soon retire and begin receiving his government pension. He had a list of health troubles, for which he was being treated at his local hospital. He had never invested in construction in Senegal and his contributions to the family home in Dakar, although regular, were less substantial than remittances sent by his siblings, who were actively preparing for their return. Walking through his neighborhood near Paris, Kadar's path was punctuated with greetings from neighbors. After someone greeted him as "professor," Kadar shook his head and lamented that all his friends were in France now; in Dakar, he knows hardly anyone. The status and social recognition he enjoyed in Paris evaporated when he set foot in his "home" country.

How and where parents imagine possible futures for their families had a direct impact on how (much) they invest in kinship- and class-making in Dakar. The frequency of trips to Dakar and how much they send in remittances or invest in an eventual return to Senegal all shaped migrants' and their children's interactions with relatives on trips back to Dakar. Malik's parents proudly reported that, even if they could not always afford to send the whole family, they made a point to send him and his sister to Senegal each year. Whereas, when I met Miriama, it had been nearly three years since her last trip to Dakar. She had never been to Senegal alone and she resisted her mother's suggestion that she might one day go by herself.

The forms of stability (and precarity) that migrants experience in France shape their intimate relations with kin abroad. Racialized processes of middle-class decline in France radiate outward, affecting the ways that relatives in Paris and Dakar weave family connections in their efforts to achieve desirable status positions, in Senegal and abroad. Rama's annual contracts repeatedly exposed her to the prejudices of the job market. They "will never hire an African lady to teach the language of Molière," she complained, bitterly reflecting on her difficulties being selected in the annual competition (*le concours*) to enter the ranks of French public-school teachers. She and her husband imagined moving back to Senegal for retirement or even before, if they found a way to make a living there.

Although Malik's parents continued to invest in their status in France, putting money aside to one day buy a home near Paris, their annual trips back to Senegal and remittances made up a far more significant portion of their budget than what Miriama's father spent on his transnational connections. The fruit of Malik's parents' investments was clear in the boy's familiarity with his relatives' lives in Senegal. Malik knew the names of his cousins who lived there and even the name of the talibé boy to whom the household offered midday leftovers. He could describe the rhythms of daily life at his grandmother's house and his place in it, explaining, for example, that every afternoon, his grandmother gives him "some money so [he] can buy a snack at the boutique." In Dakar, he and his sister moved autonomously around their grandmother's neighborhood.

Miriama was not so familiar with her grandmother's home and her father's family. She had stayed with her mother's kin on her last trip back, when she was eight. On both sides, her grandparents' homes in Dakar housed so many relatives that she had trouble remembering people's names and how she was related to them. At her father's mother's house, she often played with two cousins who were roughly her age, and she had a close relationship with one adult cousin (see Chapter 5). But her interactions with most of her relatives in Dakar were marked with polite distance.

This distance was particularly clear in the chores that Miriama's relatives expected (or did *not* expect) her to do around the house. Throughout Africa, tasks like running to fetch an ingredient, serving cold drinks to guests, helping prepare, and cleaning up after meals are chores that reliably fall to children, especially girls (Lancy 2012). Senegalese adults characterize these tasks as critical to children's upbringing (*éducation*), in that they teach young people to be attentive to the needs of others, so that, in the future, they might take part in relations of intergenerational reciprocity, supporting their elders and the next generation. Adults encourage children to show deference to older people by physically moving to carry out tasks at their elders' bidding. Perceived as central to children's moral education, among Senegalese, sometimes strict directives are taken to be signs of care and investment in a child's future.

At eleven, Mariama and Malik's peers in Senegal already managed significant household chores on their own. Malik described with awe his girl cousins in Dakar who could already prepare *ceebu jën* (Senegal's national dish of rice and fish) for the entire family. His grandmother discouraged him and his sister from helping in the kitchen, afraid it would be dangerous for them. While many tasks were out of his reach, there were certain chores at his grandmother's house that were considered Malik's responsibility when he was visiting. His relatives knew, for example, that they could trust him to run errands to the corner shop. After the meal, Malik and his sister took part in clearing away leftovers and it was Malik's job to put out the bowl of fruit. These tasks allowed him to, symbolically, at least, take up a child's role by working for (and showing deference to) his elders.

At her grandmother's home, there were no tasks that reliably fell to Mariama. She never went to fetch a glass of water for guests. Instead, she often found herself seated next to guests, being served cold by her adult aunt. When the time came to set up for the meal or to clean up after, Miriama seemed oblivious to the tasks at hand and none of her relatives asked her to help. Instead, her aunts systematically called for Miriama's younger cousin Binette, who lived in the house. While Binette carried out housework, Miriama lounged on the couch, playing games on her phone. Migrant children's behavior reflects on their parents (see Yount-André 2022), and Mariama's cluelessness to the tasks a child her age might take up reinforced her father's image as an "intello," who had lived so long in France that he had become disconnected from "Senegalese values."

Migrant parents' relationships with kin in Dakar shape their children's interactions with these relatives. Miriama's father struggled to find his place among his relatives in Dakar. He was visibly uncomfortable during long hours of catching up. He repeatedly slipped away to another room, to return half an hour later. His was not the triumphant return of a migrant eager to show off the wealth he earned abroad, but one who struggled to dodge requests in socially respectable ways. Interactions surrounding money were awkward, as if Kadar's contribution to and place in the family was not clear to anyone, least of all to him. The first time I came to visit them around lunchtime, Kadar suggested, at first, that we go out to a restaurant, something I had never done with a family in Senegal or with his family in France. After hushed conversations between Kadar and his sister, she prepared pasta for us, separate from the rice-based dish she prepared for the rest of the family.

With her father's place in the family up in the air, Miriama's position vis-à-vis her relatives who lived in her grandmother's house was equally uncertain. Senegalese are proud of the hospitality (*teranga*) they extend to visitors. But accepting this hospitality also implies a distance, which was clear each time Miriama's aunts failed to ask her to help. Miriama remained a guest at her grandmother's house. Although she forged relations with certain relatives, the wider family network as mediated by her father was unsure and sometimes tense terrain.

Transnational families' experiences on trips to Dakar are mediated by the affective and economic investments that adult migrants have maintained over their time abroad. This shapes the ways that migrants' children are received by their relatives in Dakar and the efforts their kin make to integrate them into the family. A lack of job security meant that Rama's family lived a precarious existence in France, yet she and her husband devoted significant resources to trips back. As they waited to see whether they might one day be able to move to a nicer neighborhood in Paris, it also seemed plausible that they might move back to Senegal. Instability might mean limited means, but this does not equate to a divestment in transnational relations. Rather, in the case of Miriama's father, it was precisely his comfort and stability in France that made it difficult to imagine ever going back to Dakar.

## Class Mobility and the Risk of Reracialization

The difficulties Senegalese parents face in transmitting their relative privilege to their French-born children lays bare that, for visible minorities, "deracialization" (Brodkin 1998) rooted in education or class status can *always be undone* when the stakes of belonging rise. Integration is a moving target, bound up with shifting political-economic tensions and ideas about secularism, Islam, and immigration. Middle-class decline in France shapes transnational kinship relations in, sometimes, counterintuitive ways. Like many young graduates in France, educated Senegalese increasingly experience ever longer periods of precarity, before (hopefully) one day securing a permanent contract. Paradoxically, this instability pushed Malik Sy's family to invest *more* money in their transnational kinship relations in Dakar than did Miriama's father, whose stability in France meant that he would likely finish his days in his neighborhood outside of Paris.

Miriama's father and Malik's mother were both highly educated Senegalese migrants. But over the twenty years that separated their arrivals in France, the value of a French diploma had plummeted and tensions had escalated surrounding Islam and immigration. Kadar had arrived at the end of the era of the African intellectual and benefitted from the prestige associated with this person-type in the years following Senegalese independence. Rama arrived in Paris after twenty years of tightening immigration policy, at a time when signs of Islam had become points of societal tension. Her struggles to secure a permanent contract in France reveal how the stability and precarity that migrants experience abroad shape how people invest in status and social relations in their home and host countries.

Déclassement in Europe shapes the remitting practices of transnational middle classes, limiting the resources available for people's class-making efforts in Africa. Educated migrants' relative stability in France supported the emergence of transnational middle classes, whose privilege lies in their ability to align their consumption and communication practices with French middle-class values and (thus) demonstrate national belonging. As future opportunities in France appear increasingly uncertain, investment in transnational relations becomes a renewed priority for middle-class migrants. Teaching their children to avoid prejudice in Paris and to succeed in school, Senegalese parents hope to position their children to take advantage of opportunities, whether in France or farther afield, equipped with EU citizenship and French diplomas that are valued internationally. Meanwhile, by redistributing resources to achieve middle-class belonging in Senegal, they maintain connections with transnational family members based in Dakar, but whose kinship networks stretch across Europe, to the United States and Canada, and even China.

CHAPTER 2

# Scales of Solidarity:
# Navigating Economic Moralities

Aïda Leye smoothed her cranberry-colored skirt and shifted in her seat as she made polite conversation with our dinner host, Ndeye Sarr, in Paris's 14th arrondissement. Aïda and her husband, Christophe, had arrived from Dakar a few days before, for a monthlong visit to France. Her outfit, complete with a carefully tied *musòor* (headwrap) of the same fabric, was a splash of color amid the somber black and gray the rest of us wore, standard hues of Parisian winter wardrobes. Christophe was an old friend of Ndeye's husband, Abdoulaye, from his days back in Dakar's Baobab neighborhood. The Sarrs had organized a dinner to celebrate the couple's arrival in Paris, inviting me and Alioune, a mutual friend from Baobab who, like Abdoulaye, had been living in Paris since the 1970s.

When I joined the women on the couch, Aïda switched to French, until Ndeye nodded in my direction, saying, *"Dègg na"* (She understands). Grinning, Aïda began to test my Wolof, starting with the usual greetings and progressing through a series of increasingly complex questions. As I began to struggle to respond, Aïda switched back to French, to ask, "Do you know *teranga?*" The query concluded our impromptu Wolof lesson, segueing into a discussion of Senegalese hospitality and solidarity, versions of which I had heard many times before in Dakar and Paris. Unsatisfied with my translation of teranga as mere "hospitality," Aïda launched into a description of the Senegalese value, contrasting it to what she saw as the many moral shortcomings of the French.

"In Senegal," she explained, "we have teranga. I'm not talking about friendship, I'm talking about teranga in the true sense of the word: welcome, mutual support, solidarity. You meet people and they will talk to you, help you . . . you go somewhere, they'll invite you to eat." In France, she complained, people refuse to even engage with others, never mind offer aid. Her complaints drew the attention of the men on the other side of the room, who began to take turns offering up anecdotes that illustrated the apathy and callousness they had encountered in Paris. The speakers aligned in their moral censure of Parisians who refused to stop to give directions or who, upon witnessing an accident or crime, continued walking, refusing to even call the police. Aïda concluded that, in France, no one trusts one another. She offered an example from earlier that day, at the pharmacy. Although she had a prescription for four months' worth of medicine, the pharmacist had refused to fill it, saying that the social security office (*sécurité sociale*, France's public healthcare) would first need to approve the quantity requested. "What does social security have to do with anything?" Aïda protested loudly.

This time, however, her frustration was met by silence. Her husband broke the pregnant pause, exclaiming, "They're the ones who pay!" The Sarr's eleven- and thirteen-year-old sons looked up from their video games as the adults' voices erupted in a cacophony of explanation, opposing Aïda's assessment of mistrust and arbitrary bureaucracy. Abdoulaye and Ndeye began to explain the functioning of the French social security system to her. Alioune clarified that this procedure was necessary to impede "*les fraudeurs*,"[1] people who cheat the French system by taking state-subsidized medicine to Africa to sell.

In an instant, Aïda's audience had turned from expressing collaborative support of her moral assessments to a collective effort to disabuse her of an ill-informed understanding of France's social welfare system. Aïda's story highlighted a sign in the material world—her refused request for medicine— as an index of stingy mistrust in France. Her audience, however, took the failed attempt to fill a prescription not as a sign of moral failing, but as an index of complications inherent to French bureaucracy, Aïda's inexperience navigating it (as a visitor), and regulations to deter those who would take unfair advantage.

By referencing the figure of the fraudeur, Alioune described a stigmatized type of African immigrant in France: lower-class or undocumented—one whose economic activities take place undeclared, on "the black" (Weber 2008), and might try to profit from state subsidies. Directing Aïda's attention toward this social type, he signaled his own (perceived) position in France, as well as the threat of being viewed as a fraudeur, tacitly urging her to read her own actions through a lens of "integration," relative to the expectations of the broader French public, as well as those of middle-class Africans in France. With this brief comment, Alioune's claim of knowledge of France indirectly signaled his elder status, both in age and in time abroad, and his (perceived) integration in Paris. This discursive move, with its tacit morality, stifled further discussion (of the ways racism or sexism may have shaped) Aïda's interaction at the pharmacy. If she were to insist, at that point, she would surely sound like a fraudeur.

The five adults from Dakar first rallied around values they viewed as characteristically Senegalese—framing themselves as unified by their understandings of hospitality (teranga) and solidarity—as distinct to those of the French. But when Aïda offered up the example of a pharmacist's refusal to fill her prescription, her audience was no longer aligned with her assessment. To them, the pharmacist's actions were not evidence of mistrust and lack of *teranga*, nor were they particularly out of the ordinary. Instead, it was simply how the French healthcare system functioned, especially given the hiccups one might expect without a *carte vitale* (French health insurance card). Rules, in France, surrounding who can pick up medicine, how much of it, of what kinds, and for whom are enforced more strictly than in Dakar, where a prescription and money to pay usually suffice to access medicine, given there is (usually) no formal insurance (state or private) to bureaucratize the process.

Anonymous bureaucracy dictates healthcare in France. Voicing (even resigned) acceptance of the system, Aïda's hosts signaled that they were not new here, nor were they fraudeurs themselves. Their acceptance of state bureaucracy reflected stability in France, formal working papers, and cartes vitales. To identify "fraudeurs" as a threat reflects (verbal) alignment with France's state system and suggests that the speaker did not himself rely on the "black market" to survive. With this offhand remark, Alioune carried out substantial social work, marking class boundaries among African populations in Paris and positioning himself and his hosts therein. He simultaneously shifted the collective focus to a different scale of "solidarity" and the social types who threaten its functioning. This chapter examines how speakers shift between economic moralities in unfolding interaction and, in so doing, move between scales of solidarity (and systems of redistribution) treated as (most) relevant or legitimate in a given context.

## Boundary Work and Redistribution

Alioune's reference to "les fraudeurs" positioned him relative to an imagined immigrant other, linking an (illegal) act of material circulation (obtaining state-subsidized medicine to sell for a profit) to a certain type of African immigrant. Working on the assumption that Aïda and all of those present that evening would (should) take issue with the act of profiting from the French social welfare system, the moral stance that Alioune evoked worked to distinguish him (and his peers co-present) from stereotypes of (lower-class) immigrants in France who do not share such scruples. In so doing, he used the term fraudeur to draw an axis of difference between a law-abiding, French majority and (problematic) immigrants. He projected this contrast onto African populations in France, distinguishing fraudeurs from law-abiding (integrated) Africans, highlighting the alignment of certain immigrants (himself included) with the moral-economic priorities of the dominant group. In processes like these, language practices that reproduce economic moralities also work to divide and rank individuals and their rights to resources.

This act of boundary making, saturated with economic moralities that subtly express distance from (and tacit censure of) the informal economic activities of lower-class and undocumented immigrants, simultaneously carried out an act of scale-making. The discursive shift that followed the story of the pharmacy not only rearranged alignments among participants in the interaction (general dis-alignment from Aïda's interpretation), but simultaneously reoriented the scale of solidarity treated as relevant, from discussion of interpersonal solidarity to one of the French national redistribution system. This act of rescaling was achieved through what linguistic anthropologists Judith Irvine and Susan Gal call "fractal recursivity"—that is, the "projection of an opposition, salient at some level of relationship, onto some other level" (Irvine and Gal 2000, 38). As Aïda's listeners proposed other frames of interpretation, they simultaneously redrew the relevant axis of differentiation from one of French versus Africans (distinct in norms of hospitality and interpersonal relations) to one projected onto African populations in France, dividing them into fraudeurs and "people like us," presumably compliant with French law (see table 1 below).

Fractal recursivity, Irvine and Gal note, carries out a "perspectival" model of scaling (Gal and Irvine 2019, 225). That is to say, each time an axis of differentiation is redrawn, it is from the perspective of the comparer, the ideological projects and material stakes of their view work to "pick out the qualities and dimensions taken to be relevant for comparison" (2019, 225). Teranga and trust were not at stake at the pharmacy, Aïda's audience claimed. Instead, the pharmacist acted on behalf of the national healthcare system, funded by so-

Teranga  { "Senegalese"      ———      "French"
   ⊕    {  (in France)

|

"Fraudeurs"      ———      "Integrated"                ⊕
(Undocumented / lower class)        (Middle class)         Compliance
Senegalese               Senegalese            with French law
in France                in France             and economic
                                               moralities

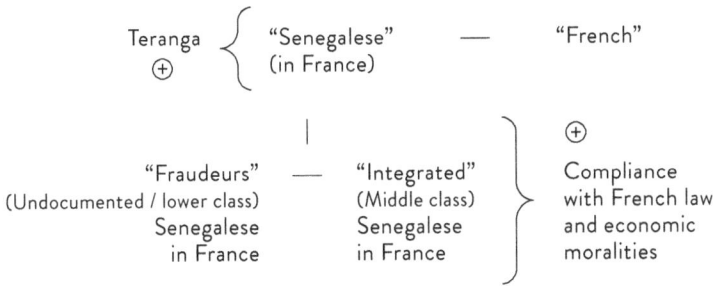

Figure 5. Fractal recursivity in discussion of "solidarity," first as hospitality (*teranga*) and second as achieved through France's national redistributive systems.

cial security, which requires the verification of numerous documents to prevent being scammed by les fraudeurs.

Not everyone in France agrees, however, about what counts as a "fraud." French ethnographer Florence Weber notes that unofficial sources of revenue, earned "on the black" and legally considered "fraud," represent a "sometimes vital" source of income for France's lower classes (Weber 2008). Not everyone sees fraudeurs as a threat, furthermore. In the cités around Paris, where Tetreault (2008) did her fieldwork, polite company simply learned to walk around the parking lots where informal dealings were carried out. Those who work or employ others on "the black," Weber notes, often do not perceive their economic practice to be illegal at all, albeit undeclared (2008, 8–12). But this diversity in the economic moralities present in France is erased in the semiotic move by which Alioune made claims at his own integration through alignment with the values of the (presumed to be law-abiding) French majority.

Whether or not an activity appears immoral (or even illegal) is a matter of perspective. It depends on the (ideological) frame used to construe it, which can vary in sometimes surprising ways. Susan Gal (2005, 31) recounts the story of a twice-stolen desk in Soviet-era Poland, where employees often pilfered from state factories (public) things they would later (privately) sell on the black market. One employee, who took a desk, intending to resell it, was dismayed to find that it was "stolen" from his truck outside his apartment, as he waited to deliver it to the intended purchaser. "By the moral rules of public and private life," Gal explains, "removing the desk from the factory did not count as theft at all, since it was merely taking from the public, the state.

The disappearance from the street, however, was something else . . . dishonest and immoral" (2005, 31).

Central to notions of economy versus morality that I explore below, it is worth citing here Gal's recursive analysis of public/private contrasts. Notions of public versus private, she argues, are rooted in a "language ideology of differentiation," which produces a series of nested contrasts, each accompanied by particular material conditions and moral expectations. Gal notes that the first man (who took the desk from the factory) and second man (who took the desk from the truck) would have agreed that there exists "a distinction between 'theft' and justified 'takings,' the first relevant to private situations, the second to public situations. They differed, however, in how they judged the nestings of public and private for the particular occasion" (2005, 31). Notions of what is moral in a given situation may vary with perspective, but individuals' perspectives also vary according to social types relevant (and recognizable) to a broader social group, including perceived sets of oppositions, like public versus private or economic versus moral.

Where one draws the public/private divide has moral and material entailments; it reflects one's (political, economic, social) position and one's material stakes in the situation at hand. So, too, the way one speaks about "fraud" of the French social welfare system reflects (and creates) one's social position in France. To treat documents required in French bureaucracy as a necessary evil, to protect against fraud, is to voice a particular (middle) class perspective, one of relative security (among immigrants in France), in alignment with French economic moralities and immigration services. Aligned with French priorities of "solidarity" at the national level, Alioune demonstrated *selective solidarity* with other Africans in France, verbally distancing himself from immigrants who would cheat the French state.

Drawing on economic moralities to strategically create similarity and difference between themselves and others in France and in Africa, the speakers gestured toward two separate notions of "solidarity" central to the material lives of middle-class Senegalese in Paris. The first is that of the French government, which frames welfare state support as contingent on immigrant "integration." The second notion of "solidarity" relevant here is that which is expected among Senegalese transnational kin, rooted in asymmetric but complementary relations that organize flows of material resources, which I describe as systems of "rank-based redistribution." These interpersonal relations of "solidarity" also have fraudeurs, who threaten the system by not fully participating, but they go by other names in the Senegalese context. Whether one is seen as greedy for a failure to give (a miser) or due to excessively ask-ing from others (a moocher), selfish "individualists" are the ones condemned in Dakar and its diaspora.

## Scales of Solidarity

Whether at the level of the state or interpersonal relations, the rights and responsibilities associated with "solidarity" cannot be extended indiscrim-inately, but are contingent on group membership. All solidarity is, in this sense, selective solidarity. With rights to resources at stake, the boundaries of belonging are often questioned—negotiations that intensify in the con-text of economic decline. As individuals and entire nations struggle to man-age increasingly limited resources, they carry out ever-more-selective forms of solidarity. Practices that index one's eligibility to benefit from relation-ships of "solidarity" may be redefined or examined with a fine-toothed comb. In France, for example, this can be seen in tightening migration re-strictions since the 1970s and in policies on secularism that place increasing pressure on Muslims to embody integration (see Chapter 1). Selective soli-darity may be imposed in a top-down fashion—through rules and regula-tions or visa refusals at the Préfecture de Police. But Alioune's warnings of frauders point to the ways these processes are also internalized by those they (threaten to) categorize, circulated in moral stories that caution new arrivals to mind and maintain the distance between you and certain "types" of Africans abroad.

Although Aïda accused the French of lacking virtuous "solidarity,"[2] this is paradoxically the same term the French state uses to describe the sorts of relations the social welfare system forges among residents of France. The European Union and the French state both characterize solidarity as a fun-damental value and guiding principle of their migration policies, elaborated and protected in the EU's Charter of Fundamental Rights (European Union 2010). French integration policy categorizes solidarity as a key French value that immigrants must uphold. At civic-training sessions, new immigrants are shown a video titled "Living Together in France," which outlines solidarity as key to fraternity. The film's narrator explains that, by paying taxes, French residents participate in "national solidarity," which (he reminds us) permits the functioning of state services like hospitals and schools (Janbon and Wallon-Leducq 2004).

The Senegalese state similarly uses the term "solidarity" to refer to government programs that distribute resources to those in need, like the Ministère de la Famille et des Solidarités (Ministry of Family and Solidarities). But, in everyday talk, Senegalese speakers rarely use the term "*solidarité*" to describe redistribution by the state. Instead, Senegalese describe solidarity as achieved through private, interpersonal interactions. With uncanny regularity, speakers in Senegal and its diaspora elaborate the notion of solidarity, as Aïda did, through the metaphor of food sharing and the idea that, wherever you go in Senegal, "they'll invite you to eat." Alimentary idioms frame solidarity as a relationship realized through spontaneous, if systematized, acts of (often face-to-face) exchange, unlike the solidarity of European welfare states, which is written into law and organized by anonymous government institutions.

The French term solidarité may be glossed in Wolof as *dimbalante* (to help one another) or *jàppalante* (literally to hold or to catch one another). Both terms use the suffix "ante" to communicate reciprocity in the acts of helping or holding. Jàppalante, like the notion of "lending a hand" in English, communicates the idea that a task requires the combined efforts of many, like "solidarity" offered in the form of gifts and monetary contributions at baby-naming ceremonies. The sort of mutual aid conveyed by the term dimbalante, meaning "to help one another," which requires no event or task as its cause, presumes and entails an asymmetrical relationship between giver and receiver. Solidarity in this case presumes and entails hierarchical relations, in contrast to the equalizing ideals of solidarity in European social welfare states.

These two systems of "solidarity" thus operate from very different starting points. France's public system of solidarity actively works to create *similarity* across diverse groups (demanding immigrant integration and enacting redistribution through taxes and social welfare), whereas systems of rank-based redistribution emphasize *difference*, distinguishing people who are otherwise similar in order to organize and encourage the flow of resources from those higher-ranked or better off (however marginally or momentarily) to those of lower status or (apparently) less wealth.

In Senegal and throughout Africa, social life is explicitly organized according to multiple, mutually imbricated hierarchies of gender and generation, caste and class. Studies of intersectionality have highlighted the ways that individuals' lives everywhere are organized according to overlapping inequalities of race, class, and gender (Crenshaw 1991; Collins 2002). But the

hierarchies associated with rank-based redistribution are distinct in the ex-
plicitness with which contrasts between individuals are emphasized and how
these status differences are expected to motivate material exchange. In Senegal, asymmetries are expected and required for money to change hands as
material "help." To achieve material exchange, status differences are highlighted, created, and drawn upon in unfolding interactions.

Judith Irvine (1974, 1989, 1990) has illustrated how linguistic and monetary exchanges in Senegal are underpinned by the assumption that "people
are inherently dissimilar" (2001, 35) and that everyday verbal and material
interactions in Senegal systematically divide participants into positions of
high and low rank. In Wolof, she explains, even the most abbreviated greeting is inherently hierarchical "because the mere fact of initiating a greeting
is itself a statement of relative status" (1974, 175). Linguistic and material exchanges presume and entail inequalities between interacting participants.
The normative expectations that organize exchanges between individuals of
high and low status (elders and juniors, men and women, wealthy and poor,
migrants and those left behind) function (ideally speaking) according to parallel logics, in which low-ranking individuals work for their superiors and
those of high rank must, in turn, support their dependents. The solidarity
achieved through this system of rank-based redistribution aims at equity, not
equality.

In French-state discourses and discussions in Senegalese households in
Paris, social actors communicate economic moralities that trace boundaries
of belonging in French society and in Senegalese kinship networks alike,
shaping the rights to resources that belonging can afford. The families of
university-educated Dakarois in Paris strategically shift between contrasting notions of solidarity and the moral logics that underpin them. These
efforts to simultaneously demonstrate integration in France and continued
commitment to Senegal result in shifting stances to habitual, everyday ethics. Speakers' moral stances have material consequences, alternately reproducing different social groups and scales of redistribution.

## Economic Moralities

At their most basic, "economic moralities" are normative expectations
regarding material exchange, obligation, and entitlement. These ideological
positions, which endow acts of material exchange with social meaning and

ethical valence, represent a form of "semiotic ideology"—that is, "basic assumptions about what signs are and how they function in the world" (Keane
2003, 419). If "language ideologies" (see the Introduction) are common-sense
ideas about language that regiment how social actors interpret talk and written language, semiotic ideologies expand this concept beyond language to
encompass discourses that organize multimodal semiotic processes. The notion of "economic moralities" I put forth here, then, focuses our attention
specifically on the material entailments of moral frames embedded in broader
semiotic ideologies, urging us to examine how assumptions about "what signs
are" organize the circulation of material resources, explaining and justifying their uneven distribution.

Like language ideologies, economic moralities encompass the conscious
and unconscious. Speakers may draw on them in conversation with varying
degrees of awareness. Economic moralities may be located in explicit pro-
nouncements of virtue or tacitly communicated through talk explaining
acts of giving, taking, and sharing. Speakers who *describe* acts of exchange
simultaneously *prescribe* how material circulation ought to take place,
offering explanations for their actions and evaluating others' behavior. As
they align with or distance themselves from the individuals and acts
they describe, speakers situate themselves relative to others in political-
economic hierarchies.

My analysis of economic moralities builds on scholarship in economic
anthropology, on what E. P. Thompson (1971) and James Scott (1976) named
the "moral economy" more than fifty years ago. While seminal works on
"moral economy" defined the concept in opposition to the (a/immoral) market economy, more recent anthropological research has focused on the ways
moral orders shape all forms of economic practice. Examinations of moral
logics that animate economic processes in banks, businesses, and state governments have highlighted the multiplicity of ethical positions that coexist
in even the most neoliberal capitalist systems (Leins 2018; Bear 2015; Muehlebach 2012).

The normative positions that I characterize here as economic moralities
could also be (and have elsewhere been) analyzed as examples of moral economy. But I suggest that the heuristic value of inverting the focus of Thompson and Scott's now classic concept is twofold. First, it reminds us that
moral-economic positions are always multiple and contested, subjective and
shifting. Rather than an object out in the world, as we often (falsely) imagine
"the economy" to be (Murphy 2017), thinking in terms of economic *morali-*

*ties* urges us to think about how economic processes emerge from everyday negotiations of normative positions, to highlight the material consequences of even fleeting moral stances and vice versa (see Zuckerman 2020). Second, directing our attention to moralities rather than economies helps us avoid inadvertently reproducing dichotomous portrayals of "moral economies" as opposed to some "real" or unmarked economy. Instead, it invites a cross-scalar analysis of the ways that social actors alternate between diverse moral positions, reproducing economic practices across contexts and scales.

I approach material circulation and the speech acts that mediate it as integrated semiotic processes, using the idea of "language materiality" (Shankar and Cavanaugh 2012) to draw attention to the mutual imbrication of linguistic and material practices. Shankar and Cavanaugh define language materiality as a field of inquiry focused on "both the materiality of language, as well as how the language and material may interact to create meaning and value" (2012, 355). Examination of economic moralities orients our analysis to the metapragmatic talk that mediates the redistribution of resources writ large, allowing us to analyze, side by side, the moral logics that mediate acts of food sharing, gift giving, and monetary forms of support. Focusing on "moral metalanguage"—that is, reflexive characterizations "embedded in the formal properties of transactions" (Keane 2008, 33) that mediate everyday acts of exchange (like snack sharing)—as iterations of economic moralities, we can trace links between families' "ordinary ethics" (Lambek 2010; Das 2015; Kremer-Sadlik 2019) and moral discourses that shape entire societies' "cultures of circulation" (Lee and LiPuma 2002).

Linguistic anthropologists have investigated the semiotic processes through which speakers link events across time and space, using the term "interdiscursivity" (Agha and Wortham 2005) to describe connections between stretches of language (discourse), whether written or spoken. Focusing on interdiscursive links forged through economic moralities foregrounds (otherwise obscured) articulations between scales of redistribution. In directing Aïda's attention at the moral-economic logic of the social security system, the other Senegalese adults oriented themselves toward the moral priorities of the French state. They thus marked the limits of their sense of moral-economic solidarity with other Africans in France, distinguishing themselves as integrated by distancing themselves from les fraudeurs. Shifting between moral-economic stances, the speakers positioned themselves first as Senegalese, unified by notions of teranga and in their criticism of anonymous social relations in France, then as *integrated* immigrants in France, familiar (and importantly, compliant with) French state bureaucracy. This shift in moral-economic stance entailed a scale-making project, by which speakers adjusted their moral expectations to the functioning of the national solidarity system.

Economic moralities link forms of language materiality across scales. These scales, Carr and Lempert argue, are semiotic achievements, "not given but made—and rather laboriously so" (2016, 3). That is, the French social se-curity system, like systems of rank-based redistribution in Senegal and its diaspora, depends upon the semiotic work of scale-making to reproduce the scale, maintain its functioning, and the legitimacy participants assume it to have. The functioning of France's social-welfare system depends on a critical mass of the population compliant with the system who would condemn acts of "cheating." Interpersonal reciprocity in Senegal, meanwhile, depends on highly codified, if often contested, moral ideas about who should "feed" or otherwise support whom (and the threat of gossip and criticism if one falls short of these ideals).

Carr and Lempert point out, further, that "there are no ideologically neu-tral scales" (2016, 3). All acts of scale-making do so from a specific vantage point, such that the "people and institutions that come out 'on top' of scalar exercises often reinforce the distinctions that so ordained them" (2016, 3). Ex-amining interactions like the one that opened this chapter, in which speak-ers shift between economic moralities, reveals emic rankings of systems of exchange, shedding light on the ways social stratification is reproduced and transformed as individuals draw on and respond to diverse moral stances. Like all values, economic moralities are bound up with processes of hierar-chical ordering. In the words of French anthropologist Louis Dumont, "to adopt a value is to introduce hierarchy" (1980 [1969], 20).

Although acceptance of French bureaucracy does not appear to be a par-ticularly moral stance, the French state imposes specific forms of economic solidarity, the conditions of belonging explicitly organized according to spe-cific moral logics. Filtered through anonymous bureaucracy (Herzfeld 1992; Hull 2012), however, the economic logics of the "modern" state purport to be divested of morality. The economic moralities of so-called "modern" socie-ties are, furthermore, premised on comparison to the values of "traditional" or otherwise "non-modern" groups. Economic moralities in the "modern" French state are founded on a public/private distinction and the expectation that economics are (or should ideally be) separate from the private (especially religious) beliefs and values of any individual or family. This division, essential to state functioning, is underpinned by an evolutionary narrative, which claims that a "Great Transformation" (Polanyi 1944) took place as exchange shifted "from socially embedded to disembedded and abstracted economic forms" (Maurer 2006, 15). This notion of the economy as a space (that ought to be) inhabited by "rational" economic actors is rooted in the Enlightenment project of filtering ethics out of economics, to make this latter a "rational" science, fit for the public sphere.

These discourses simultaneously distance the strategic calculations of "homo economicus" from morally charged relations of family, love, and care (Cole 2014; Coe 2013; Zelizer 1985). Modern assumptions that a division exists between economic and ethical spheres are not neutral characterizations, but represent a particular moral stance, linked to hierarchical configurations. The supposition that market economies are not bound up with morality is a basic premise of the "moral narrative of modernity" (Keane 2013), which reproduces inequalities that are crucial to global capitalism (Keane 2013, 2007; Asad 2003; Austen 1993; Maurer 2006). Bruno Latour argues that a separation between economics and morality requires the social work of "purification." He reminds us that if "the adjective 'modern' designates a new regime, an acceleration, a rupture, a revolution in time," it simultaneously defines "by contrast, an archaic and stable past" (Latour 1993, 10). The modern narrative "involves winners and losers," in that it situates modernity "within a normative, and often desire-saturated, view of history" (Keane 2007, 83; 2013, 160).

According to modern economic moralities, the emancipated subject should not be indebted to extended kin or obliged to engage in the ("irrational") material exchanges through which they are enacted. Instead, modern kinship is organized according to bourgeois individualism, with the nuclear family as its basic socioeconomic unit. Polygyny and high fertility are deemed "traditional" familial arrangements. Children's value in a modern family is not calculated in the economic terms of household labor or the eventual promise of filial piety, but in terms of affective, sentimental value (Zelizer 1985). Moral narratives of modernity produce a "largely tacit set of expectations about what a modern, progressive person, subject, and citizen, should be" (Keane 2013, 160). The failure to embody these characteristics is treated as "an ethical failing" that poses a threat to individuals and entire societies, as in the "danger that headcovering seems to pose to the French" (Keane 2013, 161).

Drawing together diverse moral logics under the analytic of economic moralities underscores the ways that "modern" economic logics, which purport to be divested of moral subjectivity, naturalize evolutionary ideologies that reinforce inequalities between Africans and Europeans, as well as between (lower-class) "immigrants" and successfully "integrated" foreigners. These moral ideologies orient processes of scale-making and the economic practices they encourage and denounce, marking certain acts of exchange (like informally selling products) and engagement with certain types of "economy" (like the informal economy, or "black market") indexical of one's failure to integrate.

When written into law and socialized through state education and immigration systems, economic moralities become difficult to recognize as moral positions at all, such that the legitimacy of national scales of redistribution appears obvious. Yet redistributive scales at the national level require reproduction in social actors' everyday lives. They depend on the ways that people perceive and engage with state laws, which laws they view as true obligations, and which are mere formalities that "people like us" do not (have to) follow. Without formal institutional backing, (how) do transnational Senegalese families reproduce systems of rank-based redistribution? Some version of this question is at the root of much literature on remittances and transnational connections, asking whether (and if so, how) children raised in the diaspora grow to maintain transnational affective and economic relations with relatives in their parents' countries of origin. I suggest that to make sense of the ways that migrants' children understand and engage with economic moralities, we must look to everyday forms of material exchange, especially food sharing, through which children in Senegalese families come to understand material rights and responsibilities more broadly. The following section examines the reproduction of economic moralities that underpin rank-based redistribution in Senegalese families, focusing on the ways that speakers draw monetary exchange into analogous relation with practices of food sharing, through explicit language and more tacit means.

### Food, Money, and Morals

Aïda's description of teranga, which concluded with a brief reference to solidarity as illustrated through invitations to eat, makes reference to a well-worn metaphor in Africa likening the act of food sharing to other forms of material (and monetary) exchange. Across the African continent (and beyond— see Berman 2019) speakers draw explicit parallels between acts of food sharing and virtuous solidarity in monetary terms (Osseo-Asare 2005; Shipton 2007; Ferguson 2006; Buggenhagen 2012; Yount-André and Zembe 2023), laminating the economic moralities that organize the circulation of food and money. In semiotic language, these moral narratives create similarity—an iconic relation—across material domains, forging (interdiscursive) links across contexts that work to shape material practices. Feeding others is said to demonstrate generosity and largesse, taking up the moral behavior and material responsibilities of a high-ranked benefactor. Sharing food is a means of supporting dependents and investing in "wealth in people" (Guyer and Eno Belinga 1995; Bledsoe 1980; Kusimba, 2020), which connects individuals in networks of interdependency. Exchanges of food may provide the foundation for other forms of material exchange, such as monetary support or gifts (Riesman 1992; Bledsoe 1990; Shipton 2007; Piot 1999; Ferguson 2015).

In Senegal, anyone present at mealtime is invited to "*kaay lekk*" (come eat) at the communal dish. Impromptu guests, even those who arrive after a

Figure 6. Eating around a communal dish in Dakar. The circular form makes it possible to squeeze in more guests even after the meal has begun. Photo: Yount 2011.

meal has begun, can always be squeezed in, the circular form of a dish of rice and sauce infinitely divisible. Senegalese say that anyone, even passersby, who observe you while eating should be invited to come eat. Practically speaking, when people eat in the privacy of their homes, the number of passersby is relatively few, limited to a regular handful of neighbors and relatives. On the days of weddings and baby-naming ceremonies, however, guests do spill out into the road, hosted on rented folding chairs under tents. At these events, hosts never know exactly how many people to expect and may prepare for many impromptu guests and passersby, be they well-wishers from the neighborhood or *griots* who saw an opportunity to make some money singing the new couples' praises.

Applying Nancy Munn's (1992) action-focused theory of value to her fieldwork in Senegal, Beth Buggenhagen (2012) describes the ways women in Dakar strive to create relations of reciprocity by sharing meals and offering gifts of cloth at these events (see also Moya 2017). At feasts and family celebrations, she explains, individuals worked to extend "the rights and obligations of kin to non-kin and thereby enlarged themselves in space and time" (2012, 154). Speakers describe food sharing as a virtuous means of circulating wealth and use food sharing as a metaphor to describe and encourage wealth redistribution more broadly. This is particularly significant in African contexts in which the accumulation of capital is not unequivocally valued, but might rather be construed as morally suspect, the result of malevolent acts.

Jane Guyer argues that, among Africans, the store of wealth is often not an end in itself, but rather a "medium for relational life" (2004, 70). As such, individual accumulation can provoke negative reactions, including "the alienations of social relationships, theft, witchcraft accusations, or magical attack" (Newell 2012, 4). Newell explains that, in Côte d'Ivoire, "any dramatic increase in wealth was evidence to people's friends and family members that they were not fulfilling their social obligations to share income" (2012, 4). The notion that, in order to avoid money's corrupting qualities, wealth must circulate constantly is a theme throughout the Africanist ethnographic record (Geschiere 1997; Newell 2012; Buggenhagen 2012). The accumulation of wealth in the absence of circulation, or, in the alimentary metaphor, eating without sharing, is thus potentially sinister. James Ferguson points out that, in Africa, eating is widely associated "with both political domination and sorcery" (2006, 75). He explains that Bayart's concept of "la politique du ventre (the politics of the belly)," is particularly salient within this moral cosmology, according to which the corporeal accumulation of wealth can signify nefarious power obtained through witchcraft.

Senegalese describe eating alone as selfish and even dangerous. Children are told to share their food with anyone present and to never eat in the street, to avoid inciting onlookers' jealousy. Such public consumption could expose them to harmful spirits (*jinne*), such that they might fall victim to the "evil eye" (*cat*—Gamble 1957, 75). In parables and everyday discussions, the failure to share food due to inattentiveness or, worse, deliberate deception is treated as an example, par excellence, of greed. The Senegalese play "L'os de Mor Lam," for example, describes the selfish Mor Lam, who waits impatiently for his wife to cook him a beef shank. Rather than share the meaty and marrow-filled bone with the unexpected guests who arrive at mealtime, he chooses to fake his own death. As playwright Birago Diop (1977) states in the play's introduction, Mor Lam was "his own prisoner, without generosity . . . He dies" (ellipsis in original).

The message that selfishness can result in social death is also directed at children in Senegal. A fourth-grade reading manual published by the Senegalese Ministry of Education includes a story titled "L'avare et le pique-assiette" (The Miser and the "Moocher," literally "the meal thief"—Bocoum, Mbengue, and Mododi 1997, 68). It tells of a couple of misers, husband and wife, who never hosted guests and lived "like foreigners within the village" (Bocoum, Mbengue, and Mododi 1997, 68), and a moocher, who went from house to house at mealtime, shamelessly arriving just before the meal was served and leaving afterward. The story begins as the moocher finds his way to the misers' home at mealtime. When the miserly wife finishes cooking, she leaves her husband to deal with the moocher, hides in the kitchen to eat alone, and then leaves the house. Like Mor Lam, the miserly husband in this story also decides to fake his own death, to free himself from the unwanted presence of his mealtime guest. When the miser was suddenly "resurrected," at the moment of being lowered into his grave, he said only, "I was hungry, and this man kept me from eating" (69).

The story leaves the students with a question. Which of the two committed a worse crime? An Aristotelian puzzle of ethics, virtue must be sought in the middle-path between the moocher's excess and the misers' insufficiency. It is important to note, here, that it is not just the moocher (like the welfare queen) who is portrayed as potentially to blame. The misers, who kept to themselves, are also presented as at fault in this children's story, morally suspect, not only for their refusal to invite the guest to eat but also because they acted "like foreigners" in their village. The avoidance of invitations is treated here as paramount to a desire to avoid sharing. Hiding alone in the kitchen to eat, the miserly wife embodied a stereotype of selfish greed, resources amassed but not redistributed.

The social pressure to share resources in Senegal, so intense that it brings characters in fables to fake their own deaths, is enacted in moments of food sharing and (metapragmatically) discussed through the metaphor of food. Selective solidarity, although practically inevitable for anyone with limited resources, is also unspeakable. Avoidance of situations where one might be expected to share is itself treated as morally suspect, tantamount to refusing to share.

### Political Economies of Sharing Food

Offering food to impromptu guests at mealtime, emblematic of Senegalese teranga (hospitality), is an example that speakers in Senegal and its diaspora contrast broadly with the practices of Europeans or white people (tubabs). As one man from Dakar put it, if you go to a European's home at mealtime, "he'll give you a newspaper to read, he won't call you to come eat." This characterization erases, of course, all the contexts across Europe in which hospitality is central to social relations (see Herzfeld 1980, 2012). But the question of whether one would invite an unplanned guest at mealtime speaks to broader divisions in expectations of food sharing, which came to public attention in 2022 with a viral thread known as #Swedengate. A Reddit user described being over at a Swedish friend's home at mealtime, and, when the friend was called to dinner by his mother, "He told me to WAIT in his room while they ate." Internet users around the world expressed shock and dismay, recounting examples that illustrated how obligatory sharing food with guests is in their cultures.

News sources that picked up the story noted that criticism for the Swedes came, especially, from people from countries in the "so-called Global South" (Habib and Gharib 2022).[3] Reacting to the event, scholar of food studies Krisnendu Ray noted that while hospitality exists in all cultures, in some groups, the moral imperative to feed others is stronger, something he attributed to proximity to poverty and famine, the "memory of hunger [creating] pressure to be hospitable" (cited in Habib and Gharib 2022). I use this example to contextualize the Franco-Senegalese case, not to suggest that some fundamental "cultural" difference divides global opinions on hospitality but, rather, to underscore the ways political-economic context articulates with social norms of sharing food.

The places in the world where people live in close proximity to famine, or have a "memory of hunger," are predominantly (although not exclusively) formerly colonized nations. Famine, as Amartya Sen (1981) demonstrated, is often not caused by a lack of food available but is the result of political-economic inequalities and inadequate distribution in a capitalist system in which inflation and stagnating wages mean that (rural, poor, non-white) populations face starvation, even when there is no shortfall in food production. In West Africa, the archeological record indicates that famine and long-term food insecurity were consequences of European colonialism, which "undermin[ed] the ability of many Africans to feed themselves" (Logan 2016, 519). Overexploited and structurally adjusted, after decades of austerity measures, formerly colonized nations (where feeding guests appears most vital), often lack robust national healthcare or social welfare systems to protect those in need.

Internet users and scholars who defended the Swedish position suggested that the practice of not inviting child-guests stems from hosts' desire to avoid interfering with the other family's dinner plans and a mutual desire to avoid being (or making someone feel like) a burden. The act of feeding a guest is thought to create a debt or obligation. This, of course, is precisely why people in places like Senegal (and elsewhere in Africa—see Piot 1999; Ferguson 2013, 2015) feed guests and make gifts of food, to start in motion an exchange of hospitality and forge social bonds through debts exchanged and never fully repaid. In Sweden, however, scholars and casual observers both describe a desire to avoid debt among families. "If your children eat at my place a lot," Swedish food historian Richard Tellström explained, "then you will be in debt to me, and that should be avoided because it is bad for our relationship as adults" (Ledel 2022). Anthropologist Gustav Peebles (2022) explained that Swedes see debt as limiting personal freedom. In this moral-economic logic, it is preferable to avoid interpersonal debts and let the "anonymous state to hold the tethers of debt," distributing resources "'rationally' instead of via patronage" (Peebles 2022).

In Senegal, avoiding interpersonal debts is nether realistic nor venerable and the state's redistributive function has been depleted by decades of austerity measures. Swedish social preferences for avoiding interpersonal debts through food sharing exist, of course, within a notoriously robust national social welfare system. Herein lies a crucial difference. Proximity to poverty may well encourage generosity, but social norms about sharing resources are also bound up with ideas about whose responsibility it is to care for those in need, itself contingent on what systems of solidarity are available and what consequences (legal, financial, mystic) are imagined to befall those who fail to redistribute fairly.

Food sharing does not, of course, vary in any direct or predictable way with the economic and redistributive systems of a given country or culture. But they are entangled. I suggest that the ways we socialize children into food sharing practices reflects (and creates) our perceived positions in the economic systems and distributive mechanisms available in the place(s) we live.

Moral narratives surrounding food sharing matter because they link the language materiality of everyday moments of commensality between children and caregivers to relations of material exchange that extend beyond the household. Mealtime everywhere is a site for socialization into the moral expectations of a given society (Pan, Perlmann, and Snow 1999; Blum-Kulka 1997). Moral instruction is affective and embodied, a fundamentally social process (Ochs and Izquierdo 2010). It depends on a child's capacity to enter into joint attention with other people and to respond to social engagement and prompting (Keane 2016). As a daily form of material exchange, which results in pleasure and shared gratification (but also conflict and frustration), food sharing is a key moment in the reproduction of economic moralities. People remember lessons that mediate their access to food, bound up with embodied experiences of both hunger and belonging. Co-commensals negotiate self-interest and collective entitlement, autonomy and interdependence, through mealtime interaction (Fischler and Masson 2008; Paugh and Izquierdo 2009; Anving and Sellerberg 2010; Karrebaek 2012).

French anthropologist Jacquline Rabain showed how Senegalese caregivers link people relationally through talk surrounding food (1979). Rabain's transcripts from Wolof villages fifty years ago resemble ritualized exchanges urging children to share food that I observe still today in Dakar and its diaspora: "Who gave you [that cookie]?" Rabain quotes a father asking two-year-old NDeri, noting his focus on *who*, not what or how much the child had (1979, 68). The child's response (*Mère*) was followed by a question, "You won't give me any?" (Tu ne me donnes pas?). In another example, an old woman teased a child about food the researcher had brought, saying, "Where is my portion of what Jacqueline brought you?" (1979, 65). Showing how caregivers collaborated to urge children to willingly share food, Rabain argues that food functioned as a "mode of learning exchange" in Wolof society, socializing children into a highly codified system of practices organized according to gender, age, and caste.

As children learn to share food, they develop the language skills to navigate these (and other) acts of material exchange. Even in places where indiscriminately sharing food is socially valued, people manage to find ways to "keep while giving" (see Weiner 1992). Bambi Schieffelin (1990) described how children in Papua New Guinea learned to competently share through repeated linguistic routines of teasing, shaming, and direct instruction surrounding food sharing. Her study on Kaluli children importantly showed how, in learning to share food, children also learn culturally appropriate ways to *avoid* sharing. More recently, Elise Berman theorized how children in the Marshall Islands learn how to share food in ways that "produce" aged positions, sometimes flagrantly transgressing social expectations to share, something allowed of children, because "children have no shame" (Berman 2019, 4). Immaturity, embodied in the transgression of social rules about sharing food, allows children to do things adults cannot, playing a key role in "family economic transactions and social relationships" (2019, 86).

There are not many socially appropriate ways to avoid sharing food in Senegal. When a child is seen dividing up bits of bread, cake, chips, or candy, a circle of extended hands emerges around them. Children tug at their shirts, repeating "*May ma, may ma*" (give me some) to demand their portion. The right to redistribute is usually reserved for those children who are "big" enough (in age and maturity) to diligently divvy up the snack. Even so, children develop a sense for the ways the place and time that one chooses to eat a snack can impact the amount they have left for themselves, in the end. Navigating circles of requests, children develop a sense for how and when crowds of askers may be avoided and when it is impossible to discreetly limit the portions one must dole out.

## Contrasting Registers of Redistribution

Beyond the explicit language of morals in narratives that treat food sharing as indexical of economic solidarity, economic moralities draw acts of material circulation into analogous relation through more tacit means, as well, via the linguistic and semiotic practices used to mediate material exchange. These interdiscursive links connect children's everyday acts of food sharing to adults' practices of rank-based redistribution. To make sense of how this happens, we must return to Irvine's observations about the verbal and semiotic registers[4] speakers draw on in unfolding interactions to establish asymmetrical but complementary relations, which organize language and material exchange.

In her seminal work on Wolof language ideologies, Irvine (1974, 1989, 2001) revealed the ways that speakers in Senegal draw on contrasting verbal registers to establish unequal positions of rank, which mediate the circulation of material resources. She identified an axis of contrast that Senegalese villagers described as distinguishing the speaking styles of members of high- and low-ranking hereditary occupational orders (commonly glossed as castes). She notes that Senegalese represented "griot speech" (*waxu gewël*) as impulsive and hyperbolic, whereas they described "noble speech" (*waxu géer*) as a laconic, terse way of speaking. Irvine then revealed that Senegalese villagers regularly took up speaking styles reflexively associated with caste in order to mark subtler differences of rank (Irvine 1989, 2001). For instance, a noble might use "a 'griotlike' style of speaking when addressing a noble kinsman from whom he or she wants to ask a favor" (Irvine 1990, 136). Griot and noble speech, Irvine argues, "invoke a kind of metaphor of high and low ranks" that can be used to "define (in this case) an act of petitioning and to make the petition persuasive" (136).

Long before children are expected to provide or petition monetary support, they competently respond to moral metalanguages of exchange that underpin rank-based redistribution in acts of snack sharing. Elsewhere, I have analyzed in detail how two siblings in Dakar drew upon semiotic styles that reflected noble and griot speech registers (Yount-André 2016). Drawing on these contrasting registers, the children invoked a shared language ideology that provided a metapragmatic characterization of the event at hand and the relative ranks of the two children, unequal in terms of age and gender. The children organized the redistribution of their chips without explicit discussion, drawing on verbal and embodied registers that adults in Senegal use to negotiate offerings of monetary support between differently ranked individuals.

Siblings Fatou (age nine) and Karim (age four) often divided up gifts of food brought by adults who were visiting the house without dispute or even discussion. But when I offered each child an identical snack of chips and juice, my gifts provoked a lengthy redistribution process. When they received equivalent portions, they piled all the food together on the older sister Fatou's lap. After a slight squabble in which one bag was ripped open, Fatou directed her younger brother to pick up the chips spilled on the chair, and finally gave him a portion of the chips. Whereas Senegalese caregivers might hand gifts of snacks over to one child who would divvy up the food among all children present or transfer it to another child to distribute, I had (inadvertently) allocated the snacks based on what Paugh and Izquierdo (2009, 191) call the "moral ideology of equality between siblings," which prevails in middle-class America. According to this cultural logic, once equal or at least "fair" portions were achieved, the snacks could have been eaten. Instead, the chips continued changing hands for nearly two minutes after I passed them out. Karim handed his juice and chips over to his older sister, ultimately leaving the interaction with only a torn bag splayed open on his palms, covered in chips collected from the spill. By pooling and asymmetrically redistributing their resources, the siblings cooperated to achieve the unequal social positions that organize relations of rank-based redistribution in Senegal.

Faced with material conditions that positioned them as equals, the siblings took up contrasting communicative styles, assuming asymmetrical positions even before they pooled their resources. As soon as I pulled the snacks out of my bag, Karim's speech became high-pitched, loud, fast, and emotionally charged, vocal qualities characteristic of griots and other relatively low-ranked speakers. This contrasted sharply with his older sister's smiling but terse thanks for the gifts. If Fatou had delivered her thanks in a high-pitched and energetic fashion like her brother, the interaction might have ended there. My role would have been that of an older sibling who evenly distributed the food among the children.

But with her calm demeaner, Fatou made a bid at another interpretation: I was *not* their older sibling, but an adult who had brought gifts of food from outside (*sarice*), and whose role was thus to transfer the resources to the children but not to divvy them up. She took up a verbal register and embodied presence that highlighted her status as the eldest child, indirectly indexing her right to redistribute the snacks (which now required that her brother hand the chips in his possession over to her).

Karim thanked me excitedly, dancing around the room and happily stuffing chips into his mouth. Praising me for being "nice," the boy treated me (for that moment) as his direct benefactor. Fatou, meanwhile, sat in silence, anchored in her chair, visibly waiting to open her chips. Karim's frenetic movements, dance steps, and antics of impulsively gobbling chips all correspond with Irvine's descriptions of the physical movements Senegalese villagers associated with griots. Whereas Fatou sat motionless, embodying the physical behaviors of a high-ranking patron at public event. The soft, low tones of her voice contrasted with the loud shrillness of her younger brother's verbal style in this interaction. Juxtaposed with his sister's behaviors in ways that echo the asymmetrical roles Senegalese adults embody through noble and griot registers, Karim's hyperactivity and high pitch appears to index his low-status position as the younger sibling.

These contrasting verbal registers may be seen more broadly in moments of snack sharing among children in Senegal. Among children and adults alike, the act of redistributing resources itself presupposes and creates unequal relations between giver and receiver. When a circle of children emerges around a child who is redistributing bits of their snack, the low-ranked (in this event, at least) askers embody the volume, excited movements, and repeated requests of griots. The (high-ranked) distributor, meanwhile, rests still and silent, face screwed up in concentration, trying to make equal pieces that will satisfy their friends and simultaneously keep some for themselves.

## Economic Moralities Across Contexts and Scales

If recent critiques of scholarship on moral economy concur that the term has been used to describe such vastly diverse contexts that it has lost analytic traction (Fassin 2009; Hann 2018; Carrier 2018), the capacious notion of economic moralities proposed here does not at first appear to arrange things at all. Where these critics proposed to "clean up" the term with a more precise definition of what might "count" as a moral economy, I propose a somewhat different tack. Rather than focus on morals embedded in economic systems, reliant on scholars' etic definitions of "moral economy," the inversion of this classic concept I propose here directs our attention toward the ways economic processes are achieved through everyday negotiations of morality.

Speakers draw on economic moralities in everyday interactions, establishing and (re)negotiating the moral frames they use to make sense of acts of material exchange. In the example of the chip sharing, this could be seen in the way the elder sister influenced the redistribution of the chips by using a terse, laconic speaking style. This verbal register tacitly called upon her younger brother to recognize her status as eldest (and thus her right to redistribute), compelling him finally to put all the food in her possession so that she might be the one to divvy it up. The contrasting semiotic registers that the children took up served to link the interaction, both in linguistic form and its material results, to interactions among Senegalese adults who use similar verbal registers to petition for and give monetary support. These language practices interdiscursively link acts of exchange across contexts and scales, asserting some sort of similarity (iconicity) between events to influence how the interactions unfold.

When speakers voice economic moralities, they use moral claims to "orient, compare, connect, and position" themselves relative to various social groups, carrying out scale-making projects (Carr and Lempert 2016) in their efforts to juggle moral priorities and achieve a favorable status in the various socioeconomic networks in which they take part. As speakers shift between moral priorities, they also shift between group alignments and belongings, moving between scales of solidarity. Attending to economic moralities urges us to take seriously the moral-economic processes achieved in the household between children and caregivers, to consider how they prepare the semiotic and material grounding for economic practices beyond the household.

## CHAPTER 3

## "Sometimes Too Generous":
## Reciprocity and Avoiding the Wrong Crowd

R ama Sy extended her fingers one by one as she listed the rules of eating around the communal dish: "You eat only what's in front of you, children wait to be served, they can't take meat from the center of the dish, the littlest has to hold the platter so that it doesn't turn." On weekends, she made deliberate efforts to familiarize her eleven- and nine-year-old with communal eating, organizing a weekly Senegalese meal with their relatives in and around Paris. Together, the adults who grew up in Dakar guided the children in the etiquette of sharing a communal meal, which would delight relatives in Senegal on the next trip back. "I just teach them, and then," Rama paused thoughtfully, "I don't know what it brings them." In any case, she concluded, "my children are generous." So generous, she continued, they could sometimes be "even a little *too* generous!" With equal parts annoyance and pride, Rama described how her son, Malik, "empties her refrigerator" to share with the "kids downstairs" in the courtyard of their apartment complex. She comically recounted the regularity with which arguments arose over his desire to take groceries from their apartment to redistribute outside.

If the previous chapter was about how speakers use economic moralities to position themselves in conversation, this chapter begins to explore how one's position shapes, in turn, the moral expectations that motivate exchange and value-laden interpretations of these acts in stories told afterward. In household conversations about the ways children share food, symbolic notions of position (one's status in hierarchies of class, race, migration trajectory) are entangled with position in a physical sense (the places one lives, visits, and shares food). Together these elements provide clues that allow children and adults in transnational families to understand and negotiate the economic moralities at play in a given context.

## The Place of Food Sharing:
## Contextualization Cues and Economic Moralities

Senegalese in Dakar and Paris alike treat acts of sharing food as textbook examples of hospitality (teranga) and generosity (*tabe*). They associate these virtues not only with morality, but also with status. Among children, sharing food is linked to maturity—being "big" in terms of age. Adults and children both perceive older children to be more willing to share and better able to divide food up equally (Yount-André 2016). For adults, sharing food demonstrates that one is "big" in status, hosting mealtime guests an index of material means and largesse (Buggenhagen 2012).

Speaking with Rama a few months into my fieldwork, I was familiar with adult migrants' accounts of their deliberate efforts to teach their children "Senegalese values" by teaching them to eat around a communal dish and urging them to systematically share their snacks with other children present. Beyond cooking and eating Senegalese food, parents specifically emphasized their efforts to teach their children to share food the way they had growing up in Dakar. Youth cited expectations to systematically redistribute their snacks as an illustration of how life in their homes was just like in Senegal (*comme au Sénégal*).

Notions of place were central to my participants' conceptions of the moral expectations that mediate food sharing, and economic moralities more broadly. The idea that in different geographic contexts people hold distinct ideas about how the resources should be redistributed appeared obvious in families with whom I worked, supported by well-worn stereotypes among Senegalese about the ways African notions of "solidarity" diverge from those of "tubabs" (white people), like those discussed in Chapter 2. Places, specifically Senegal and France, thus functioned as metonyms for idealized and opposed value systems. These presuppositions gave me a quick way to explain a basic premise of my research: moral expectations regarding the circulation of resources are multiple and sometimes contradictory. But dichotomous representations of morality in Africa versus Europe also mask subtle elements of context that shape the ways economic moralities emerge as relevant.

Examining how people interpret acts of exchange in unfolding interaction can show us how place coexists with questions of who is present, why participants are gathered, and how they mark the event through talk. Together, these elements make up a series of potentially relevant signs that frame the ways children and adults construe an event, making sense of what type of interaction is taking place and how to respond.

One need not be physically in Africa for "Senegal" to signal a certain type of interaction and the norms of exchange that accompany it. By organizing "Senegalese meals" in Paris, Rama's family intentionally used place to signal the conventions for sharing food they hoped would hold sway. For children, family gatherings around a platter of ceebu jën were rich with "contextualization cues" (Gumperz 1982) that helped them anticipate the sorts of food sharing that would take place. Long before the communal dish was served, adult voices speaking more Wolof than French would set the tone for the evening, providing children clues for the sorts of behaviors their parents would expect. For Malik, it would be difficult to sneak a premeal snack without offering a portion to each of his cousins. Spontaneously divvying up his treats, however, he knew could earn him praise from the adults, who were particularly oriented toward food sharing as a mark of precisely the sort of generosity they hoped to cultivate in their children.

Rama's declaration that her children were "even a little *too* generous" announced a departure from parents' usual tales of laboring to impart the virtue of teranga to their children in France. Rama's comment pointed instead to the potential risks associated with sharing. With this narrative twist, Rama shifted from characterizing herself as a virtuous Senegalese mother toward a more complex story of her struggles to navigate value-laden interpretations of her and her children's everyday behaviors in France.

### The Perils of Misplaced Generosity

Rama's story hung in tension with stereotypes of food sharing as unconditionally venerable, emphasizing the moral meaning of sharing to be contingent on context. With an exasperated laugh, she claimed that her children's snack sharing "drives her crazy" and simply "wears her out." After each confession of frustration, she offered information about where, how, and with whom Malik shares. These details outlined the stakes that Rama perceived to be at play in the spaces outside their apartment in Paris, hinting at her difficulties in bringing up preadolescents in France, where they were racial and religious minorities.

Place was key in Rama's narrative, not only in terms of their geographical position in France (where groceries were expensive and their belonging in question), but specifically the space of the common courtyard outside their apartment. Rama complained that her children constantly take groceries from "here" (their apartment) *downstairs* to share with children *outside*. "As soon as they get something," she explained, they immediately plan how to divvy it up downstairs, claiming ice cream bars for "this person, and that person, and that person" before the box is even opened. Speaking in the present tense, Rama described an ongoing struggle that regularly reaches a point at which she must put a stop to Malik's liberal redistribution, because she "[doesn't] buy groceries for everyone outside!"

The Sy family lived in a state-subsidized housing complex (HLM) in Paris's 19th arrondissement, an area known to have a high density of immigrant families. Although some public housing units in Paris are not readily distinguishable from the outside, theirs was a visually marked "*barre HLM*." These austere cement high rises, constructed *en masse* in the 1970s to house immigrant workers and their families, are now viewed as eyesores and are gradually being demolished in cities throughout France. Their architecture, arranged around a common courtyard, has become iconic of "les cités," housing projects that dominate France's impoverished suburbs (banlieues). In French media and public imagination, banlieues like Seine-Saint-Denis are regularly presented as ethnic enclaves, where immigrant parents raise delinquent children.

Towering over neighboring buildings (where residents pay three to four times more in rent), barre HLMs bring stereotypes of the banlieue into central Paris. In the halls of Rama and Malik's building, I regularly passed women in headscarves and men in the flowing *djellabas* and kufi caps emblematic of Muslims in France. The smell of cuuraay incense lingered in the hall after West African women in brightly printed wax fabrics left their apartments. On the rare occasions that I saw Rama burn cuuraay, she carefully put it out before the smell impregnated her clothes. This was one of many efforts she made to distance herself from stereotypes of "*bledards*," naïve immigrants said to act as if they had just arrived from the village, even if after many years in Paris. Derived from the Arabic word "*bled*," meaning country or village, in the French imagination "bledard" is linked to images of Muslim immigrants from former colonies, whose accented French and "traditional" clothing are assumed to be evidence of a failure to adapt to life in the metropole.

In conversation, Rama and her husband, Alpha, verbally distinguished themselves from their neighbors. They regularly mentioned that they both held master's degrees from francophone universities, noting that many immigrants in Paris still struggle to speak French. The couple took pleasure in recounting the luxury they enjoyed on trips to Dakar. Rama commented that, in France, people assume that their summer trips to the "bled" were characterized by hardship but, in fact, their quality of life was substantially better in Dakar than in their cramped Parisian apartment (cf. Bidet 2021). Each summer, they spent a couple weeks at Alpha's parents' spacious villa, which was equipped with all the modern amenities. Rama rolled her eyes saying that the Playstation at his grandparents' house may well be Malik's favorite part of going to Dakar.

While their working-class neighbors appeared to have no qualms displaying evidence of their country of origin or Muslim religion, Rama and Alpha diligently minded boundaries between their private lives and public forms of self-presentation, to align themselves with French ideals of immigrant "integration" described in Chapter 1. Rama described consciously dressing differently in her apartment than in public spaces in Paris. Although she often wore an ankle-length wax housedress while we chatted in her apartment, she always changed into jeans or another (in her words) "normal" pair of pants before leaving home, even if only to run brief errands. But the class distinctions that middle-class parents work so diligently to maintain become more difficult to police as their children get old enough to venture into the neighborhood alone.

Outside their apartment, it was harder for Rama to make sure that Malik avoided looking and sounding in ways that were associated with "second-generation immigrant" youth. North and West African youth (especially boys) who grow up in public housing complexes are often assumed to be prone to violence, delinquency, and drug use. These assumptions are bundled together in social types like *"mec de la cité"* (lit. a "guy from the cité") or "racaille" (lit. "trash" or "scum") or, more recently, someone with a *"wesh wesh"* style.[1] Tetreault (2015) explains that these labels bring to mind images of tough young men dressed in polyester track suits, their accented French and heavy use of slang associated with illicit activities and violence. Known for loitering *"dehors"* (outside) and claiming *"la rue"* (the street) as their domain, racaille are presumed to render public spaces dangerous (Tetreault 2015, 168).

Although Rama and Alpha had found an apartment they could afford in central Paris, far from Paris's most volatile banlieues, their residence in an HLM nonetheless brought them into close proximity with people who fit the stereotypes of bledard and racaille. To enter Rama and Malik's housing complex, visitors used the intercom to scroll through a list of residents' names, predominantly of North and West African origin. After the heavy lock on the front door clicked open, one passed through a dimly lit entryway and then through a metal gate, into a large courtyard enclosed by four fifteen-story buildings. Signs hung above basketball courts indicating the directions to buildings A through D. In the evenings, a group of young men congregated in the space between the front door and the metal gate, leaning against the cement wall or squatting on the steps to the courtyard. Absorbed in discussion or the rap music they played from their phones, they hardly seemed to notice those of us entering or leaving the apartment complex.

During my fieldwork, stigma surrounding "second-generation" immigrant youth took on new meaning in Malik's life, both due to his age and the historical moment during which he was entering adolescence. At eleven years old, Malik had just finished primary school. As his features gradually lost the soft roundness of childhood, the threat of being associated with unflattering images of young black men quickly became more tangible. At the start of the school year, Rama was particularly concerned that Malik might start off on the wrong foot with the teachers at his new middle school. Having taught in French public schools herself, she had seen how teachers who had previously struggled with difficult students could be quick to judge minority children, writing them off as troublemakers. "It starts at school," she explained, "teachers with prejudices about black kids. Then the kids are frustrated, they quit school and sell drugs." This, she asserted, was the plight of the "kids downstairs" who lingered in the entrance of their building.

During Malik's first week of school, a note from his teacher about a scuffle at school with a boy named Mohammed seemed to confirm her worst fears. Malik tried to reassure his mother, claiming that he had done nothing to provoke Mohammed's aggression and repeatedly assuring her that, in the future, he would be sure to "avoid the wrong crowd" (*éviter la mauvaise fréquentation*). From the eleven-year-old's mouth, this phrase rang of adult concerns, evidence of prior conversations in which Malik's parents had attempted to convey to him the risk of associating with youth who might prove to be bad influences.

For Malik, the transition to middle school had been accompanied by a significant change in his classmates. In Paris's less affluent arrondissements, like the 19th, the populations of public middle schools and high schools had a disproportionate number of children from immigrant households, many of whom lived in state-subsidized housing. Teachers were often wary of working at these schools, known for behavioral troubles. Despite the French motto of "*liberté, égalité, fraternité*" emblazed on all public school buildings, once children entered adolescence, public schools increasingly became spaces of forced segregation. As Malik navigated the new social space of middle school, his parents' admonishments reminded him that it was his responsibility to sort potential friends from those who were likely to get him into trouble.

After school, Malik had to continue carefully avoiding "the wrong crowd" in the common spaces of his apartment complex. His mother anxiously surveyed the movements of the "kids downstairs" in the entryway until she could sense the time of day when their numbers would swell from the harmless two or three in the afternoon, to a group of twelve or fifteen that spilled out into the courtyard as the evening light faded. Their persistent presence perturbed Rama, for whom these youth served as a reminder of omnipresent stereotypes about Black boys and the threat that her son might get caught up with delinquents and drug dealers.

Although Rama had never seen drugs being sold in the courtyard, the nightly scent of marijuana wafting from the corners of the courtyard led her to fear the worst. French films regularly feature images of cités as hubs for drug trafficking—spaces where the leaders recruit youth to do the dangerous footwork of making deliveries, under the premise that, if caught, as minors, their punishments would be less severe. But, in recent decades, penalties have stiffened for male juvenile delinquents, particularly for racial minorities (Terrio 2009). French law now allows prison sentences for minor infractions like loitering in public spaces of stairwells or the entrances to buildings (Ossman and Terrio 2006).

These legal penalties became increasingly harsh over a period of time when the notion of "immigrant delinquent" solidified as a social type in France. By 2005, when rioting overtook suburban areas outside cities throughout France, so-called "second-generation" youth became widely associated with the burning of cars and violent destruction of public property. When then Interior Minister Nicolas Sarkozy referred to the rioters as "racaille," while he was criticized for using the derogatory term in public address, it demonstrated the extent to which the trope had become normalized in the French language.

Ten years later, at the time of my fieldwork, fears of fundamentalist Islam were layered onto these pernicious images of minority youth. After gruesome attacks on Paris in January and again in November of 2015, city residents learned that the terrorists who had carried out the killings had been radicalized French nationals. In the days following these attacks, Parisians watched, on-edge, as images of the accused attackers—all of North or West African descent—circulated repeatedly in the media. After the November attacks, police raids in the banlieue of Seine-Saint-Denis reinforced the idea that les cités were breeding grounds for not only delinquent racaille but, furthermore, for Islamic fundamentalists. As stereotypes of minority youth were loaded with ever-more-malicious associations, for youth like Malik this meant that avoiding being grouped in this disparaging category was a high-stakes occupation that saturated their daily lives.

### Deictic Distance: Navigating Commensality and Contagion

For Rama, the threat of racaille was, quite literally, too close to home. Just entering or leaving their apartment complex drew Malik into close proximity with the youth who loitered near the gate. When he was younger, the spacious courtyard had seemed a luxury to Rama. Backyards are virtually nonexistent in Paris. The city's population density and high cost of rent make spaces where children can play rare. It still pleased Rama to watch her children meet their friends on the basketball court below their apartment, where she could lean out over their balcony to greet the other parents. But as Malik got older, the ways he used the communal space had shifted. He rarely played basketball beneath their window now, preferring to wander the courtyard with his friends into spaces out of their parents' field of vision.

When describing her frustration with her children's generosity, Rama used words that highlighted the distance that separated her from these acts of food sharing. She introduced her complaints by announcing that her children take her groceries "downstairs to give to the kids." She only used the word "friends" once to describe the children to whom Malik redistributed snacks. Instead, she called them simply "the kids downstairs" (*les gamins en bas*), or even the "people outside" (*les gens dehors*). In her story, each

mention of the recipients of Malik's benevolence was accompanied by spatial language that disassociated her from the sharing event.

Words like *here* and *there* are terms that linguists call "deictics" or "shifters": expressions whose meanings shift depending on the context of their use
(Hanks 1990; Silverstein 1976; Wortham 1996). Spatial deictics allow speakers
to locate themselves physically relative to the events they describe, situating
the storytelling event with respect to the narrative they recount. In Rama's
story, her repeated use of the spatial deictics *here* versus *downstairs* or *outside*
(the courtyard) served to divide up the social world of their apartment complex. As we sat upstairs, Rama gestured toward her refrigerator a few meters
away, referencing the snacks she bought for her children, not "everyone outside." The warmth of the apartment and Rama's hospitality materialized,
then, in aperitif snacks she had served when I arrived and provided a foil to
the cement courtyard below. "Outside" (dehors) was a space beyond her control, a territory informally claimed by racaille who linger there, in Rama's
narrative and in the French language more generally (see Tetreault 2015).

Rama's description also distinguished the courtyard of Malik's
childhood—a place of friendship and play—from the courtyard of his adolescence: a space filled with strangers he encountered outside his mother's
watchful gaze. At that moment in Malik's life, the courtyard could represent
either peril or play in Rama's eyes. But in recounting Malik's tendency to redistribute snacks outdoors, her focus was on the courtyard as a distant space
filled with unfamiliar youth. The idea that Malik shared his food there perturbed her more than the cost of the ice cream bars or the simple fact that he
had begun to venture into corners of the courtyard that she could not see.
Unlike mere physical proximity or a passing conversation, eating together
could provide the basis for friendship between Malik and the "kids downstairs," as Rama had called them, using the same term she used to ask me if
the youth who loitered in the entryway were already out when I had arrived.

Commensality, or the act of eating with others (Fischler 2011), is a means
through which people create and maintain social relations, but also transform and curtail them. Eating together can create similarity between co-
commensals, likened as members of the same social group (even if only
informally or briefly), while distinguishing them from others who were not
invited to take part. In many places, commensality is even said to generate
family relations. Janet Carsten (1995) tells us, for example, that Malays view
those who eat at the same hearth to acquire the same "blood" over time, even
if not otherwise biologically related.

Anthropologists like Marshall Sahlins (2013) call this the "consubstantial effect" of commensality. By eating the same food, co-commensals are thought to share the same substance or essence. True on a cellular level (the bodies of those who eat together are constructed, in part, from the same biological materials), in social life this effect is endowed with symbolic meaning through culturally specific narratives that surround acts of eating. Stories of kinship or friendship forged through food sharing guide our interpretations of co-commensals, allowing us to view those who eat together as being the same "type" of person, be it as friends or relatives, classmates, or people of similar background or class status.

For children, who often have little control over who joins them at the dinner table, sharing snacks is an important way to forge friendships (Berman 2014; Comoretto 2015). Swapping snacks and divvying up their food allows children to claim autonomy, independently weaving social connections and positioning themselves in the social hierarchies most relevant to their lives. It was commensality's potential to forge social relations that allowed Malik to see an unopened box of ice cream bars as social currency on the courtyard. This was also precisely what bothered Rama about these sharing events.

Commensality can also represent a threat of contagion. If directed at the wrong people, food's capacity to conjure connection could associate Malik with youth who would negatively influence his behavior. Unconvinced by his promises to "avoid the wrong crowd," Rama tried to limit his snack sharing, attempting to exert some control over the social relations he might forge in hidden corners of the courtyard. In her complaints that Malik could be "too generous," Rama expressed her fear that he was not yet equipped to engage in the selective solidarity that living in Paris required. Even in the lives of children, economic moralities are bound up with other moral priorities, many of which are not obviously related to the ways resources are distributed.

## Competing Moral Priorities

Rama's narrative highlighted the ways that expectations among Senegalese, that children systematically share their snacks, could sometimes prove ill-advised in Paris. Most of the Senegalese families I knew had some version of this story. One mother described having told her daughter to *stop* sharing food at preschool (*la maternelle*). During recess in France, children eat individually packaged snacks their parents pack, like madeleines or squeeze pouches of applesauce. In her first weeks of school, the girl had dutifully been divvying up her treat among her friends, leaving her with little more than crumbs. As her mother recounted the story to the hilarity of their relatives, the five-year-old grinned sheepishly, remembering her blunders in the first weeks of maternelle, two years prior. Her aunts, who had children of their own, immediately recognized how sharing too much could make a child appear naïve and foreign in France. Wiping tears of laughter from her eyes, one imagined aloud the girl's schoolmates thinking, "That Senegalese girl is really nice—easy to take advantage of!"

As common as stories of excess generosity proved to be among Senegalese families in Paris, they emerged only in specific contexts. Their humor required a sympathetic audience who could appreciate both the virtues of systematically sharing food and the pragmatic complications it presented in France. Even in Senegal, expectations that people be ready to share their food if others so much as notice them eating can sometimes prove onerous. These situations were often the subject of jokes about miserly adults' or naïve children's clumsy attempts to hide their food. Even people who have never left Senegal are often aware that Europeans do not share food as one might in Senegal. But the idea that a Senegalese person abroad go so far as to *discourage* their child from sharing could seem scandalous to those unaware of the undesirable social connotations of misplaced generosity. Among Africans in France, parents' suggestions that a child ought to limit their sharing could expose them to critique that they had "become European," raising their children to be "selfish tubabs." Even Rama encountered resistance when she recounted the above narrative.

I recorded Rama's story in the presence of her husband, Alpha, and his "cousin" Oumar (a childhood friend), who had dropped by their apartment before the children returned home from school. As Rama described how Malik's habit of sharing his afternoon snacks "wears [her] out," Oumar repeatedly chimed in, offering up an alternative moral evaluation. When she complained that her children's habits sometimes cause her to "freak out," Oumar protested, "that's sharing that they're learning!" Ignoring his comment, Rama continued to explain her frustrations. But Oumar persisted, speaking over her to clarify that this sharing is what they will later "continue with their family."

Although she remained calm and courteous, Rama's dismissals of Oumar's interjections became increasingly brusque, her annoyance apparent in her tone. She had little patience for his explanations that her children's snack sharing illustrated generosity, having herself enumerated these very points only moments before. Oumar's suggestion that the children's openhanded redistribution presages the generosity they would show their parents later in life, provided a subtle critique of the irritation Rama expressed about the sharing.

If Oumar had been Rama's elder, she may have simply fallen silent when he interjected with reminders of the virtues of food sharing. Instead, she resisted his moral interpretation of her story, denying him the floor each time he interrupted. At one point, she repeated the word "but" four times in a row to prevent him from finishing his thought. Oumar, the son of one of Alpha's father's friends, was not one of the relatives with whom they gathered weekly for Senegalese meals. According to Rama, he had a reputation for being a contrarian. He furthermore knew little about the difficulties of raising preteens in France, having sent his three-year-old son back to Senegal to live with his wife's family.

With his own child growing up in Dakar, Oumar could afford to focus on the moral meanings of food sharing most common there. Whereas Rama and Alpha were invested in equipping their children to satisfy expectations of "good children" among Senegalese relatives as well as authority figures in France, who held significant influence over their futures. Although he was still young, Malik's capacity to "avoid the wrong crowd" had serious implications for Rama and Alpha's class ambitions in France. A few critical missteps could call into question his parents' diligent efforts to demonstrate their integration into the French middle class.

In everyday acts like sharing a snack with a friend, Malik had to navigate prejudice against minority youth in France to avoid being grouped alongside stereotypes of delinquent youth in la cité. And yet, attempting to avoid sharing his food was not a safe option either, particularly given the emphasis that Senegalese place on openhanded redistribution of food as a sign of one's moral fiber. Children growing up in transnational Senegalese families in Paris must develop nuanced understandings of the ways that place is bound up with a number of other potentially relevant signs to frame interpretations of a given act of food sharing.

Questions of where, with whom, and in what context all work together to create an interpretive framework that allows participants to determine what sort of event is taking place and calibrate their expectations accordingly. But participants rarely have the benefit of a clear moral consensus before they share food or otherwise redistribute resources. Instead, multiple moral interpretations coexist and compete.

To resolve her struggle with Oumar over the moral meaning of her story, Rama returned to the message of her children's generosity with which she had begun. Stating that they were "just like that" (generous). She wondered aloud if it was a result of their upbringing, eating around the communal dish, or something they had inherited from her and her husband. Framing generosity as a family trait, Rama shifted back to a narrative that portrayed her as a moral Senegalese mother, who cultivated her children's virtuous behavior through mealtime socialization. She then urged me not to take her word for it but to ask Malik directly when he got home from school. "He'll tell you," she assured me.

### Similarity and Difference at Snack Time

To Rama's dismay, when the eleven-year-old returned home, he bluntly denied *ever* sharing snacks with other children in Paris. Confused, he stammered, "I think they all have enough to eat." His stunned mother reminded him of all the food he pilfered from their refrigerator. "You don't do that?" she persisted. "Maaliiik!" Rama drew out her son's name, her tone hanging between teasing and pleading. She reminded Malik of details about how he redistributes snacks until he reluctantly agreed that he *sometimes* takes a little food downstairs to share with his *friends*, minimizing the amount that he shared, he conceded begrudgingly, as though being reproached for this behavior. Although he had not been present when his mother described how he distributes food to the "kids downstairs," Malik emphasized the word "friends" as if he anticipated Rama's warning to avoid the wrong crowd. Regular scolding had made these snacks a sore subject for the boy, who had done all he could to avoid the topic entirely.

Malik's reluctance to admit to sharing in France contrasted starkly with his eagerness moments before when describing how he gives food to children who beg in the street in front of his grandmother's house in Senegal. Malik explained to me that on his annual trips to Dakar, every day at 4:00 p.m.,[2] his grandmother would give him money to go to the corner shop (*la boutique*). There, he would buy a pack of Biskrem cookies and a bottle of Gazelle pineapple soda. On his way home, Malik told me, he would offer a few cookies to the children begging in the street, before going inside to eat his snack.

Why did this story of distributing cookies in Dakar seem to Malik to be a more readily recognizable (or worthy of recounting) example of sharing?

Whether or not an act is "generous" is clearly subjective. But Rama's and Malik's contrasting stories suggest that whether an event even counts as "sharing" may also be a question of perspective. Rama's and Malik's accounts provide a lens into the ways economic moralities become relevant in real time, both in mundane acts of material exchange like a snack swap and, equally importantly, in the stories we tell to make sense of those events.

Malik's story of distributing snacks in Dakar resembled, in many ways, the exchanges in Paris that his mother had described. In both accounts, the boy handed out snacks, bankrolled by his (grand)parents, to children outside his own or his relatives' home. And yet, it seems obvious that offering food to beggars and giving an ice cream bar to a friend represent distinct types of events, which presume different social relations and give rise to divergent expectations regarding how the event should unfold and what should happen afterward.

On the one hand, Malik's story of giving in Senegal depicted an act of charity, *sarax* in Wolof. Almsgiving is the fourth pillar of Islam. In Dakar, child beggars called *talibés*, like those Malik described, are among the most common recipients of charitable gifts. Talibés are Muslim child-disciples, sent by their families (often from rural Senegal) to study the Qur'an with religious leaders in the capital. Once there, children as young as six or seven are routinely obliged to spend their days begging for money and food in Dakar's dusty streets, an activity that leaves them filthy. Their destitution is palpable in their dirt-powdered skin and their oversized clothing, faded and torn.

Charity is founded on an unequal relationship between giver and receiver. Talibés' abject poverty and pleas for spare change beg passersby to take up the role of benefactor. Often, on a daily basis, adults in Dakar give money and leftover food to talibés. Some households make arrangements with a specific child, who waits nearby as the family eats, ready to salvage whatever is left after the meal has been cleared. At Malik's grandmother's house, they gave leftover rice from their afternoon meal to a talibé whom Malik called "Little Lamine." Malik regularly mentioned Lamine in our discussions of his trips to Dakar, dismayed and intrigued by the plight of the child who roamed Dakar's dangerous streets with no adult supervision.

Like fasting during the month of Ramadan or praying five times daily, children are not yet expected to give offerings of sarax. Yet, the talibés who line the thoroughfares of every neighborhood in Dakar make sarax a highly visible part of children's daily lives. Even young children in Senegal are able to explain the moral logic behind sarax. Nine-year-old Arame, for example, told me that it is important to give money to people who cannot repay you, because the poor person will give you a blessing in return. Explaining that the recipient would utter, "May Allah give you even more money in return," in her own words Arame articulated Bonhomme and Bondaz's observation that almsgiving "cannot be reduced to a sporadic transfer between a giver and a receiver" (2017, 346), but always presumes God to be an invisible third party in a triangular form of gift exchange.

Rama's story, on the other hand, described more closely an expectation of what anthropologists would call "reciprocity." Unlike charity, reciprocity designates a mutual form of exchange, in which participants (ideally) alternate between the roles of giver and receiver. These roles may alternate on a short timescale, like dinner guests who return an invitation to cement the friendship. Or they may shift over the course of one's life, like intergenerational cooperation in families, in which children may be expected to feed their elders and the next generation, but only once they are grown. The timing of a return gift reflects the type of relationship participants share and can create a sense of closeness or distance.

Key to the reciprocal giving and taking of food, like other transactions that Sahlins referred to as "generalized reciprocity," is the idea that the gift is "putatively altruistic" (1972, 193). For an exchange to feel like reciprocity, one cannot be too overtly focused on an eventual return. As Marcel Mauss famously pointed out, however, gifts are never totally disinterested. But we learn to act as if they are.

Mauss described gifts as functioning according to a tripartite structure, in which people feel an obligation to give, receive, and reciprocate. But to create friendship through reciprocity, especially among peers, participants work to minimize this tacit obligation, erasing the instrumentality of the relationship and the back-and-forth exchange of social debts. In Senegal and France alike, givers often avoid bringing up the possibility of a return at the moment of doing someone a favor. Givers minimize the burden associated with giving to put recipients at ease. This social work is written into everyday politeness formulas: in French, "*de rien*" is the standard response to "*merci*." Meaning literally "of nothing," this phrase minimizes the effort required to offer assistance, highlighting the gift as freely given.

When the alternating asymmetries of reciprocity become habitual, gifts can seem so routine they appear invisible. Until, of course, someone begins to feel that the giving and taking no longer sufficiently even out and calls for a reevaluation of the relationship. For Malik, engaged in the tricky process of friendship-building amid the volatile social terrain of adolescence, exchanges of snacks with other children in the courtyard represented normal, everyday gestures of friendship. He spoke of his acts as if they were insignificant and easily forgotten, certainly not worth telling in the presence of a foreign anthropologist and her audio recorder.

Although his parents worked hard to distinguish themselves from their neighbors, when Malik spoke about his friends in the courtyard, most salient were their commonalities. They lived in the same apartment complex and went to the same school. They all wore jeans and T-shirts or athletic gear. While some of their parents had audible accents, the children all spoke the Parisian French of (lower) middle-class youth. The food they shared reinforced their similarities. Identical, individually packaged snacks passed from one child's hand to another, which they ate together, side by side.

In urging him to recount his own generosity, Rama put Malik in an awkward spot. Telling the story she requested would once again open him to his mother's warnings about which youth to avoid. It would furthermore require him to forgo humility, emphasizing only his end of these give-and-take relations. This characterization of their everyday exchanges would distinguish him from his peers, calling into question their similarity and the equality of the social connections he cultivated through commensality.

But not all instances of food sharing are examples of commensality. Not all gifts entail expectations of a return. When gift recipients are unable to later assume the role of giver, uneven exchanges highlight *differences* between participants, rather than similarities. This was obvious in Malik's account of feeding beggar children in Dakar, who would obviously never return his gifts of food. Rather, Malik's offering would likely inspire more requests from talibés, who came to expect the child's generosity around four o'clock. Unlike the commensality he shared with his friends in Paris, in Dakar, Malik physically distanced himself from the talibés after distributing cookies. The cool calm of his grandparents' tiled kitchen, where Malik ate the rest of cookies in privacy, marked the material gulf that separated his life from the experiences of the talibés forced to beg and eat under Dakar's punishing sun.

### Between Stigma and Prestige

Taken side by side, Rama and Malik's stories illustrate how various "types" of food sharing come to appear distinct through value-laden narratives, in which speakers outline the economic moralities they deem relevant in a given context. If charity and reciprocity appear to be two distinct types of exchange, it is because we have heard different stories about each. Engaging in and talking about these as distinct events, social actors learn to separate unfolding interactions into recognizable sharing events, tied to specific sets of expectations.

Although sharing food with his peers in Paris—who, as Malik noted, all had enough to eat—appeared rather unremarkable to the boy, the material inequities that characterize life in Dakar provided a salient context for his own narrative of redistributing snacks. In Senegal, poverty was on display in a way to which Malik had never been privy in France. Children, even younger than he, begged for food alone in the street. For Malik, these talibés became a stirring symbol of his own privilege. Walking before them at snack time, a full package of cookies in his hand, the boy had the means and desire to redistribute.

It is worth noting that youth who grow up in Dakar do not usually share their snacks with talibés in the road. Adults in Senegal generally forbid children from eating in the street, which precludes talibés from being accidentally included in other children's acts of food redistribution. But as Malik carried his daily ritual of a 4:00 p.m. snack from France into his life in Senegal, he improvised on examples of virtuous acts of giving that he had observed in his grandmother's home. Like his grandmother, who offered meal leftovers to Little Lamine, Malik allocated a portion of his snack—the food over which he had control—to the talibés.

As they travel between France and Senegal, children like Malik alternate between positions of stigma and prestige, experiences that shape the ways they understand acts of resource redistribution and the moral notions that mediate it. Children who are used to receiving public aid in France realize that, in Dakar, their families appear wealthy, able and expected to redistribute money and gifts. Poverty that is so palpable in Senegal makes plain the geographic hierarchies that organize migration and flows of resources in transnational families.

In everyday interactions like sharing snacks, children must reckon with the assumptions that their interlocutors, on both continents, hold about the places they live and visit. Although speakers often describe economic moralities as though they vary from one country to the next in a categorical manner, in everyday life, moral notions about resource redistribution coexist and compete. Speakers' efforts to combine or contrast them are evidence of their attempts to create social closeness and distance in the transnational social spaces they inhabit. Rama's worst assumptions about the racaille who loiter in the courtyard entered into tension with Malik's quest to make friends through snack sharing. In Senegal, pejorative portraits of migrants and their children are equally present, but there the assumption is of wealth with suspicions of selfishness.

The following summer, Rama and Alpha booked a few nights for their family at a resort on Senegal's Petite-Côte, an area south of Dakar known for its luxurious beaches. On Facebook, Rama posted a photo of her children at a beachside restaurant that served delicacies like prawns and lobster, foods that are beyond their means at restaurants in Paris. Malik held out his drink and flashed a peace sign at the camera as he leaned in toward his sister, Diary, smiling. The palm trees that lined the coast behind them in the twilight hinted at the sound of the waves in the distance.

Shifting from the stigmatized position of an "immigrant" in France to the prestige of being a "migrant" in Senegal in the space of a five-hour flight is difficult no matter how old you are. It does not escape children that the luxury they enjoy on trips to Senegal is accessible to them because their relatives live in a "poor country." In Malik's story, he was able and willing to give, which allowed him to reckon, in a gratifying way, with the ambivalence this observation provokes. Framing himself as benefactor, the boy presented himself to me as virtuous and "big" according to the moral expectations in Senegal. But what happens when migrants and their children encounter requests to redistribute that surpass their means?

# CHAPTER 4

## "What Did You Bring Me?": Narrating and Evading Material Expectations

Trips to Dakar are often extremely expensive for Senegalese visiting from Paris, far beyond the cost of a flight between the two capitals. I have heard of families of four who spent close to ten thousand euros on a three-week trip to Dakar. Migrants' relatives in Senegal anticipate their return with high hopes of financial support and *sarice*, gifts from abroad. In Senegalese households in France, few topics spark such animated discussion as do family and friends' expectations of gifts. Talk of return trips to Dakar—and justifications for the infrequency of these visits—often inspire a chorus of complaints among Senegalese adults. Speakers share their stories of audacious requests, aligning with others' frustrations about demands for support in Senegal that exceed their revenue in France.

Children growing up in Paris repeatedly overhear adults' critical refrains, until they can anticipate a story's punch line, accustomed to the contexts in which solicitations arise and the social relations (or lack thereof) that mediate them. For adults who were raised in Dakar, stories of exorbitant expectations stand out against a backdrop of hundreds of other requests that go unremarked, so natural that they rarely merit recounting. Low rank confers rights to financial support in Senegal, especially from high-status migrants assumed to have access to great wealth abroad. For migrants' children who have only limited personal experience in Dakar, however, taking part in adults' conversations about gift requests is a complex task. To contribute a relevant anecdote, they must describe a request presumptuous enough that adults from Dakar would find it brazen as well. Otherwise, they risk appearing spoiled and selfish or revealing their incomprehension of the expectation in Senegal that others have a right to ask for support.

Conversations about the gifts that migrants distribute while visiting Senegal (sarice) shed light on the ways that youth growing up in France become aware of and embody, or resist embodying, status positions in systems of rank-based redistribution among Senegalese. As migrants' children recount stories of gifts offered in Dakar or requests that went unfulfilled, they situate themselves relative to the moral expectations that endow acts of redistribution with meaning in their transnational families. Jeering at the absurdity of a request or expressing frustration at incessant demands, the words they choose reveal a youth's tacit assumptions about how resource redistribution ought to take place—perspectives that do not always align with those of their parents and other family members who grew up in Dakar.

## Migrants' Gifts and Rank-Based Redistribution

Badara Sarr had only been to Dakar three times in his eighteen years, but he felt familiar with his parents' country of birth thanks to the steady flow of relatives and friends from Senegal that his family hosted for a meal, or sometimes for much longer visits. He understood the Wolof his mother used when speaking to him, even if he usually responded in French. If he concentrated, he could follow adults' fast-paced debates about current events in Dakar. During these conversations, as his two younger brothers sprawled on the floor, immersed in video games, Badara had begun to take a more active role in hosting visitors. Sitting on the couch near his father, he joined in adult discussions when he could, tucking his phone under the fold of his athletic shorts, where he could check it discreetly.

During my fieldwork in 2014, Badara was sharing his bedroom with his cousin Ousmane, who had moved to Paris from Dakar the previous autumn to study engineering. Although he was only a few years older than Badara, Ousmane often took a didactic tone when explaining life in Senegal to his French-born cousin, his accented French a testament to his recent arrival from Dakar. Having lived in Paris only a few months, the young man had yet to return home as a "migrant," yet he spoke knowingly of the sizeable expectations that would await him there. For those back in Senegal, he explained, "as soon as you're here [in Europe], you're good. They don't know that there are difficulties here, too. So, you inevitably have to bring something. They'll look at you like, 'What are you going to give me?'"

This phrase seized Badara's attention. After listening in silence for more than five minutes, his mouth twisted into a look of distaste as he chimed in, "What did you bring me?" Ousmane nodded vigorously, apparently pleased with his pupil's comprehension. He eagerly repeated, "What did you bring me?" as if in agreement, but Badara's look of aversion made plain that the cousins attributed this question with contrasting meanings. They uttered the same phrase word for word, but Badara was visibly bothered by these requests, as if evidence of his Senegalese relatives' problematic behavior. Ousmane, meanwhile, went on explaining these expectations of gifts, elaborating on the notion that, in Senegal, living abroad is presumed to be evidence of economic means.

There is no general term in Wolof that corresponds with the word "gift" in English or "*cadeau*" in French. The word sarice refers specifically to a gift offered in the context of one's return, something "one brings back from a trip or a simple errand" (Diouf 2003, 305). Dakarois claim that, like other ritualized forms of giving, social expectations surrounding sarice gifts have intensified over time (see Buggenhagen 2011). A Wolof instructor in Dakar explained that sarice once described "little things we bring back for children" after a trip downtown. Today, however, the term usually refers to more consequential gifts (clothes, smartphones) that migrants bring from abroad for adults and children alike.

The sort of gift one might offer as sarice varies with the distance and duration of a trip, as well as the social relations between traveler and beneficiary. An outing downtown would not merit a gift of sarice among adults, though an adult might bring back some candy or cookies for children. Offerings of sarice, like most forms of material circulation in Senegal, are organized according to the expectations of rank-based redistribution described in Chapter 2. Sarice are gifts that people of relatively high rank, especially (though not exclusively) migrants, offer to those of lower rank, notably those back home. For migrants, their age, marital status, and occupation are factors in determining what sort of sarice one may be expected to offer on trips back home.

Adja, a twenty-five-year-old woman who had been living in Paris for seven years explained, for example, that if she visits her uncle in Dakar, she would not give sarice, because, "children aren't expected to do this sort of thing." In this case, she clarified, she would be considered a child, since she is young and not yet married. "When you're married," she continued, "people assume you're better off." In Senegal, to get married is to assume a new position in socioeconomic networks. Getting married indicates that one has the resources necessary to take up the adult responsibility of supporting dependents. Senegalese claim that men have a moral and legal obligation to provide for their wives and children. For women, too, marriage can provide a means to social adulthood. Presumed to have gained access to her husband's assets, a new wife is expected to redistribute these resources to care for dependents of her own, especially her parents and family of origin.

After a moment of reflection, Adja commented that, now, when she returned to Dakar, her relatives' expectations had changed. Although she was still a student, more people expected sarice each trip. But, she added, "sarice is a favor, not an obligation." Like marriage, migration is thought to mark a transformation through which one "grows up" in the eyes of those back in Africa. Young people who left Senegal as students, reliant on family to pay for their flights and university fees, can return as adults, ready to ease their elders' burden by contributing to the household budget. Even if a migrant does not actually have more money than before, returning from abroad, they gain social status and influence. But this status must materialize through generous acts of redistribution upon returning. Failure to offer money and gifts on par with family members' expectations can spark accusations of greed or laziness.

In Senegal, sarice gifts and the monetary support that migrants distribute are carefully monitored, taken as evidence of givers' wealth and power, as well as their love and commitment to their relatives. People in Dakar recall with clarity past gifts that migrants have brought them. Children eagerly point out notebooks and articles of clothing they received when migrant relatives came to visit. Conspicuous attention to migrants' gifts is not limited to intimate exchanges among relatives. New possessions spark the curiosity of onlookers who wonder about the origin of what (they assume) must have been a gift. A new smartphone or tablet, for example, points clearly to one's connections abroad.

Through these gifts, migrants' family members gain reputations as people who are well cared for by their relatives abroad. The influence that this status confers in Dakar is linked back to specific migrants through language tracing gifts' origins and praising migrants' generosity. For adult migrants, this scrutiny of the resources they redistribute can be a source of tremendous pressure, but also pride. The anxieties that gift giving can provoke are accompanied by the potential to "grow" through migration, one's status transformed through acts of material redistribution. For migrants' children, however, these interpretations can seem quite foreign.

Morally charged expectations of gifts and the speech acts that surround them represent common points of tension in transnational families. Economic moralities that underpin acts of gift giving also shape the language practices that carry out and construe these exchanges, influencing how one speaks about a gift or the giver's generosity, whether one might make a request, and how one expresses thanks. Divergent expectations regarding these language practices are at the root of Badara's and Ousmane's distinct reactions to the imagined question, "What did you bring me?"

In Wolof, one might teasingly ask a close friend, "What did you bring me?" but in many contexts, this demand would seem impolite. Senegalese describe such explicit requests as demonstrating a lack of the virtue *kersa*, meaning self-control and reserve. Asking for sarice, like asking for money, is associated with low-ranking *griots*, who are among the only Senegalese besides beggars who ask directly for money. High-ranking *géérs*, in contrast, are said to demonstrate such kersa that, out of restraint, they would struggle to ask for help, even if legitimately in need. Senegalese view griots' explicit requests to be an integral part of their low rank, which entails a right to compensation for the service and deference they provide their higher-ranked patrons. The frank language that griots use to ask for gifts and their elaborate praise of others' largesse function, furthermore, to ensure the circulation of resources in a community. At events like baby-naming ceremonies, for example, griots use a megaphone to announce the gifts received for all to hear, specifying the quality of cloth offered and the precise sum of monetary offerings. Praising guests, one by one, for their generosity, griots' public announcements generate social pressure to give, encouraging competitive giving and escalating expectations (Buggenhagen 2012; Moya 2017).

To request a gift is to address one's interlocutor as a potential benefactor and, thus, as someone of higher rank than oneself. For a petition for support to be persuasive, furthermore, a speaker must embody other subtle signs of low rank. People who hope to request aid show deference by doing things like addressing their interlocutor with kinship terms for elders, like "big sister" or "uncle," or by assuming the conversational role of "asker," because the act of initiating a salutation and asking after one's interlocutor's health and family generally falls to the younger speaker or the person of relatively lower rank (Irvine 1974). These practices are not part of any conscious "rules" of etiquette for requesting support, but are implicit indicators of status, which draw attention to a person's intent to ask a favor and create the impression that the request should be taken seriously. Indeed, Judith Irvine has shown that speakers struggle to request financial support if they are unable to secure the lower-rank conversational position by *asking* questions rather than responding. Studying conversational roles in Wolof speech, she discovered that when high-ranking géérs (nobles) occasionally took up the role of "asker," they effectively prevented their interlocutors from soliciting material support. Regularly petitioned for aid herself, Irvine realized that by employing géérs' "self-lowering strategy" and continually inquiring after her interlocutor's health, family, work, and day, she was temporarily able to avoid requests for monetary support.

Senegalese claim that, like other offerings of material support, children are not yet expected to give sarice but, as we will soon see, migrants' children regularly encounter appeals for gifts on trips to Dakar. Like Badara, these youths often struggle to make sense of the amount of attention their relatives pay to sarice. Even the thanks they receive can seem unpleasant to young people who are unaccustomed to the long-winded accolades of generosity common throughout West Africa. Migrants' children shift awkwardly in their seats when praise for their kindness goes on too long for comfort, their polite smiles fading into looks of confusion.

Throughout sub-Saharan Africa, money and gifts are explicitly described as a gauge of the givers' power, influence, and generosity. As such, they merit verbal praise from those of lower rank. These performances of gratitude show deference, marking the receiver as deserving of resources and subtly encouraging the giver to continue redistributing. Expectations like these are epitomized by griots' stylized ovations. Griots' elaborate proclamations of generosity establish the power and largesse of their high-ranked benefactors (the longer and louder the song, the more prominent the patron). Although only griots are paid to perform praise songs at ceremonies, their elaborate linguistic stylings provide a template for speakers of all castes. For instance, a géér may speak in the loud, fast-paced, emphatic style typical of griots in order to ask a favor from a higher-ranking relative (Irvine 1990). Taking up a position of deference relative to their addressee, these language practices legitimize the request for material support. Similarly, within transnational families, the verbal stylings of griot speech shape the ways that non-migrant relatives express their gratitude. Family members honor migrants as high-ranking benefactors and perform their own deference by repeatedly extolling migrants' kindness and largesse, asking that Allah bless the giver. Through lengthy praise of migrants' generosity, relatives in Senegal demonstrate themselves to be deserving of support.

In Europe and North America, in contrast, speakers tend to downplay or ignore the distribution of material resources among family members (see Coe 2013; Zelizer 1985, 2000). Compared to griot-like performances of gratitude, even heartfelt thanks in the "West" are relatively succinct. Speakers learn to highlight a gift's value in terms of its thoughtfulness, rather than the money spent, taught (in French as in English) that "it is the thought that counts" (*c'est la pensée qui compte*). According to this logic, excessive attention to gifts can appear distasteful, as if evidence that the receiver is motivated by a calculating self-interest, rather than care. Although in other settings in Europe and North America financial calculation may be positively valued as the mark of a "rational" economic actor, among family and friends it is perceived to cheapen or negate the love that the giver and receiver share.

Guided by the notion that money cannot (or should not) buy love (*l'argent n'achète pas l'amour*), speakers in Europe and North America learn to minimize the importance of the material resources invested in family relations, verbally extracting the (base) material from (virtuous) relations of love. This stands in stark contrast to the logic prevalent in Africa that voicing one's appreciation for the material support is a necessary acknowledgement of the giver's status and the humble receiver's rightful claim to resources. In transnational families, divergent expectations concerning the language that mediates gifts and the moral narratives that undergird them can create points of tension, giving way to disagreements over the messy details of reckoning with relatives' expectations of support.

### Unraveling Virtue

When discussions in Senegalese households move from the theme of relatives' audacious requests to stories of what one actually gives (or refuses to give) on trips to Dakar, the tone of the conversation shifts. Gone are the choruses of laughter and heads bobbing in unison, replaced by more hesitant accounts, as speakers carefully search for the words to describe how they give or avoid doing so. In the Sarr household, after awaking Badara's attention to the discussion of sarice gifts, Ousmane continued his authoritative (albeit secondhand) account of the stress that offering sarice entails. His uncle, who had made the journey back to Senegal many times in his forty years abroad, interjected curtly, "It doesn't stress me out anymore." Ousmane stopped short.

All eyes turned to Abdoulaye, awaiting explanation. "For me, it's done," he continued, "I've already given." Abdoulaye's declaration seemed to directly oppose Ousmane's claims, yet his nephew immediately concurred. Aligning with his uncle, Ousmane confirmed that the older man had now "made it through." As Abdoulaye elaborated, his nephew echoed him in supportive repetition, confirming and clarifying the older man's remarks.

In familial settings, listeners routinely chime in to offer input or contest another's interpretation, asking questions and interrupting others' thoughts. Rather than "telling a story *to* another," in these mundane discussions, speakers are often "telling a story *with* another" (Ochs and Capps 2001, 2). In these interactions, which Elinor Ochs and Lisa Capps call "living narratives," the direction of a story and its content are not predetermined by a single narrator but emerge gradually, shaped by all conversational participants. As such, the moral of the story is not always clear but materializes in the collective act of telling. In transnational families, this means that people who are differently positioned in terms of age, wealth, and time spent in Senegal influence one another's accounts of giving, shaping how speakers voice their interpretations and which conclusions appear to hold sway.

Together, uncle and nephew characterized the expectation to distribute sarice gifts as associated with a temporary life stage. Gift flows not only mediate the relative status positions of adults and children but also signal an adult's transition to elder status. When one reaches a certain age, diminishing flows of material support can signal an attempt to "retire" from certain obligations to provide for dependents, becoming an elder. With these specifications, Abdoulaye's initially provocative dismissal transformed into a description of the conditions that structure his gifts of sarice.

"It doesn't stress me out at all anymore when someone says, 'What did you bring me?'" Abdoulaye continued. "I say, 'What did you bring me when I was leaving?'" *Yombal* is a term in Wolof that describes the sort of gifts one offers travelers before they leave on a voyage. Although Abdoulaye juxtaposed sarice and yombal as if they represented gifts and return gifts, these two forms of exchange do not necessarily function this way. The word sarice is more commonly used than yombal. While sarice has evolved to include the products that migrants bring back from abroad, in Wolof, yombol has a hackneyed ring. Senegalese explain that this term evokes images of the olden days, when one might have offered provisions to a person leaving on a long voyage on foot or horseback. If, in Senegal, sarice is on everyone's lips at the moment of a migrant's return, the disuse of the word yombal illustrates an asymmetry between these two forms of gift, founded on the presumption of unequal positions of migrants and those back home.

Abdoulaye responded to his own hypothetical question. "What did you bring me when I was leaving? *Nothing*? Well then, in that case, you—" he paused, just short of announcing the imagined askers to deserve no sarice. "Well," Abdoulaye continued, "the people I owe something to don't ask for it," subtly pointing to his relatives' restraint (*kersa*) and thus high status. Ousmane jumped in, adding "You don't wait for them to ask," specifying that it is not that Abdoulaye's family no longer expects gifts, but that his offerings precipitate their requests. "Yes," Abdoulaye confirmed, "but those who ask—" he again hesitated, reluctant to declare the hypothetical askers undeserving. His nephew finished the sentence, "It's not obligatory." Abdoulaye nodded, repeating, "It's not obligatory."

Abdoulaye then took a philosophical tone, announcing, "We have obligations. The obligation to be human." Elaborating, Abdoulaye outlined a taxonomy of giving, classifying cases in which one is called to give and ordering them into hierarchies of obligation. The obligation to be human, he explained, "means that you know that you are indebted [*redevable*] to certain people and you also know that there are people in need who, if we don't assist them, will never be able to make it without our help." Distinguishing one's responsibility to provide for dependents from requests from those in need, Abdoulaye began to break down the common refrain that Senegalese systematically give. People must judge for themselves what they can afford to give, he continued, keeping in mind, on the one hand, that "you necessarily owe something to someone," and, on the other, that, in Senegal, "you find situations so catastrophic" that it would take everything you have to help them. "And when you come back, what are you going to you do?" he asked, flustered. "Are you going to restart from zero? Is that reasonable?" His volume rose as he repeated, "Is that reasonable? No. I have a wife and children. It's not possible."

Contrasting his obligations toward his wife and children (those to whom he owes something) with the requests he receives from those in need, Abdoulaye voiced, in frank terms, the need for selective solidarity. To fulfill their moral obligations to dependents, adults must limit the material aid they supply to others. Carefully selecting those to whom one gives is, thus, not evidence of selfishness but a responsibility shared by all adults. In Senegal, where one regularly encounters situations of dire need and monetary support can often mean the difference between life and death (Foley 2009), this sorting resembles a sort of triage. As Abdoulaye shared his tactics for managing the sorting process, his agitation laid bare the discomfort this sort of decision entailed, even after decades of making trips back.

Abdoulaye articulated the need to strategically limit giving support more bluntly than most Senegalese, but the basic ideas he put forth were common. Many expressed this necessity through parabolic stories that ended with a somber moral. A Senegalese student in Paris described, for example, a woman in Dakar who, aware of her family's privilege, gave all she had to beggars. When the women fell on hard times, however, she regretted not having been more generous toward her relatives, who offered support only begrudgingly. An explicit description of the need for selective solidarity amounts to an admission that one sometimes avoids giving. Even Abdoulaye's frank resolve waivered each time he began to specify the circumstances under which he would refuse to give. Concluding his explanation, Abdoulaye explained that it is up to each of us to decide to whom we owe something and to whom we do not. In the case of the latter, "If he asks me, I won't give," he finally affirmed, only to immediately soften his stance, "well, I'll try to make a little gesture." Despite his initial declaration that he no longer gives, Abdoulaye gradually made clear to whom he gives, in what circumstances, and why. In justifying why he does not give to *everyone* who asks, Abdoulaye implicitly communicated the value of giving to those in need.

### Involuntary Sarice

Concluding his lecture, Abdoulaye fell quiet and his gaze turned to his son. I asked whether Badara, too, had felt pressure to give on trips back to Dakar, and the young man and his father agreed that, so far, he had been spared (*épargné*). "It'll come!" Ousmane intervened, "It'll come!" If his cousin had been spared requests in Dakar, it is because, at eighteen, he is, "still little." But once he starts working, Ousmane cautioned, "People will learn that Badara has a job and then, 'Oh really?'" Playing the role of a person who had heard that Badara was employed, Abdoulaye interjected, "You have a job? Help me, I'm your cousin from—" Badara then interrupted, smiling to indicate that he too knew the routine, "and I've seen you maybe one time when I was—" Jumping in at Badara's hesitation, his father added loudly, "Or even that you've never seen!" Ousmane repeated, "That you've never seen!" Uncle and nephew repeated "That you've never seen!" five times before Badara concluded, "For right now, I've been spared. Afterward, we'll see, but," looking toward his father, "I heard what he said."

In this playful story, the three men collaboratively imagined a future moment when Badara would cross a threshold into adulthood in a way that appeared obvious to those in Dakar: by earning resources of his own to redistribute. After their laughter died down, the men concurred that if Badara were to return to Senegal today, though still in high school, he would already receive requests to give. "I'm eighteen now," Badara explained, demonstrating to his father and cousin his maturity and comprehension of the social roles that mediate redistribution in Senegal. Unlike Adja from Dakar, however, who described herself as a child at twenty-five, given that she was an unmarried student, Badara (born in Paris) defined adulthood according to the age of legal majority in France. Ousmane countered that before he receives requests for money, people in Senegal would likely ask Badara to give in a way deemed appropriate for youth, asking that he leave them an article of clothing that he had worn during his visit.

If starting to work, getting married, and migrating are considered quintessential signs that one is prepared to take up adult responsibilities, in Senegal, requests to give often precede these transformations. Family members and friends nudge children to give, testing how much young people are able and willing to offer. Sharing snacks is a routine event when even young children take up the role of benefactor. Older children are sometimes asked to give away more substantial belongings, like clothing or accessories, to friends and relatives. Unlike adults' obligation to provide for dependents, however, one is at liberty to decide whether to hand over a requested possession. Yet, the habitual nature of these requests means that youth in Senegal grow up with regular opportunities to redistribute items from their wardrobe and to benefit from others who have generously parted with their things.

For migrants' children, requests to make gifts of their personal possessions are far more one-sided. Youth in France described how their cousins in Africa would sometimes admire their clothing while they were wearing it, fingering the fabric as if imagining how it might feel to wear, in an attempt to choose what to request at the end of the trip. I have encountered these sorts of requests myself in Dakar, which varied from a coaxing compliment—"*Sa t-shirt bi rafette na. Khanaa bii moom nga koy may.*" (Your T-shirt is nice. I'm sure you were keeping it just for me.)—to a subtle nod toward my sunglasses, followed by a wink, as the hopeful beneficiary quickly pointed at herself. Always made with a grin, it was easy to treat these requests as compliments, more than earnest solicitations.

I asked Ousmane whether the people really mean it when they ask visitors to make gifts of their possessions. "They mean it!" Badara answered loudly. Talking over his father and cousin, Badara announced that he had an anecdote that demonstrated just how serious these requests are. Repeating the word "listen," until the other men fell silent, Badara recounted a story of his last trip to Dakar, five years prior. Before leaving Paris, he explained, "We had done a lot of shopping," buying new clothes that, he had assumed, would serve him for the coming school year. "We went to Senegal, and Dad—" "Yes?" his father interjected, curious. Badara continued with a grin, "He waited until we went to the beach and said to uh, what are their names?" His father chuckled, recognizing the story. "My cousins," Badara continued, recounting how his father had told three of his cousins "to go help themselves in—" He paused. "In your suitcase?" I asked. Nodding, Badara continued, "to go take, uh, he gave them—" Stumbling, Badara restarted multiple times, struggling to put his father's actions into words. Interrupting Badara's awkward efforts, his father asked, "And were you upset with me?" Shaking his head, Badara confirmed that he was not and Abdoulaye chuckled, saying, "voilà," with a shrug.

Over the course of telling, it became clear that Badara's story, which he had introduced as an illustration of his relatives' expectations of gifts, was truly an account of his father's behavior. He described his father waiting until he and his brothers had gone to the beach, a detail that gave the act an air of suspicion. Badara then said that his father had told his cousins to go "help themselves" in his suitcase. With the knowledge that Badara was not conscious of the event taking place, this phrase evokes an image of the three cousins rummaging through Badara's new things as if at a garage sale. Badara cut himself off twice just before specifying *where* cousins were allowed to "help themselves." Nodding in confirmation after I supplied the word "suitcase," he said only that his father had told them to "go help themselves in—" and "to go take—" hesitating each time his phrase required a possessive adjective, to indicate that they were helping themselves in "*his* suitcase" or taking "*his* things."

At the end of the narrative, Badara's opinion on the gift was not entirely clear. The punch line of his story was smothered by the fact that, in telling it, Badara was obliged to concede that it was not a story of the exaggerated expectations of his relatives in Senegal but rather an account of how *his father* had encouraged his cousins to take his clothes. After reassuring his father that the act had not upset him, Badara specified that he had found it a "little odd." His use of the past tense in this phrase contrasted with his declaration immediately following that he "thinks" (in the present), that it was good that his father had organized the exchange without his knowledge, because otherwise "it could have made [him] sad." In this way, Badara communicated that he was now mature enough to understand his father's actions.

Abdoulaye then reminded Badara that, upon returning to France, they had bought him new clothes. Abdoulaye had only given away things that they could later replace, drawing attention to the reality that Badara could access European clothing more easily than his cousins. Abdoulaye then specified why he shared Badara's things with these cousins, in particular, highlighting the similarity and the proximity between Badara and his cousins. They were "boys his age" Abdoulaye explained, with whom Badara "had spent the vacation." Then he said, "And we were going home." The act of returning to France draws attention to the fact that the boys live on different continents, a critical status asymmetry.

Badara and his cousins were equal in most ways, except in geographic hierarchies. The asymmetry between the children was materialized in the act of returning to France, and it was at that moment that Abdoulaye offered Badara's clothes to his cousins. Mauss noted, "The unreciprocated gift still makes the person who has accepted it inferior, particularly when it has been accepted with no thought of returning it" (2002 [1950], 83) The timing of the gift, offered just before Badara left Senegal, prevented its reciprocation. The significance of this act, positioning Badara as higher-ranked than his Senegal-based cousins, would thus persist after their departure.

In the story of Badara's begrudging gift of sarice, his father's actions—both in the past and in the moment of storytelling—made clear certain normative expectations concerning material obligation and entitlement. In giving away his son's things, Abdoulaye communicated the importance he attributed to the gesture of leaving possessions with kin in Senegal. His actions in the story demonstrated a sensitivity to notions of asymmetrical positions salient in Senegal, treating geographical hierarchies that divide migrants in Europe from those in Senegal as salient even among children, such that these inequalities might motivate certain forms of rank-based redistribution.

In recounting the story, Badara both expressed his past confusion at his fathers' actions and asserted that his present, narrating self could now see the merit of the act. Despite his claim of alignment with the economic moralities his father had enacted, the act of narrating the story appeared to disturb Badara's understanding of the rights of individuals and the sanctity of one's private property. His hesitation before announcing that they had taken *his* things sheds light on Badara's struggle to understand the moral logic at play as he grappled with diverse notions of possession and the rights that family members might have to one another's belongings. Through the act of storytelling, Badara processed his past experiences in Dakar, making sense of the expectations of rank-based redistribution that motivated his father's actions as he attempted to present them to his audience. Shaped by his father's questions and comments, his story also carried out interactional work in the narrating event, demonstrating to his father and cousin his mature understanding of the moral expectations that surround gift giving in Senegal.

Badara's example demonstrates the complex task that telling a story in the presence of relatives from Senegal can represent for migrants' children. No matter how familiar youth may be with adults' accounts of giving gifts in Dakar, recounting their own experiences is another task entirely, which requires them to anticipate the economic moralities their listeners might find relevant and articulate them in their own words. This exercise shapes the ways youth understand and engage with the expectations to redistribute that they encounter in Senegal, coloring the language they use to describe them. Outside the earshot of kin, however, youth often voiced sharper critique of the material expectations they encounter in Dakar. Yet, even in storytelling events unmediated by the moral gaze of Senegalese relatives, youth wrestle with multiple moral stances in their attempts to describe the complex stakes of gift giving in Dakar.

### Dodging Moral Pressures

Aminata, a twenty-two-year-old who grew up between Paris and Dakar, spoke to me bluntly about her frustrations with the requests for gifts and money she encounters in Dakar, asserting nonchalantly that she had no moral qualms with refusing to give. Born in Paris, Aminata spoke Wolof fluently, having lived with her parents and sisters in Dakar between the ages of five and ten, after which her family returned to France. She characterized this period in Senegal as having affected her and her three sisters differently, describing the sister who was in middle school at the time as having been the most marked by the experience. Aminata called her "the most Senegalese" of the four daughters, explaining that this sister had later married a man in

Dakar and now lives in Senegal near her in-laws, whom she dutifully show-
ers with gifts.

In an interview in 2014, Aminata characterized her own moral stance
toward giving in opposition to her sister's, describing moments when her
frank refusal to give to relatives in Dakar sparked confrontations within her
immediate family. Aminata outlined two tactics that she had developed to
circumvent requests for support in Dakar, only one of which was a socially
acceptable means to avoid giving in Senegal. And yet her stories also demonstrated a nuanced understanding of moral expectations that mediate redistribution in Africa. At moments, her firm stance yielded, revealing her
sense of responsibility to give, despite her bold claims.

"Other than my smile, I have nothing to give," Aminata claimed to have
unequivocally explained to her mother before setting off on a trip to visit kin
in her maternal grandparents' village. When her mother responded dubi-
ously, Aminata defended her position asking, "When I'm struggling in
France, did these people pay my rent? Will these people help me?" When her
mother confirmed that they would not, "Well, voilà," Aminata replied, "From
that point on, it's clear." Aminata balked at the obligations that fall on migrants within the moral logic of rank-based redistribution. Highlighting her
own struggles to make rent in Paris, in the story, she reminded her mother
(and me in its telling) that she was simply not in a position to provide material support. She asserted, furthermore, that mutual support among relatives
ought not to be a unidirectional flow from migrants toward those back home
but rather a more reciprocal exchange of resources.

Stating her intentions clearly to her mother did little, however, to miti-
gate relatives' expectations once back in the village. At her uncle's home,
Aminata narrowly avoided pressures to give. The visit concluded with an
extended farewell, during which each move to leave was met by more talking. Goodbyes in Senegal, particularly if parting ways with someone one sees
rarely, often include the hosts' repeated blessings and thanks for the visit.
Handshakes stretch on so long that guests are sometimes left standing, holding hands with their hosts, as the latter repeatedly praise their generosity
and kindness. At this moment, visitors who are richer or otherwise of higher
rank, might discreetly slip a folded bill into their host's hand, a token of gratitude and acknowledgement of relative rank. At her uncle's home, after her
mother and sister had both discreetly offered monetary gifts, Aminata described a moment when the expectation that she give, as well, had become
palpable. Yet, stubbornly refusing, she continued smiling and shaking hands

as if unaware. Fed up, her sister slipped a 2000 CFA franc bill (roughly $3.50) into her hand to give to their uncle. Aminata did so and the sendoff quickly concluded. Once outside, her sister angrily demanded that Aminata pay back the 2000 francs, as if it were a loan. "Excuse me!?" Aminata mimed her shock, "You toss me a bill and I'll give it," but no repayment would be involved.

Aminata laughed, remembering her sister's frustration. "I have no scruples about that!" she declared. "In fact," she explained, "I'm not even touched. I have no obligation to fulfill, none. I don't see why I should give them something when they don't deserve it." In her value-laden language of "scruples," "obligation," and being "deserving," Aminata pointed at the tensions between the economic moralities that she and her sister had each stubbornly maintained on that trip. She specified that it was the social pressure to give that bothered her—the tacit expectations made evident, but rarely explicit, through language. She hated the idea that distant cousins or aunts can "come out of nowhere" and "sing for you" (sing your praises). "Sing like a griot?" I asked. "Oh yes, yes, yes," Aminata assured me. "It's so embarrassing."

Aminata described a scene that had taken place during a trip to Senegal five years prior, which had revealed to her how speech acts mediate redistribution. Out one day in Dakar with her aunt and sister, Aminata explained that "a lady came to sing our praises, our grandmothers, our grandfathers. And I just stood there." Aminata stared blankly ahead, miming her confusion. "I didn't get that we were supposed to give her something." On her left side, she felt her aunt giving her "these big nudges." To escape the performance, they would need to hand over some cash. Unaware, Aminata and her sister stood awkwardly listening until, finally, their aunt took money from her own pocketbook and handed it to the woman. "Ohhhhhh!" Aminata exclaimed wide-eyed, mimicking her realization that they were "supposed to give her money?" Her embarrassment had hung with her, realizing afterward that, at the center of attention, her ignorance had been exposed to all by the praises that the woman sang loud and clear, followed by her own failure to react.

This moment of verbal and material exchange made clear to Aminata how speakers in Senegal implicitly solicit monetary support by taking up a low-ranked linguistic role like that of griots. Annoyed to discover the requests hidden in songs of praise, however, her response had been to hone her skills of avoidance. Aminata described this moment as having taught her to dodge tacit requests by playing dumb or, in her words, "playing crazy"—that is, acting totally oblivious of others' expectations. Her extended family in Senegal already treated her like a "tubab [white person] who doesn't understand any-thing," she asserted. But being "the house tubab" came with certain benefits, allowing her to "mind [her] own business." She confessed that sometimes in Senegal, she had even pretended not to understand Wolof. "I just looked at them with a really blank stare. I really played the idiot," Aminata explained. "You have to pretend, otherwise you can't get by."

Aminata's tone shifted as she described a second strategy of evasion that she employed in Senegal. Softening her stance against giving, she claimed that, "When people are nice and don't insist," she gives willingly. But, other-wise, she "hides behind" her status as a student. Subtle reminders that one is a student and thus not yet a gainfully employed adult, are a common means by which young people in Senegal limit others' expectations of material sup-port. Describing it as "hiding behind" her position as a student, Aminata spoke as if this were another means to skirt expectations to give. Among Sen-egalese, however, reminders of one's student status communicate in clear terms one's relative immaturity and low rank, and thus legitimate inability (for the time being) to support others.

Aminata's unequal presentation of her strategies for evading requests communicated her recognition that, in the eyes of her Senegalese relatives, the two tactics held substantially different moral weights. Anticipating the moral censure she might receive if other Senegalese heard about how she "played crazy," Aminata's description of this strategy was filled with justifi-cations and callous claims of her lack of concern with others' evaluations. Aminata's brief mention of "hiding behind" her status as a student was not accompanied by any further explanation. Instead, in her narrative, it marked a move toward acknowledging and aligning with her relatives' economic mo-ralities in Dakar. "At some point, I'll work and I'll do it [give] because you have to," she concluded, "but it will annoy me, because I don't like being forced to give." Aminata's assertion that she would never "get by" if she tried to give every time she was asked resonates with Abdoulaye's discussion of the need for selective solidarity. However, in contexts in which Abdoulaye would make a "small gesture" in lieu of directly refusing and the géérs that Irvine studied might use a self-lowering strategy, Aminata lacked socially ac-ceptable strategies for avoiding or delaying requests. For the moment, "play-ing crazy" was a tool she needed in these situations to dodge the demands that otherwise appeared unmanageable.

Making reference to her status as a student is a strategy of selective solidarity that corresponds with normative expectations of rank-based redistribution, whereas her strategy of "playing crazy" represents a refusal to engage with these economic moralities at all. Self-lowering strategies merely delay expectations of support. Aminata's feigned obliviousness, however, would preclude any promise of future socioeconomic relations by excluding her as a functioning member of Senegalese society. Repeatedly delaying gifts may be frustrating for those who rely on them, but for people in Senegal, a blunt refusal to acknowledge one's position in the reciprocal kinship relationship appears truly shameful. When I asked adults in Dakar whether they had heard of "playing crazy" to avoid requests, they lowered their eyes and shook their heads in disappointment, before confirming that they knew, of course, that some people behave like this. Children in Dakar looked ahead solemnly, confirming that they had often suspected migrants' children of pretending to be clueless to get out of work or avoid conversation.

### Anticipating Adulthood

When I presented these cases to an audience at the École des hautes études en sciences sociales (School for Advanced Studies in the Social Sciences) in Paris, a Senegalese doctoral student asked whether I had not also met Senegalese in Paris who demonstrated "true" solidarity? Despite their bluster, both Aminata and Abdoulaye communicated the discomfort they experienced when they had to avoid giving and ultimately concluded that they would give whenever possible. Although they described evading requests in more candid detail than most Senegalese felt comfortable doing, their blunt descriptions of the need for selective solidarity make plain the tricky negotiations required of all Senegalese who navigate solicitations for support that surpass their limited resources.

On trips back to Dakar, migrants are often overwhelmed by requests for financial aid, realizing quickly that it would be impossible to give each time asked. But deciding when, to whom, and how to give (or not to give) represents a complex cultural calculation that encompasses questions like: Who has the right to ask for support? For whom does one have a responsibility to provide? By what strategies might one avoid giving? In everyday life, these questions are negotiated in unfolding interactions—social actors have little time to compare different possibilities or measure one's status relative to one's interlocutor in multiple imbricated hierarchies.

Despite her brazen rejection of her relatives' expectations of gifts, like Badara, Aminata demonstrated an awareness that the obligation to give sarice is linked to adulthood and the economic stability that allows one to support dependents. Justifications of her behavior illustrated a nuanced understanding of the moral expectations to give and the speech acts that mediate them. In these examples, young people raised in France described situations in which they struggled to give according to the normative expectations of their families, whether due to naiveté or outright resistance. Their stories show that the line between ignorance and willful avoidance to be blurrier than relatives in Dakar may imagine.

Badara's father and Aminata's aunt and sister each implicated these youth in relations of material exchange with kin in Senegal, obliging them to give without their consent or awareness. Although, at first, these migrants' children may not have understood the moral logic that drove their involuntary offerings, having been made to go through the motions of gift-giving had marked them. Carrying the confusion and frustration they felt at those moments in Dakar with them back to Paris, in storytelling events, sometimes years later, the youth worked to make sense of the moral logic that had motivated their relatives' expectations. Families' stories of these interactions shape youths' moral understanding of these events. Even their refusals to align with the economic moralities of rank-based redistribution were structured by an awareness of the moral expectations that underpin these socio-economic relations.

The stories of Badara and Aminata, two youth on the verge of adulthood, were shot through with ambivalence regarding the responsibilities that accompany growing up in multiple national contexts, encountering new expectations that they only partially understood. As migrants' children, in Dakar they faced expectations to give that surpassed the requests that youth growing up in Senegal are likely to encounter. Although relatives in Senegal may recognize that migrants' children often fail to grasp the intricacies of rank-based redistribution, they also worry that they might, as Aminata had, take advantage of their status as foreigners to deliberately avoid giving. The threat that migrants' children refuse to acknowledge moral expectations to provide material support shapes the way that kin in Senegal attempt to guide them in taking up appropriate positions of rank.

## CHAPTER 5

# Transnational Cross-Cousins:
# Selective Kinship on Social Media

Mariama could count on one hand the number of times she had met Souleymane, one of her cousins on her dad's side, who was married and worked as a journalist in Senegal.[1] Mariama's father and Souleymane's mother were siblings, of the same mother and father, in a family of eleven children who had grown up together in Dakar and moved abroad, with some subsequently returning to Senegal. Attending middle school just outside of Paris, Mariama's life was separated from her adult cousin by age and geographic distance. Yet the two shared a special bond, materialized through messages on social media and exchanges of sometimes substantial gifts.

Scholarship on transnational families has regularly examined the remittances that adults abroad send to children living in their country of origin (Hondagneu-Sotelo and Avila 1997; Schmalzbauer 2001; Parreñas 2001; Coe 2011). This chapter highlights an inversion of this process: adults in Senegal who work to create and reinforce transnational relations with (and through) children growing up in France. Focusing on kinship relations between children in France and their family members in Senegal provides insight into the everyday exchanges through which transnational families attempt to ensure the social and material reproduction of households in Africa. It analyzes the evolving relationship between eleven-year-old Mariama, in Paris, and Souleymane, her thirty-five-year-old cousin in Dakar, who devoted substantial effort and resources to establishing close ties with his younger cousin.

Approaching material circulation and kinship-making as mutually imbricated processes, I demonstrate how Senegalese forge and reinforce links with *certain* family members, in efforts to favorably position themselves in socioeconomic networks of transnational kin. I argue that, by drawing on behaviors associated with "cross-cousin" kinship relations, which have historically shaped marriage choices in West Africa, these transnational kin forged emergent family relations that linked individuals across national borders, even in the absence of marriage. This cross-cousin relationship provides an example of a more general practice in which transnational families draw on and transform kinship categories that have long organized intimate and economic relations in Africa, to establish and reinforce relationships with kin abroad.

I trace the ways in which children in France used social media to maintain relationships with relatives in Senegal and examine how adult caregivers shape these relations by orchestrating material exchanges and characterizing behaviors as evidence of specific kinship relations. Senegalese adults create cultural "scaffolding" around children, facilitating exchanges that structure and encourage children's participation in various social practices. I suggest that, at the time of my fieldwork, Facebook was a social media platform particularly well-adapted to the work of scaffolding. At that moment, Facebook facilitated multigenerational exchanges among relatives in a space where youth demonstrated a sense of ease and ownership relative to their parents. Tracing exchanges of gifts and Facebook messages among transnational family members, I explore the constraints and affordances (cf. Gibson 1979; Manning 2012; Miller et al. 2016) of Facebook as a medium of kinship-making to consider how children growing up abroad come to understand having family relations in Senegal and the economic expectations these roles entail. I do so by paying careful attention to the economic moralities that family members voice when interacting with kin and characterizing familial relations.

Members of transnational families draw on multiple, sometimes contradictory, ways of understanding familial relations and the material expectations they presume and entail. In Paris, Kadar's kinship strategies and economic practices, for example, were guided by his desire, on the one hand, to present himself as a "modern" individual, integrated into France, and, on the other, to favorably position himself in relations of reciprocity and exchange with kin in Senegal. An examination of everyday processes of kinship-making and the economic moralities that underpin them illustrates how individuals reinforce and transform socioeconomic relations that link Senegalese across continents, reproducing households in Africa in ways that are imbricated with former European metropoles and new frontiers.

Faced with prolonged economic crisis, money and gifts sent by relatives abroad have become a critical source of support for many families in Senegal (Hannaford 2017; Buggenhagen 2012; Melly 2011; Foley 2009). Although remittances are widely regarded as one of the more reliable sources of income in this context of financial insecurity, flows of resources from abroad are routinely interrupted and discontinued. Economies in Europe and North America also face economic downturns, and family members in Senegal live with the fear that, over time, migrant relatives might "forget them," meaning that their remittances slow to a stop.

Whether and how migrants—and their children—recognize kinship relations with those in Africa is critical to the material reproduction of Senegalese households. Family members in Senegal show a vested interest in the ways in which the next generation perceives the moral stakes of resource allocation. Children thus provide a privileged view into the uncertainty and mutability of these links, shedding light on the efforts of families in Africa to enact and maintain links with family members abroad.

A growing body of scholarship examines children and youth as agentive actors in transnational processes, focusing largely on those who have themselves migrated or, alternatively, on children "left behind" in their parents' country of origin (Orellana and Reynolds 2008; Coe et al. 2011; Coe 2013; Thorsen 2006; Cole and Durham 2008; Maira and Soep 2005; Hashim and Thorsen 2011; Boehm 2012). These child-focused studies have demonstrated how young people motivate adult migration and remittances, functioning as "pivotal points" (Olwig 1999) in transnational families. Less is known about the role that children growing up abroad might play in the reproduction of transnational kinship relations. Migrants' children have historically been examined relative to questions of assimilation into the host country, and often analyzed as "second-generation" immigrants (Bankston 1998; Portes and Zhou 1993; Portes and Rumbaut 2001). This chapter examines the ways in which children growing up abroad may influence the social and economic practices of individuals in their parents' country of origin, both through their own agentive participation in transnational relations and as a locus of adult efforts to establish and reinforce links between individuals in Africa and abroad.

In what follows, I first examine contrasting notions of kinship relevant to members of these families, in order to consider the many economic moralities that together give meaning to interactions between transnational kin. I then turn my attention to Mariama and Souleymane's relationship, to examine how children in France experience and understand kinship relations that span continents. I show how her father and cousin structured Mariama's experience of transnational kinship, analyzing how Senegalese adults attempt to shape children's perceptions of kinship and the ways one "ought to" share resources with geographically distant family members.

## Transnational Cross-Cousins

In English, we would call Souleymane and Mariama "first cousins" and, in French, "*cousins germains.*" But in Senegal, like much of Africa, there are distinct kinship terms for "parallel cousins," meaning the children of siblings of the same sex, and "cross-cousins," or the children of siblings of the opposite sex (Fox 1967, 185). In Wolof, one's parallel cousins are simply called "brother" and "sister" (*mag* and *rakk*), while the terms "*sang*" and "*jaam*" index a distinct relationship between cross-cousins. The word "sang," which literally means "king" or "master" in Wolof (Moya 2017, 130), suggests that matrilateral cross-cousins are the "masters" in their relationship with their patrilateral cross-cousins, who, in turn, are their "slaves" (*jaam*). Mariama was the daughter of Souleymane's mother's brother. In Wolof, she was his sang.

Mariama's father Kadar moved to Paris in the 1970s to go to university. He had lived in the French capital and its nearby suburbs ever since, teaching physics and chemistry in a public high school. He married Mariama's mother late in life, introduced by their family members in Dakar. They lived together briefly in the suburbs of Paris but divorced soon after Mariama was born. I met Kadar's ex-wife on multiple occasions but had privileged access to Kadar's interactions with Mariama and his family members in Senegal. As the oldest of eleven siblings, Kadar had hosted each of his brothers and sisters in the French capital at one time or another. Some came for brief visits, while others stayed long enough to find a place of their own, embarking on their own migration journeys. Kadar spoke fondly of Souleymane's mother, Fama, describing her as his only little sister who lived in France and saying that she had, like him, originally moved to attend university.

At the time of my fieldwork, most of Kadar and Fama's siblings were scattered throughout Europe, though three lived in Dakar. Fama lived in a small city in the French Pyrenees, and one of their brothers lived near Kadar in a suburb of Paris. Three siblings lived in Italy and one sister in Spain. One brother was deceased, and another lived, unemployed, in their family home in Dakar. Two of Kadar's sisters also lived there, taking care of their aging mother and the children of two of their sisters who lived in Europe. Souleymane was born in Dakar and raised in their family home, cared for by his maternal aunt after his mother migrated to France. At the time of my fieldwork, he lived in a separate apartment nearby. In Senegal, where the majority of jobs are located in the "informal" sector and characterized by their precarious nature (APS 2015), Souleymane's position as a journalist at a major newspaper provided him with economic security unavailable to most Senegalese. His French language skills and formal education similarly signaled his privileged class status. Formal francophone schooling, like the language skills it teaches and necessitates, also indexes class, signaling that one's family has the means to pay school fees.

An analysis of Mariama and Souleymane's relationship in the context of their transnational family sheds light on everyday kinship-making processes that shape and are shaped by resource redistribution on a global scale. It demonstrates the continued salience of long-standing kinship strategies, showing how practices that have permitted Africans to weather economic volatility for centuries are now carried out, in part, through social media.

## Cousin Marriage and "Modern" Morals

In Wolof society, as in many areas where a specific term designates cross-cousins, this relation is often described as the preferential conjugal unit. As such, women—said to rank lower than their husbands in gender hierarchies—ideally marry men who are their "slaves" in kinship terms (Diop 1985, 60–65; Moya 2017). These overlapping hierarchies counterbalance each other to establish a union that is, symbolically at least, egalitarian (Diop 1985, 65). The cross-cousin relationship allows individuals to renegotiate and play with symmetry and asymmetry in their relative social roles. Rank relations among cross-cousins are often the topic of lighthearted play. Indeed, cross-cousins are known for mischievous and even profane joking relationships, which, in any other context, would cause offense (Diop 1985, 60; Radcliffe-Brown 1940; Mauss 1928; Lévi-Strauss 1945; Launay 1977, 2006). In Senegal, relationships between jaam and sang cross-cousins are said to be playful and flirtatious, founded on systematic teasing, and associated with specific obligations. On the days of religious celebrations, jaam perform the role of a slave by cooking and "animating" the event, even theatrically washing their cross-cousin's feet (Moya 2017; Diop 1985, 60).

## Meta-Semiotics of Kinship and Marriage

Linguistic anthropologist Asif Agha distinguishes between kinship terms (kinterms) and kinship behaviors: that is, the "behaviors performed through the use of kinterms or behaviors construed through the use of kinterms" (2007, 344). Practices such as gift-giving, for example, may constitute kinship behaviors when construed through kinterms that group them alongside other practices associated with familial relations. Decoupling kinterms and kinship behaviors sheds light on the ways in which children in the Senegalese diaspora who speak no Wolof may nonetheless take part in relationships that family members in Senegal understand in the terms of Wolof kinship. Mariama, for example, knew only a few phrases in Wolof and was not familiar with the kinship terms jaam and sang.

The distinction between kinship terms versus behaviors also sheds light on the ways individuals improvise on and transform family relations, allowing for an analysis of emergent and metaphoric forms of kinship (or "fictive kin") alongside conventional familial relations. Agha points out that, although individuals' actual behaviors do not always conform to the kinship norms they are thought to share, "acquaintance with norms also makes possible effective forms of tropic improvisation" (2007, 340), through which individuals play with and reconfigure kinship norms in their efforts to achieve specific interactional aims and carry out the social work of relating.

Second, Agha's reflexive model highlights the ways in which meta-level semiotic discourses imbue kinship relations with values "construed society-internally as a higher-order index of other facts about persons" (2007, 345, 358). He points out that the social meanings of kinship vary within each society, relative to "social domain (practices, groups, institutional frameworks)" (2007, 340). As such, various familial forms come to be associated with specific groups of people and are thought to be linked to notions of class membership, urban or rural residence, and modern versus traditional values. Agha's approach encourages a focus on the uptake or the pragmatic effects of various kinship behaviors, taking into account the possibility that the perspectives of those engaging in and interpreting the relation overlap only to a certain degree.

In Senegal, representations of cross-cousin marriage vary with socioeconomic class, age, and geographic location. While these unions were relatively common among the generational cohort of Senegalese now aged sixty or older (Neveu Kringelbach 2016, 157; see also Dial 2008, 74–9), urban youth are sometimes unaware that marriage is associated with the cross-cousin relationship at all. Senegalese villagers and inhabitants of lower-class urban areas may still describe it as the ideal marriage unit (Moya 2017), but I have heard middle- and upper-class urbanites describe cross-cousin marriage as a "traditional" practice limited to villages and discouraged by Islam. In France, cousin marriage is associated with the bygone kinship practices of aristocratic families. In Europe and Africa alike, this type of relation can mark couples or entire groups as "backward," insufficiently "modern," or, for immigrants in France, unsuccessfully "integrated" into French society.

Mariama's father, Kadar, like many Dakarois in Paris, regularly criticized African immigrants who arranged marriages for their children between cousins or with partners from their parents' village. Despite Mariama and Souleymane's genealogical position as cross-cousins, marriage was not, to my knowledge, an explicit topic of discussion or even the subject of teasing among family members. Souleymane was already married to a woman his age, whom he planned to join in Montreal the following autumn. Furthermore, Senegalese urbanites such as Souleymane increasingly aspire to companionate, monogamous marriage[2] and cross-cousin unions have become rare (Neveu Kringelbach 2016, 157).

Normative evaluations of cousin marriage as a problematic relic from the past construe this kinship practice according to a "moral narrative of modernity" (Keane 2013; Latour 1993, chap. two). Central to these narratives are morally charged expectations of kinship and how relatives "ought" to share resources. According to these economic moralities, the emancipated modern subject should be autonomous, not indebted to far-flung kinship networks.

Modern notions of kinship position the nuclear family as the basic socioeconomic unit, whereas polygyny and high fertility are associated with "traditional" familial arrangements (Déchaux 2003; Cole 2016; Radcliffe-Brown and Forde 1950). Jennifer Cole points out that "romantic love, companionate marriage, and the nuclear family all emerged with—and signify—modernity, while the pragmatic demands of extended families, custom, and material concerns are said to characterize more traditional societies" (2016, 202). If modern marriage is ideally a pact between two individuals founded on romantic love, cross-cousin marriage rings of obligation: a strategic decision made by extended families. Africanist scholars have pointed out that the notion that economics should ideally be separate from intimate familial relations hinges on a "discursive and cognitive split of emotions and material resources that is particularly salient in the West" (Coe 2013, 59), but that is not relevant in many African contexts (see also Cole 2011). Cati Coe asserts that, in West Africa, "a person's distribution of his or her resources is taken as his or her level of affection for others," in contrast to the United States and Europe, where "the distribution of material resources between family members is downplayed" (2013, 28).

Scholarship on family in Europe and the United States has repeatedly demonstrated that, in reality, kinship arrangements diverge significantly from idealized notions of nuclear families (Déchaux 2003; Gulløv and Winther 2015; Ochs and Kremer-Sadlik 2013; Gillis 1996). But the ways in which individuals evaluate and experience kinship are nonetheless shaped by normative images of family, institutionalized in law and everyday language. Keane explains that narratives of modernity produce a "largely tacit set of expectations about what a modern, progressive person, subject, and citizen, should be" (2013, 160). Failure to embody these characteristics is treated as "an ethical failing" thought to pose a threat to individuals and entire societies. Immigrants are under particular pressure to demonstrate membership in their host country's "community of value" (Anderson 2013) lest they be perceived as unable (or worse, unwilling) to live up to modern ideals. Immigrants' kinship practices are scrutinized as measures of their belonging in the host society.

## Kinship and Rank-Based Redistribution

Economic moralities of rank-based redistribution presume and entail inequalities, which direct the flow of material resources (Irvine 2001; Buggenhagen 2012, chap. 2). In cross-cousin relationships, jaam (slaves) are expected to "work" for their sang (washing their feet or helping cook), who, in turn, provide the former with gifts and support. This relation is contingent upon age, however, in that children are not expected to engage in the (often flirtatious) behaviors of cross-cousins. Overlapping hierarchies of age can sometimes reverse the direction of gifts between cross-cousins, as in the case of an adult jaam who provides a child sang with gifts.

Growing up and gaining status in Senegal are interpreted according to economic moralities of rank-based redistribution. To be an adult depends less on age than having the material means to marry, take care of children, and otherwise support dependents (Cole 2011; Bledsoe 1990; Durham 2000, 2004). Migrants similarly achieve status in Senegal by distributing money and gifts. In their transnational family, Kadar's and Souleymane's positions as successful adults were thus contingent on their ability and willingness to redistribute their resources. To position oneself favorably in transnational kinship networks while simultaneously demonstrating belonging in one's host country, migrants must carefully construct their kinship relations, taking advantage of overlaps and ambiguities between diverse meanings of family.

## Kids' Kinship and Facebook Families

The ways children understood their kinship relations often diverged from their parents' perceptions. Even those children who understood Wolof spoke of their family members using French kinship terms. Most professed ignorance when I asked about Wolof kinship relations that lacked an equivalent term in French (such as sang and jaam). At Senegalese social gatherings in Paris, adults from Dakar attempted to locate themselves relative to other Senegalese. Prodding their interlocutor's past, they searched out connections in meandering conversations that regularly uncovered long-forgotten social links and sometimes even kinship relations.

Adults laughed in delight when they unearthed an unexpectedly close connection, while their children disengaged, expressing boredom with theatrical sighs. Kids responded to these discoveries with skepticism, unconvinced that their parents had stumbled on "real" family relations. Mariama expressed ambivalence regarding her father's interpretations of family, sometimes questioning Kadar's representations of kinship. For example, Kadar once revealed to me that a Senegalese mother and daughter in Paris whom he had originally introduced to me as "family friends" were in reality their distant cousins. When I asked Mariama later if she was aware of this relationship, she reacted dismissively, explaining that the girl was not her "real" cousin. In contrast to her father, who used the term "cousin" to reflect a distant but nonetheless genealogical kinship relation, Mariama interpreted this kinterm as a form of metaphorical or "fictive" kinship.

Mariama's perceptions of who constituted kin became clear when, at my request, she drew a picture of her "family tree." She began by confidently adding her father's siblings to the tree, hesitating only on the names of one aunt and one uncle whom she had never met. When she looked to her father for clarification, he began guiding her through their kinship connections, listing his siblings, then nieces and nephews, one by one. Mariama, meanwhile, continued mapping the family tree as she saw fit, ignoring her father's genealogical list, asking him only to repeat himself when she arrived at names she was less sure of. Kadar carefully named family members and related details of their lives, while Mariama quickly exhausted her knowledge of family connections and grew bored of the task. Sidestepping her father's long-winded explanations, she contented herself to write only "grand-mère" and "grand-père" in reference to Kadar's parents, resisting my suggestion that she ask her father their names. Instead of listing her cousins under the names of their parents, as she had done for herself and her own parents, Mariama listed them all together at the top of the page, explaining that she had "a lot of cousins." She asked me multiple times if I really wanted her to list all of them, reiterating that she has a very big family.

Mariama spoke of her cousins as if they made up an unwieldy list, impossible to keep track of. This dismissive portrayal contrasted with the importance she attributed to her relationship with Souleymane. She hesitated before adding Souleymane's name to her list of cousins, as if his inclusion on this list required explanation. "And who else," she wondered aloud. "Ah, Souleymane!" she remembered. Mariama then paused before writing his name, specifying, "But him, actually, he's a journalist. But he's still my cousin." As she wrote his name next to those of cousins closer to her age who lived in her grandmother's home in Dakar, Mariama verbally distinguished Souleymane as an employed adult, only to then reiterate his genealogical status as her cousin. Indeed, Mariama and her father regularly singled Souleymane out among her cousins, drawing my attention to their exchanges of gifts and regular communication.

### "Friends" and Family: Media and Materiality of Cultivating Closeness

My attention was first drawn to a special relationship between Mariama and Souleymane when Kadar told me that Mariama's cousin had promised to buy her an airplane ticket to Dakar during her school vacation. A testament to Souleymane's desire to cultivate a relationship with his cousin, this gesture would facilitate Mariama's familiarity with Dakar and her kin there. Later, when I inquired about the possible vacation to Senegal, Mariama expressed doubts that the promise would materialize.

Her father responded with surprise, bordering on indignation. When Mariama justified herself, saying that sometimes people "just say things like that," her father reassured her, saying that if Souleymane had offered her a trip to Dakar, he would make good on his promise. Later, when I asked Kadar whether he thought that Souleymane would indeed buy the ticket, he suggested that it did not matter whether Souleymane bought it or he (Kadar) did, because Souleymane could pay him back once in Senegal. Regardless of whether, in the end, it was Souleymane or her father who financed the ticket, for Mariama, her trip would be a gift from her cousin.

Mariama described her close relationship with Souleymane to me during a guided "Facebook tour" I audio-recorded. On her Facebook page, Souleymane was the first "friend" she showed me, her attention drawn to his page by a private message he had recently sent her. She scrolled quickly through a chain of messages they had exchanged and flipped through his photographs, describing when he had posted them. She then perused her personal inbox, skipping over long chats with friends from school to show me other messages she had sent to family members abroad. Most had responded succinctly— one line of thanks to Mariama's happy birthday message, for example. Others had sent no response at all.

Mariama then showed me her Facebook "wall," which included posts in which people in Senegal had "tagged" her. By adding Mariama's name to the caption of an image or article they posted, these Dakarois linked their post to her Facebook profile. She confessed that she was not always sure why they had tagged her in posts of photographs taken in Dakar or of comics about buying sheep for Tabaski, the Islamic festival Eid al-Adha. She explained that she did not know exactly how she was related to many of these young people in Dakar, but knew them to be family. Mariama's Facebook exchanges with Souleymane were among the most substantial and regular she had with family members. Most of her relatives who had Facebook profiles were older than her. The communications they shared were brief and indirect, unlike the personal messages she shared with Souleymane.

The following summer, Mariama and her father traveled to Senegal while I was in Dakar carrying out fieldwork. There, I was able to meet Souleymane at the home of his maternal, Mariama's paternal, grandmother. The large family home had many bedrooms, financed by remittances that Mariama's father, Souleymane's mother, and their siblings had been sending from Europe since the 1970s. After introducing myself to Souleymane, I told him that Mariama had often spoken about him back in Paris.

I mistakenly referred to him as her "uncle" and Souleymane kindly corrected me, saying that even if she sometimes calls him her uncle, he is actually her cousin. Having overheard my error, Mariama rushed toward us, insisting that she does not mistake him for her uncle; she knows very well that he is her cousin! Mariama and her father then joined our conversation, Kadar teasing her for the attention she pays her cousin and telling Souleymane that Mariama found him very "classy." Kadar chuckled playfully as he described their preparations for the trip, saying that Mariama had insisted on buying a special gift for Souleymane. Kadar teased his daughter, reporting that she "loved Souleymane so much that she wanted to spend one hundred fifty euros on a shirt for him." She selected this gift because, Kadar reported, she knew that he always wears chic button-down shirts. Souleymane's collared shirts visibly distinguished him among their relatives in Dakar, most of whom wore T-shirts or wax-print fabrics. In the heat of Dakar's summer, Souleymane's shirts, like his closed shoes, indexed his socioeconomic and professional status. Among Kadar's nephews in Senegal, he was the only one who held a salaried position in Dakar's formal sector.

On returning to Paris, I learned that Souleymane had given Mariama two hundred euros just before she returned to France. Offered just before their interactions were again stretched across a transnational expanse, Souleymane's gift appeared to be an effort to encourage Mariama to remain in contact. Indeed, back in Paris, Mariama spent most of the money replacing her flip-phone with a new smartphone, which allowed her to communicate with family abroad through Facebook, Skype, and WhatsApp.

### Facebook Scaffolding

A site of regular familial exchange, Facebook fosters the kinship work I have called "scaffolding," in which adults strategically engage children's participation in kinship activities and attribute the act of relating to the child. Borrowing from cognitive psychologists' work on language acquisition (Bruner 1978), linguistic anthropologists use the term "scaffolding" to refer to mediating activities that social actors carry out to support "authorized knowledge, or that information which is deemed by the community and the institution to be legitimate" (Bruna and Gomez 2009, 157). Ochs and Schieffelin (2009) provide the example of a caregiver who constructs a tower, allows a child to place the last block, and then describes the construction as the child's doing. They point out that, through the work of scaffolding, caregivers portray children to be more culturally competent than their behaviors would otherwise indicate. By celebrating children as skillful social actors, through scaffolding, adults place a tacit emphasis on behaviors they value.

Facebook was a social media platform particularly adapted to scaffolding work among transnational families: first, because (at the time of my fieldwork, at least) it was a multigenerational platform that fostered kinwork,[3] and second, because (at that point), children demonstrated a sense of ease and ownership on the site (relative to adults). While Facebook's most avid users at that time were still young people, among the Senegalese with whom I carried out my fieldwork, the site's user base was undergoing a generational shift. Parents in their forties and fifties were increasingly creating profiles and joining their children on the site. As such, Facebook was a new (and ultimately short-lived) space of intergenerational interactions where children had direct access to international family members.

As the site's popularity extended across age cohorts (see Miller et al. 2016), interactions with family members became an increasingly important use of the platform. The site developed to foster this engagement, encouraging users to signal who among their "friends" are family members. Unlike Twitter or Instagram, where one might create a public profile that reveals little about one's family life, Facebook encourages users to create a personal profile, sharing information on their relationships and announcing events like marriages and births.

Daniel Miller and his colleagues (2016) have documented the ways in which Facebook users internationally use the platform to consciously form family ties and to connect with distant relatives they may have never met face to face. In Facebook-mediated kinship relations at that time, children possess particular agency as a result of their familiarity with and regular use of the site. In most cases, the children I worked with had joined Facebook before their parents. Mariama, for example, joined four years before her father finally created his own profile. Having observed (and been part of) the development of the platform and its usage, youth demonstrated a sense of authority on the site relative to their parents, who often struggled to understand the utility of its various functions. When he began using Facebook, Kadar had trouble grasping what to post where. He repeatedly addressed specific friends in the space for general comments on a photograph. Because he did not "tag" the friend in question, notifying the user that he had mentioned them, Kadar's personalized questions often remained unanswered, hidden among the comments his photograph had inspired.

Children were socialized into Facebook's various functions both by engaging with their peers on the site and by talking about these interactions. They developed an understanding of Facebook codes of usage through discussions analyzing the ways in which interactions on Facebook had unfolded (see Gershon 2010). Children developed a Facebook-specific vocabulary (posting, tagging, messaging) that made clear the various possible forms and functions of communication on the platform.

These social media skills positioned children in transnational families to take agentive roles in interactions with kin. While telephone conversations and Skype calls with relatives in Dakar were primarily organized by her father, it was Mariama who would inform Kadar about recent exchanges on Facebook. Unlike calls or chat-based applications like WhatsApp, which mediate exchanges between dyads or preselected groups, Facebook's timeline creates a "public" space between friends. Mariama was thus privy to interactions among family members that did not directly involve her, allowing her to observe exchanges that could later be of interest to her father or other family members who spent less time on the platform than she did. Facebook also allowed her to autonomously initiate interactions with kin, as she did with Souleymane, whom she had added as a friend following a trip to Dakar in 2012. But the structural affordances that permitted Mariama to engage autonomously with family members are unequally distributed among children in transnational families. Maintaining one's Facebook profile requires regular access to a smartphone, tablet, or computer. While these are common among youth and adults in Dakar, children rarely possess their own devices, leaving them dependent on older people for access to the social media platform. Children in the Senegalese diaspora often have privileged access to Facebook compared with their Senegal-based age-mates.

## Constructing Cross-Cousins

In many ways, Mariama and Souleymane's relationship diverged significantly from the behaviors that Senegalese (and anthropologists) commonly associate with cross-cousins. Mariama was unfamiliar with the kinship terms jaam and sang. She did not appear aware of the stereotypical forms of teasing that cross-cousins often engage in. Nor did Souleymane attempt to recruit her to the role of joking partner, introducing her to this mode of play. Marriage between the two was not a possibility that family members explicitly entertained. But even if Mariama never called Souleymane her "jaam," their close relationship suggests that this kinship relation offered a logical foundation for the creation of new forms of relatedness, linking them across the Senegalese diaspora.

Mariama and Souleymane were both quick to emphasize their status as cousins, not as uncle and niece. For Mariama, this meant that Souleymane was not a person of her father's generation who had the right to boss her around. For Souleymane, the concept of jaam/sang cross-cousins provided him with a means of creating a close relationship not only with Mariama but also with her father. Scholars of kinship have argued that kin strategically use marriage between cross-cousins to cement socioeconomic relations between a nephew and his mother's brother. In Wolof society, men are said to have a material obligation to provide not only for their own children but also for their sister's children (Diop 1985, 60). John and Jean Comaroff point out that a mother transmits to her children a particular relationship with her brother, which is accompanied by "ritualized reciprocal exchanges, solidarity against agnatic rivals, and, sometimes, substantial material support" (1981, 37). When a man's daughter marries his sister's son, the uncle continues to benefit from his investments in his nephew's upbringing.

An examination of the efforts Souleymane and Kadar invested in the creation and maintenance of Souleymane and Mariama's relationship shows how the cross-cousin model provided a foundation not only for a close relationship between Souleymane and Mariama but also between Souleymane and Kadar. Souleymane's mother had four other living brothers but, to my knowledge, he did not offer any of their daughters gifts as substantial and frequent as those he provided Mariama. The Comaroffs note that, although a man's mother is likely to have multiple brothers, he will "generally emphasize his close matrilateral link with only one or two of them," carving out his own kinship universe by "selectively activating a number of linkages" (Comaroff and Comaroff 1981, 33). Kinship relations are always negotiable, produced through individuals' efforts to position themselves within political-economic networks of kin. The significance of Souleymane's relationship with Mariama was the result of her role as her father's daughter, his uncle. In cross-cousin relations, she held the high status of sang thanks to this relation, essentially representing and yielding the authority of his uncle.

Establishing a close relationship with Mariama and, by extension, with her father, Kadar, allowed Souleymane to create and reinforce socioeconomic bonds with this French-educated branch of their transnational family. Like his uncle, Souleymane's formal education in Dakar had provided him with access to salaried employment in the formal economic sector. His plans to emigrate to Montreal would reinforce parallels between the two men's lives and statuses in their family, as educated migrants to francophone destinations who had the means to migrate legally and seek skilled jobs abroad.

Indeed, as tightening immigration controls and economic decline in "fortress Europe" have caused France's allure to stagnate among French-educated Senegalese, Canada has gained in popularity and prestige as a migration destination (see Hirtzmann 2013; Pâris 2014). Quebec saw an upsurge in visa requests from young French citizens who hope to relocate to this francophone area perceived to rebound more quickly than Europe following crisis (Daudens 2012; Shingler 2014). Souleymane's migration destination offered economic promise and prestige similar to that associated with France when his uncle migrated in the 1970s. Souleymane and Kadar's education and class status distinguished them from their relatives who had migrated to work in the informal sector in Spain or Italy, as well as from those who were unemployed in Dakar. Souleymane's choice to cultivate a close relationship with Mariama and her father both flows from and reinforces divisions in the Senegalese diaspora that may be observed within their own transnational family.

For his part, Kadar played a strategic role in reinforcing, broadcasting, and supporting the kinship behaviors that linked his daughter and nephew. He verbally highlighted the material support that Souleymane provided Mariama, as well as the affection she displayed for Souleymane. Even if her father never spoke of marriage, Kadar frequently teased his daughter about her relationship with Souleymane, repeatedly stating in a sing-song tone that she loves her cousin. Drawing frequent attention to the gifts the cousins exchanged, Kadar circulated an image of closeness between the two, reminding his daughter and other family members that she and Souleymane share a special bond. Kadar also paid for the sarice gift that she offered Souleymane on their trip to Dakar, treating Mariama as the gift's impetus and true giver. This meant, importantly, that Mariama benefitted from her relationship with Souleymane and (unlike Badara and Aissatou in the previous chapter) was not expected to offer money or gifts of her own possessions. Her father even demonstrated a willingness to finance the plane ticket that Souleymane had promised his daughter, transforming a verbal proposition from Souleymane to Mariama into a material debt between his nephew and himself. In facilitating the acts of exchange that linked the two cousins, Kadar actively worked to reproduce Souleymane and Mariama's close relationship.

And yet it was on Facebook, with Mariama, that the majority of their interactions were carried out, giving the girl a sense of authorship in the creation of this relationship. Bourdieu emphasized the fact that kinship relations can always be characterized in multiple ways (traced through paternal or maternal lines, for example), so that "one can always bring a remote relative closer . . . by emphasizing what unites" or "distance the closest relative by emphasizing what separates" (1990, 172). As individuals manage and manipulate the meanings and practices of kinship for personal and collective aims, what is at stake "is nothing other than the definition of the practical limits of the group" (Bourdieu 1990, 172). The identification and redefinition of the terms of a cross-cousin relationship, key to individuals' positions in socioeconomic networks, simultaneously mark boundaries of belonging between differently positioned groups of kin.

Souleymane's gifts to Mariama thus provided a means by which he could carve his own political-economic position in their transnational family, cultivating closeness through tacit reference to jaam/sang relationships without explicitly characterizing the relationship as such. These repeated material exchanges created privileged socioeconomic links between Souleymane, Kadar, and Mariama, but avoided the sometimes stigmatizing connotations of cousin marriage. They wove particularly dense connections between the francophone, educated members of their transnational family by reconfiguring long-standing kinship behaviors in ways that allowed them to position themselves as "modern" individuals, capable of integrating into Europe or North America. In so doing, Souleymane, Kadar, and Mariama carved out new forms of kinship in the Senegalese diaspora through reference to and transformation of kinship norms readily recognizable in Dakar. Mariama's obliviousness to the workings of cross-cousin relationships in Senegal was relatively inconsequential, given that the two men, both raised in Dakar, actively facilitated gift exchanges between the two cousins. Her father's and cousin's acquaintance with the cross-cousin relation made "possible effective forms of tropic improvisation" (Agha 2007, 340), which organized and provided moral justification for the flow of material resources. As the recipient of Souleymane's material care, Mariama was the locus of her father's and cousin's efforts at making and reinforcing their transnational connections. The two men thus established a cultural scaffolding surrounding her, aimed at creating a particular closeness between these two geographically distant branches of their transnational family.

## Selective Kinship in the Senegalese Diaspora

An analysis of Souleymane and Mariama's relationship as that of "transnational cross-cousins" sheds light on the ways in which individuals in the Senegalese diaspora draw on and reconfigure long-standing modes of kinship in new political-economic contexts and through new media. By engaging in certain kinship behaviors associated with jaam and sang relations, without explicit use of these kinterms, Souleymane was able to draw on this kinship relation to connect with certain transnational kin without associating himself with the "traditional" practice of cousin marriage. Decoupling kinship behaviors and kinship terms, these transnational kin improvised on the jaam/ sang relationship in ways that allowed them to position themselves favorably in Senegal and abroad.

The interactions in transnational Senegalese families examined here have revealed the ways in which children actively participate in the reproduction of transnational kinship relations and how caregivers attempt to guide children's interpretations of family by establishing cultural scaffolding around them. Facebook provided an efficient means through which to carry out this scaffolding, by giving children particular agency in the reproduction of kinship relations. Because Mariama actively maintained her relationship with Souleymane, the efforts her father and Souleymane put into establishing a closeness between the cousins were easily overlooked. As such, Mariama and her "love" for her cousin appeared to be the origin of this closeness.

The autonomy and agency Facebook grant children in transnational kinship relations are not evenly distributed across transnational families. Indeed, Facebook allows children with regular access to the social media platform, who are thus already privileged, to create and reinforce relations that accentuate extant inequalities between themselves and their Senegal-based age-mates. But viewed through the lens of economic moralities of rank-based redistribution, reinforcing these inequalities, as Souleymane did with his substantial gifts, is not in itself problematic, in that a more substantial difference of rank might motivate more significant redistribution of resources later on. Mariama's position of privilege is not problematic in that it might eventually direct the flow of resources, if (and only if), through these exchanges, Souleymane and Kadar also transmit key concepts of economic moralities of rank-based redistribution, so that her unequal position might one day move her to invest in their Senegal-based family. Investments in children of migrants are uncertain but also critical to the social and material reproduction of families in Senegal.

# Networks of Selective Solidarity: Talk of Morals, Money, and Migration

F amilies in Senegal and its diaspora treat "solidarity" as a fundamental social value, but it is impossible to give to everyone who asks. Solidarity (*dimbalante*) in the Senegalese diaspora is achieved through interpersonal acts of aid (*ndimbal*), mediated by asymmetrical relationships between migrants and those back home. "Help" generally refers to monetary support that flows in one direction: from high status to low, from migrants toward those "left behind." Middle-class Senegalese in Paris encounter solicitations for monetary aid from relatives in Dakar and other Africans in Paris. Meanwhile, their middle-class employers and children's teachers in Paris expect certain signs of "integration," which require material investments in their lives in France, their children's education, clothing, and housing. A far cry from stereotypes of immigrants who irrationally spend and profit from the system, families who invest in and aspire to transnational middle-class status must use their resources more judiciously than their French colleagues who earn the same salaries but have no transnational economic commitments.

I have used the term "selective solidarity" here to capture the social work required by the simple economic principle that social actors with finite resources must select the amount and types of material support they provide others. All solidarity is necessarily *selective*, mediated by questions of group belonging (in families, social classes, nations) in specific historical and political-economic contexts. The selective solidarity of the French social-welfare state defines deservingness relative to economic moralities of immigrant "integration" and stereotypes of immigrants' (irrational or illegal) economic practices. Class-based expectations of immigrant integration shape rights to state allocations and, more broadly, mediate access to educational and employment opportunities. These markers of middle-class status have become increasingly difficult to achieve in France over the past thirty years and déclassement disproportionately affects immigrants and their children.

Senegalese families' stories of navigating resource redistribution, in the face of moral pressures from people on different continents, demonstrate how the expectations of kinship in Africa are bound up with values of immigrant integration in Europe. As budgets are stretched thin, economic solidarity at state and family levels becomes increasingly selective. Kin in Senegal must adapt, meanwhile, by adopting flexible expectations of family to accommodate relatives abroad.

Awkward and inevitable, selective solidarity is also unspeakable. To make explicit one's strategies for selective solidarity would be an admission of practical knowledge on how to *avoid* (morally valued) forms of reciprocity. Even my interlocutors in Chapter 4 who did announce this position in brusque terms softened their stances over the course of our conversations. Abdoulaye (Badara's father) noted that, rather than rejecting outright someone's request for monetary support, he would make some "gesture" (that is, give some money), even if only a symbolic sum with a promise of more the next time. Aminata, who was still a student in Paris and had only lived in Dakar in her childhood, had tactics for selective solidarity that even she admitted would not be viewed as socially acceptable by her relatives in Senegal. Her tactic of "playing crazy" (feigning ignorance or pretending not to speak Wolof), in particular, is one more harshly judged by Senegalese audiences. Yet even she concluded her discussion of material pressures on migrants by saying that one day she, too, will give.

When solidarity is enacted through interpersonal interactions, acts of selective solidarity are immanently personal and require substantial knowledge of social norms to manage with discretion. Whether pulled off seamlessly or embarrassingly botched, selective solidarity is enacted through language or, as is often the case, carried out through a silent *refusal* to speak to and engage with others. This can be seen in Mouna's strategic calculations about where in Paris she could openly speak Wolof, described in the Introduction, as well as in the self-lowering strategies that "noble" Wolof villagers carry out through their salutations, when they meet griots in public (Irvine 1974, chaps. two and four). Another well-known example among Senegalese is the tendency for migrants abroad to, at some point, simply stop answering calls from numbers with a +221 (Senegalese) country code in the days leading up to a holiday. Such an act of baldly ignoring one's family and friends might appear to be a brazen rejection. Often, this is not the case, however. Rather, silent withdrawal is one of the few socially acceptable means by which one can communicate to family and friends that one has spent all the resources one can afford helping relatives prepare the celebration.

Language-mediated strategies for avoiding economic entanglement are rarely taken up as neutral by those who observe or hear about them. Instead, social actors evaluate and interpret their own and others' practices of material exchange—and avoidance of economic engagement—relative to ideological frames that I have been calling "economic moralities." These frames are located in the moral metapragmatics of everyday talk, cued in the subtleties of the types and terms one draws on in conversation, negotiated and communicated tacitly through the formal structures that verbal and material exchanges take as they unfold.

## The Moral Language of Exchange

This book provides an account of some of the more indirect ways that moral talk moves money. These chapters have explored how the moral language of family life works to weave the fabric of current and future economies and migration networks. These links—sometimes fleeting, others durable—are forged through the sedimented effects of everyday language that relatives in Senegal and its diaspora use to guide children in their material and affective practices.

Economic moralities focus analytic attention on the ways that moral narratives work to divide social actors (to value is to evaluate) in ways that entail a specific directionality (an "ought"). That is to say, like the modern/non-modern distinction explored in Chapter 2, moral divisions include a preferred side of the axis of distinction (depending on one's perspective, of course). The way this axis is framed reveals one's alignment with diverse economic moralities and serves to situate a person in social and economic relations at various scales, relative to multiple possible forms of belonging. Alioune's category of a frauder, for instance (Chapter 2), was an example of a social type, the use of which signaled a middle-class speaker in France who categorizes certain informal economic practices in pejorative terms. This type and the economic moralities that underpin it served, in turn, to distinguish transnational middle-class Senegalese from lower-class immigrants in France in their moral language and (presumably) material practices. It also entailed a shift in scales of redistribution that speakers treated as relevant or legitimate, from interpersonal exchanges to state-mediated solidarity.

The chapters of this book have examined how economic moralities work to establish social distinctions while simultaneously justifying material relationships between proposed categories, in ways that structure people's rights to resources. The Introduction highlighted the moral act of metapragmatic typification, examining how middle-class Senegalese divide up their social worlds in Paris in moral-economic terms distinguishing themselves from working-class ("bush-to-banlieue" type) immigrants in France. The differences they perceive between various types of African immigrants, interpreted in terms of migration trajectory and education (which is to say class status), in turn, shape the ways middle-class Senegalese move through Paris, which language they speak where, and who they talk, eat, and otherwise share resources with.

Economic moralities underpin class distinctions in France and Senegal alike. But embodied practices like speaking French fluently or proficiently eating with a fork and knife, which in Senegal are perceived to index class and formal education, in France are often taken up as signs of "integration." For visible minorities, national belonging depends on one's ability to achieve markers of French middle-classness. Fitting in is, at least in part, a question of material investment in one's host country, orienting one's communication and consumption practices to consistently demonstrate "integration" and alignment with French middle-class values. Chapter 1 explored economic moralities of class in migration, distinguishing between those I have termed "transnational middle classes," who invest in class-making in both home and host countries, from "diasporic middle classes," whose status ambitions are focused on their countries of origin and live abroad as lower-class migrants.

Practices of scale-making through language are critical to acts of selective solidarity. Chapter 2 examined how people draw on economic moralities in unfolding conversation to shift between scales of redistribution, alternating between moral positions that support face-to-face solidarity (essential to systems of rank-based redistribution) and the contractually based, publicly managed solidarity of the French state in ways that mark their distinction from (and moral critique of) the economic practices of certain other African immigrants in France. Public-versus-private distinctions, central to notions of solidarity in France, are also foundational to moral expectations of immigrant "integration." Secularism, for instance, is expected specifically in French public spaces. Even the staunchest defenders of *laïcité* agree that people can practice religion in private spaces of their home and places of worship. Notions of public and private spaces accordingly shape the social and self-presentation practices of middle-class Senegalese in Paris. We saw this in the careful ways Rama Sy described speaking, dressing, and presenting herself and her family in public in Paris versus in the privacy of her own and her relatives' apartments.

Chapter 3 explored how speakers anchor economic moralities in place through language and deictic reference. Senegalese families create spaces for the enactment of economic moralities and commensal practices common among their Senegalese relatives, articulating with ease the differences between life "here" and "there" and the importance of transmitting Senegalese values to their children. Rama also used the deictics "downstairs" and "outside" to endow social spaces outside her apartment in Paris with moral significance relative to the threat she perceived, of her children becoming entangled in the illicit activities of which she presumed the young men who loitered in the entryway of their building were involved.

Economic moralities emerge in co-constructed stories. The moral meanings of acts of resource redistribution that took place in Senegal, sometimes many years prior, are renegotiated in the emergent act of recounting. When children attempt to describe (and thus make sense of) acts of exchange they observed (or took part in) on trips to Dakar, in front of their parents and other relatives from Senegal, at stake is their ability to demonstrate themselves to have grown up and come to better understand the interactions. Chapter 5, then, showed how economic moralities of Senegalese kinship are made relevant to migrants' children growing up in France through exchanges on social media and (sometimes substantial) gifts from relatives living in Senegal and elsewhere in its diaspora.

### Investing in Transnational Children

In July 2021, I was back in the same living room in Dakar where, ten years prior, I had filmed siblings Fatou and Karim as they embodied contrasting semiotic registers to redistribute their snacks (Chapter 2). Members of the family gradually made their way into the living room to greet me. After an hour, I had yet to see Fatou, who was usually one of the first to come shake my hand and smile, agreeing that it had been too long since we had seen each other, before returning to her housework. "*Ana Fatou?*" I asked Djenaba about the whereabouts of her eldest daughter. Djenaba's response was standard, but vague, "Mu ngiy foofu" (lit. she is there). But the deictic "there" (*foofu*) suggested that Fatou was neither home nor expected back anytime soon. "There where?" I wondered. "Canada," her younger brother Karim chimed in. Studying in Montreal, Fatou was living with Djenaba's sister, who had moved there over a decade ago.

"Next it's me," said Karim with a grin. Not necessarily Canada, he explained. His mother nodded as he told me the hope is that he too will "leave" (*partir*) to go abroad, once he finishes high school. Even for those who hope to ultimately return to Senegal to work, the value of a university degree from Europe or North America far outweighs that of a diploma from any university in Senegal. For many middle-class Dakarois, youth grow up assuming that university studies also imply moving abroad. In SICAP Mermoz, ten-year-old Meïmouna pointed to her cousins in an unframed family photo taken four years prior, telling me one by one which country they live in now. Once she had identified everyone who was already abroad, the girl then proceeded to list, in the order of their birth, the rest of the cousins in the photo, indicating who would then be the next to leave. She hesitated only briefly when I wondered where they would all be going, before shrugging and answering simply, "to a country."

Among Senegal's middle classes, migrating for one's studies has been a critical means to social mobility and to avoiding déclassement since the colonial period. Recent decades have seen an overall tightening of migration restrictions in Europe and North America, paired with diminishing opportunities associated with higher education in Africa since the 1970s (Cole 2011) and in Europe for the past thirty years (Peugny 2009). But whatever the difficulties associated with studying abroad and however unsure the ultimate results, foreign diplomas remain essential to Senegalese middle classes. This is part of a broader global trend by which higher education has become ever more essential to middle-class status, though statistically less able to assure economic security on job markets inundated with skilled candidates.

Until recently, however, France was the only obvious destination for educated Senegalese youth. Today, France is—at best—one of many plausible destinations and often not the first choice of youth from Dakar. The diminishing value of French university degrees, compounded by systemic racism in France, has increasingly led Senegalese students in Paris to view France as a "first step" on a longer professional and migratory trajectory. Seated in a café down the street from the Panthéon, a Senegalese master's student at the Sorbonne scoffed when I remarked that he was following in the footsteps of Senghor. Although factually true, based on his migration trajectory and institutional affiliation, he had trouble with the comparison. Unlike Senghor, he felt no commitment to France, and he hoped to leave as soon as he had finished his degree.

Chapter 1 traced the ways that Senegalese transnational networks expanded into Spain and Italy in the 1980s along class lines. Unlike the thousands of Senegalese who decided to test their luck in these destinations as street vendors, migrant laborers, or in other unskilled jobs, for most educated Senegalese urbanites, migration to non-francophone destinations would mean abandoning their hopes of salaried employment. As the opportunities associated with a French education have dried up in Senegal, middle-class urbanites have increasingly chosen to join Murid trade networks or use other informal (undocumented) channels to get abroad (Hannaford 2017; Babou 2021). Forgoing the potential value of the educational capital they had acquired in a francophone setting, this choice amounts to accepting long-term déclassement abroad in the hopes of attaining social mobility back home through economic means. The loss of class status that an educated urbanite accepts in this case is the closing off of belonging to a *transnational middle class* in favor of more circumscribed status ambitions, focused on Senegal and (hopefully) achieved through the economic success of migration (by whatever means), aspirations I have identified as those of *diasporic middle classes* (see Chapter 1).

Other educated Senegalese urbanites, meanwhile, continue to place their bets on education as a means for mobility, shifting the geographical focus of their efforts, often toward Canada or the United States. In addition to speaking French, young educated Senegalese are increasingly fluent in English. From preschool to high school, French/English bilingual education has mushroomed in Dakar over the past fifteen years. Students who graduate from the International School of Dakar or one of the Senegalese American Bilingual Schools are prepared to go on to university programs in English, if lucky enough to be accepted to a program abroad.

Getting to the United States to do a bachelor's program is difficult for most middle-class Senegalese, for whom tuition at American undergraduate institutions is prohibitively expensive. But a lucky few manage to leverage French *license* (bachelor's) degrees to enter graduate programs or find skilled employment in the United States. For educated Senegalese who are privileged but not rich, Canada has a reputation for being a more attainable (that is, economical) destination for studies, especially for Senegalese who have French nationality. This, I was told, can provide privileged access to a skilled work visa, particularly in fields like the health sector, in which Canada needs workers. In the quest to leverage education and language skills into social mobility and (ideally) transnational middle-classness, Senegalese youth who grew up in France have a leg up on their cousins in Dakar who were not lucky enough to be born with European passports. French-Canadian bilateral agreements reserve a certain number of work and study visas for young French citizens, but not Senegalese. The paths to North America multiply for those with French passports and diplomas, reinforcing transnational connections forged along the (linguistic) geographies of colonialism, divided by global class inequalities.

Transnational families experience escalating global inequalities in their everyday lives through processes of déclassement, which disproportionately impact immigrants and their children in France. After her daughters had gone to university, Hélène Sène reflected back on how she used to assume that if she found a way to get them into a good school and the girls tried hard, there was no reason they wouldn't succeed in France. But looking back, she could see moments in her children's trajectories, close calls, when they risked being squeezed out of the educated, middle-class paths they were on. She remembered struggling for weeks to help Mathie find an internship required for her studies. Without professional networks that could open doors in her chosen field of marketing, her parents watched fearfully, realizing that failure to obtain an internship could call her success into question, no matter how well she did in the classroom.

Freelance work and short-term contracts have become the norm for even the most highly skilled of workers in France. Senegalese in Paris who have master's degrees, like Rama Sy (Malik's mom), described in Chapter 3, often still struggle to find permanent employment. Annual contracts meant that Rama had to face hiring prejudices anew each year on the job search. As they watched their children struggle with similar prejudices at school, Rama and her husband Alpha ultimately decided to send Malik's younger sister, Diary, to Dakar to go to French school there. Rama told me that Diary had wanted to go, because school was not going well for her in Paris. At some point in the French school system, Rama explained, they do *"un tri sélectif,"* literally "selective sorting," a phrase most commonly used in French to describe sorting recyclables out from waste materials, a metaphor for the sorting process in French high schools, where academically inclined students are put on a separate curriculum to those destined for more manual, "professional" careers. This, Rama noted, worked to sideline certain children and orient them toward a "garage track" (*dans des voies de garage*), an expression to describe a situation from which one sees no way out. A "garage track" in French (*une voie de garage*) referred originally to the train track running alongside the main rail lines, used only for service, which goes literally nowhere.

## Selective Solidarity to Maintain Connections

Selective solidarity is, importantly, not the same thing as cutting off support for those back in Africa, which Senegalese call "forgetting" one's family. Instead, Senegalese migrants must practice selective solidarity in order to make good on their kinship responsibilities in both home and host countries. As my interlocutors specified, some forms of monetary support are "optional," whereas others are statutory obligations upon which households depend to survive. Adult migrants must limit the support they offer strangers and distant family, in order to be able to pay their bills back in France and continue to support their children and other dependents.

When I have presented material from this book to French audiences, most readily grasp how difficult it must be for transnational Senegalese to invest in middle-class status in France while sending money back to Senegal. When I point out that processes of déclassement make it even more difficult for migrants to transmit economic stability to their children and manage their material commitments in the two countries, French audiences often guess that this could push them to stop sending remittances or to cut off contact with certain family members. My ethnographic data suggest the opposite. As economic opportunities in France diminish and their children's futures there appear increasingly uncertain, Senegalese families invest *more* time, energy, and money into relationships in Dakar.

When faced with instability and foreclosing opportunities in France, the families in this book did not cut back their remittances. Instead, many doubled down on imagined futures in Senegal. Whatever their struggles with precarity, Rama and Alpha Sy, whose lives in Paris were among the most obviously affected by déclassement, carefully maintained their connections in Dakar. When Rama saw the opportunities for a middle-class education in

France foreclosing for her daughter, she told me she decided this was "out of the question," and selected instead to send her to live with her in-laws to attend one of Dakar's best high schools.

Their continued investments and close relationships with those in Dakar allowed Rama and Alpha to feel comfortable sending Diary to live with relatives there, without her parents. With their daughter in Dakar, they now send even more in remittances and are searching for possible economic opportunities in Senegal that would allow them to return before retirement. Growing numbers of Senegalese migrants and their children are choosing to return to Senegal (or to move for the first time to their parents' country, like Diary), as depicted in the Arte documentary, *Senegal: Retour au Bled*. Dakar remains a hub that connects Senegalese across the diaspora in ways foundational to transnational kinship- and class-making projects. Even those migrants who had the most tenuous commitments to their relatives in Senegal continued to invest resources in bringing their children back to Senegal to cultivate these connections. Kadar, Mariama's father (Chapter 5), who had little ambition of returning one day to Senegal, invested nonetheless in bringing his daughter to Dakar where she could forge a cross-cousin relationship that would soon stretch from Paris to Montreal.

Close relationships forged on summer vacations when migrants' children are young sometimes provide the foundation for long-lasting closeness, renewed as children grow on each subsequent visit to Senegal. This was the case for Diary, who, like her brother Malik, had made close relationships with her relatives in Dakar on annual trips back. Other times, summer moments of closeness are not followed up with regular contact and visits. For Mariama, her Facebook-forged closeness with her cross-cousin Souleymane was ultimately ephemeral (or perhaps, has yet to be rekindled). When I sent her a text asking how Souleymane was doing, ten years after the summer I met him at her grandmother's home in Dakar, Mariama sent me an audio message, surprised that I remembered her cousin and admitting that she hadn't heard from him in years. Although she last visited Dakar only a couple summers ago, she had stayed with her mother's relatives. After her father had a debilitating stroke while she was finishing high school, Mariama had fallen out of contact with many of her relatives on his side of the family. Children's transnational practices, guided and scaffolded by their parents, are contingent on their parents' ability and means to maintain connections, as well as caregivers' evaluations of potential futures in France, Senegal, and elsewhere in its diaspora.

## Children as Transnational Economic Actors

The children of Senegalese migrants in France come to understand the economic moralities that hold sway among their transnational relatives through stories their parents recount and in moments of shared reminiscing about past trips to Senegal. But they also learn about them through interactions that leave them filled with frustration and resentment, like the moment when Badara and his brother discovered that their father had distributed their clothing to their cousins in Dakar. They come to sense different moral-economic perspectives through intense emotional experiences, such as the embarrassment Aminata described feeling when put on the spot as a woman sang her praises and she stood there, naïve and unaware that the kind words were a means of asking for cash.

Understandings of rank-based redistribution come to children in Paris in piecemeal (and often confusing) fashions. Unlike their cousins growing up in Senegal, migrants' children do not grow up divvying up food using contrasting verbal registers to mark asymmetrical status positions. The verbal registers that adults and children use in Senegal to organize redistribution are not readily recognizable to migrants' children, who have probably only seen their parents and other relatives circulate resources according to rank on a rare few occasions in their lives. Children growing up in the diaspora may arrive at young adulthood without ever having been close enough to a griot's performance to understand that the only way out of the interaction, once your praises are being sung, is to hand over some cash.

Although there is much that migrants' children do not understand about their parents' economic relations in Senegal, the confusion and frustration youth sometimes feel are often short-lived compared to the many other ways that they feel connected to relatives and later reminisce about their time in Senegal. Even those children who, at the time of my fieldwork, were the most reluctant to go back, changed their minds after enjoying beachside vacations in Senegal as teenagers and young adults. Back in France, youth who as children had bitterly complained that they did not want to return to Dakar, now post throwback photos of their summer vacation in Senegal on social media. Images of their four-wheeler trip around Senegal's Lac Rose or of them enjoying a fruit cocktail at a beachside restaurant in Dakar's high-end Almadies neighborhood communicate luxury and status and simultaneously a commitment to their family's country of origin. The ethnographic data presented here offer only a snapshot of these children's moral-economic development, which has continued to grow and to change in relationship with changing family relations and economic opportunities internationally.

Youth growing up in Senegalese families abroad are already part of transnational affective and economic circuits. Even if they do not totally grasp the moral reasoning that drives these relations, children recognize when resources circulate around them, particularly instances when money and possessions are exchanged in their name. Through moments like these, children may become aware of practices of rank-based redistribution even if they assume that it is not (yet) their responsibility to take part. Each story of exchange, each act of telling, leaves a mark on youth growing up in the Senegalese diaspora. Even those who flip-flop in moral alignments may still be engaged in a gradual process of learning the intricacies of rank-based redistribution. That is, even in acts of rebellion, like Aminata's description of "playing crazy," youth can gradually gain a more nuanced understanding of how resources circulate in the Senegalese diaspora.

Repeatedly, my interlocutors would pause, when explaining moral expectations to offer gifts or redistribute resources, to specify that children do not yet have the obligation to give material support. This moral-economic distinction has important implications for the ways that people in Senegal and its diaspora interpret one's failure to offer material support, in that young people have no material obligation to give to relatives or send remittances until they have a stable job, get married, or otherwise embody markers of social adulthood. But long before they are ever expected to give, children's lives are saturated with the moral-economic calculations. When Malik doled out portions of his afternoon snack to child beggars on the street in front of his grandmother's house in Dakar, he was faced, firsthand, with global inequalities. Recognition of his own privilege moved the boy to offer cookies to children in the street before taking the rest of the pack into his grandmother's house to eat. Badara and his brothers were confronted with inequalities of wealth and access to consumer goods in their father's explanation for why he had (without their permission) distributed their possessions to their cousins in Senegal. Mariama, too, was taking part in transnational economic relations as recipient of her cousin's gifts and by harnessing her father's resources to reciprocate with a sarice gift for her cousin.

Children in the middle-class Senegalese households I studied in Paris and Dakar were the focus of substantial investments of time, money, and energy by adults in multiple countries. In order to one day reciprocate, migrants' children must first gain a sense of their own (changing) position in asymmetrical relations that organize the circulation of resources among transnational kin. Economic moralities mediate belonging and the rights (and responsibilities) to resources it affords, in transnational families and state systems alike. These moral-economic expectations are rarely taught in any explicit manner but, rather, are transmitted indirectly in the verbal and material exchanges that make up everyday family life. The semiotic grounding for transnational economic processes is woven into interactions among children and caregivers, household talk shot through with subtle cues about who deserves access to scarce resources.

# APPENDIX 1. TRANSCRIPTS

## Contrasting Registers of Chip Sharing

1  CY: *Regardez ce que j'ai.* (2.1)
2  Karim: *Ça c'est quoi?*
3  CY: **A:m!** [hands bag to Karim]
4  Karim: *Chips:?*
5  CY: **Waaw am.** [hands bag to Fatou]
6  Fatou: °*Merci*°.
7  CY: *De rien:* **Ak!** *Attendez—* [reaching for more] (0.7)
8  Karim: *Ça c'est quoi?* [pulling at the corner of bag] (1.1)
9  CY: *C'est pour vous!* (2.0)
10  [**Am**]
11  Karim:

[high pitched, grabs second bag of chips]

12  CY: *Oui!* (0.8)
13  Karim: *Chips.*
14  CY: **A:m::!**= [hands second bag to Fatou]
15  Fatou: =°*Merci*°. [takes second bag of chips]
16  Karim: *Deux.*
17  CY: **Bëgg nga chips?** (1.5)
18  Fatou: [nods, straightening crumpled package]
19  CY: *E[::t* **bë::gg n:ga**]—
20  Karim: [Bëgg nga chips?] [high pitched squeak]
21  CY: [*Tampi*]*co::::?* [hands Tampico juice to Fatou]
22  Fatou: [Tampi]°—*Oui merci.* (1.8) [takes juice]
23  CY: **Ak**=
24  Karim: =**Bëgg ng**[a Ta:mp:i?
25  CY: [**Ak ak yo:w?**

CY: Look what I have. (2.1)
Karim: What's that?
CY: Here! [hands bag to Karim]
Karim: Chips?
CY: Yes, here [hands bag to Fatou]
Fatou: Thank you.
CY: You're welcome. And! Wait—[reaching for more] (0.7)
Karim: What's that? [pulling at the corner of the bag] (1.1)
CY: It's for you [pl.]! (2.0)
[Here]
Karim: [No:::]: yes:::::::!

[high pitched, grabs second bag of chips]

CY: Yes! (0.8)
Karim: Chips.
CY: He::re!= [hands second bag to Fatou]
Fatou: =Thank you. [takes second bag of chips]
Karim: Two.
CY: Do you like chips? (1.5)
Fatou: [nods, straightening crumpled package]
CY: And do you like—
Karim: [Do you like chips?] [high pitched squeak]
CY: Tampico? [hands Tampico juice to Fatou]
Fatou: Tampi—Yes, thank you. (1.8) (takes juice)
CY: And
Karim: Do you like Tampi?
CY: And and you?

[Karim holds out hand]
**B[ëgg n]ga Tampico?** [hands Karim
   Tampico]

[Karim holds out hand]
Do you like Tampico? [hands Karim
   Tampico]

26  Karim: **[Wa:aw]!** [high pitched] **Waaw.**
       [takes Tampico]

Karim: Yes! [high pitched] Yes.
   [takes Tampico]

27  CY: [um]

CY: Um

28  Karim: *[Me]rci, t'es gentille.* [holding
       Tampico near face]

Karim: Thank you, you're nice. [holding
   Tampico near face]

### "Sometimes Too Generous"

1   Rama: Et voilà, je leur apprends juste et
2   après maintenant, je ne sais pas ce que ça
3   leur apporte à est-ce que ça, me—mes
4   enfants sont généreux. Tu vois? *Très*
5   généreux, même un peu trop généreux.
6   Parce que tu vois ils vont prendre toutes
7   mes courses ici ils vont les amener en bas
8   pour donner ça aux gamins. Des fois ça me
9   fait péter un plomb!

Rama: So that's it, I just teach them and
afterward, now, I don't know if that
makes them, if that, m—my
children are generous. You see? *Very*
generous, even a little too generous.
Because, you see, they take all
my groceries here they take them downstairs
to give to the kids. Sometimes it makes me
freak out!

10  CY: [laughs]

CY: [laughs]

11  Oumar: C'est le partage [qu'ils] app—
12  qu'ils apprennent.

Oumar: That's sharing that [they're] lear—
They're learning.

13  Rama: [Tu vois] c'est ça.

Rama: [You see] that's it.

14  Oumar: C'est ce partage là qui—

Oumar: That's the sharing that—

15  Rama: Mais mais mais mais justement,
16  moi, ça me fatigue.

Rama: But but but but exactly,
for me, that wears me out.

17  Oumar: Mais c'est ça qui perpétuent avec
18  leur famille.

Oumar: But that's what will continue with
their family.

19  Rama: Mais oui, parce que dès qu'ils
20  vont avoir un truc—

Rama: Of course, because as soon as they
have something—

21  CY: Uh huh?

CY: Uh huh?

22  Oumar: C'est normal.

Oumar: It's normal.

23  Rama: Tu vois, euh c'est, c'est penser à
24  des copains qui sont, les copains qui sont
25  en bas.

Rama: You see, uh they're, they're thinking
of the friends who are, the friends who are
downstairs.

26  CY: Uh-huh.

CY: Uh-huh.

27  Rama: "Oui maman, euh, t'as acheté les
28  glaces? Je vais donner des glaces à untel,
29  je vais donner des glaces à untel, je vais
30  donner des glaces à untel."

Rama: "Yeah mom, uh, did you buy the
ice cream bars? I'm going to give ice cream
to him, I'm going to give ice cream to him,
I'm going to give ice cream to him."

31  CY: Uh-huh.

CY: Uh-huh.

32  Rama: Au bout d'un moment, je suis
33  obligée de m'énerver, je leur dis, "Eh! je
34  fais pas les courses pour les gens
35  dehors!"

Rama: At some point, I have to
get upset, I tell them, "Hey! I
don't buy groceries for everyone
outside!"

36  Oumar and CY: [laugh]

Oumar and CY: [laugh]

37  Rama: Tu vois? Mais, après mes enfants

Rama: You see? But, then, my children

38 sont comme ça.
39 CY: Ouais.
40 Rama: Après maintenant je ne sais pas si
41 c'est du fait qu'ils mangent au bol donc
42 le partage pour eux c'est quand même
43 normal ou si c'est un trait de caractère
44 qu'on a tous les deux, <u>son, son, leur</u> père
45 et moi.

are like that.
CY: Yeah.
Rama: Then, now I don't know if
it's the fact that they eat around the dish so
sharing for them is just
normal or if it's a character trait
that we both have—<u>his, his, their</u> father
and me.

### Badara's Suitcase

1 Badara: C'est pour de vrai, moi j'ai une
2 anec—j'ai une anecdote, écoute, écoute.
3 Quand, la dernière fois que je suis parti—
4 Abdoulaye: Mm-hm.
5 Badara: On avait fait des bonnes courses,
6 *moi* je pensais que c'était les courses
7 pour l'année, j'allais avoir euh
8 les nouveaux vêtements et tout.
9 Et euh on est partis au Sénégal, et Papa—
10 Abdoulaye: Oui?
11 Badara: Il a attendu qu'on aille à
12 à la plage, il a dit à euh à eux à—
13 comment ils s'appellent?
14 Les trois-là.
15 Abdoulaye: Heh heh heh.
16 Badara: À mes cousins.
17 CY: Oui?
18 Badara: D'aller se servir dans—
19 CY: Dans ta valise ?
20 Badara: [nods] D'aller prendre, euh, il leur
21 a donné quoi mais—
22 Abdoulaye: Et tu m'en as voulu?
23 Badara: Non.
24 Abdoulaye: Heh voilà.

Badara: They mean it, I have an
anec—I have an anecdote, listen, listen.
When, the last time I went—
Abdoulaye: Mm-hm.
Badara: We had done a lot of shopping,
*I* thought that it was shopping
for the year, I was going to have, uh,
new clothes and everything.
And, uh, we went to Senegal and Dad—
Abdoulaye: Yes?
Badara: He waited until we went to
the beach, he said to, uh, to, uh—
what are their names?
The three of them.
Abdoulaye: Heh heh heh.
Badara: To my cousins.
CY: Yeah?
Badara: To go help themselves in—
CY: In your suitcase?
Badara: [nods] To go take, uh, he gave
them like, but—
Abdoulaye: And you were upset with me?
Badara: No.
Abdoulaye: Heh, there you go.

# APPENDIX 2. KINSHIP DIAGRAMS

**DIALLO FAMILY**
**Paris, Malakoff / Dakar, Sacré Cœur**
*Introduction*

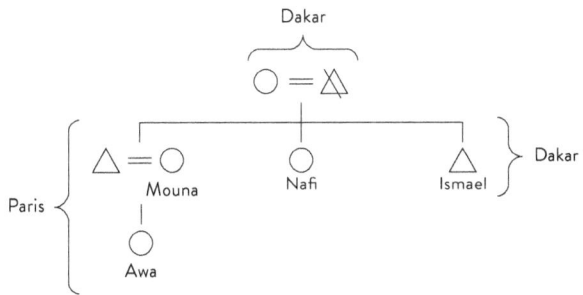

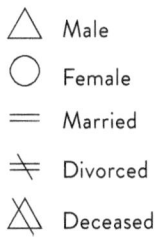

△ Male

○ Female

= Married

≠ Divorced

⩟ Deceased

**DIAGNE FAMILY**
**Paris, Kremlin Bicêtre / Dakar, Castors**
*Chapters 1 and 5*

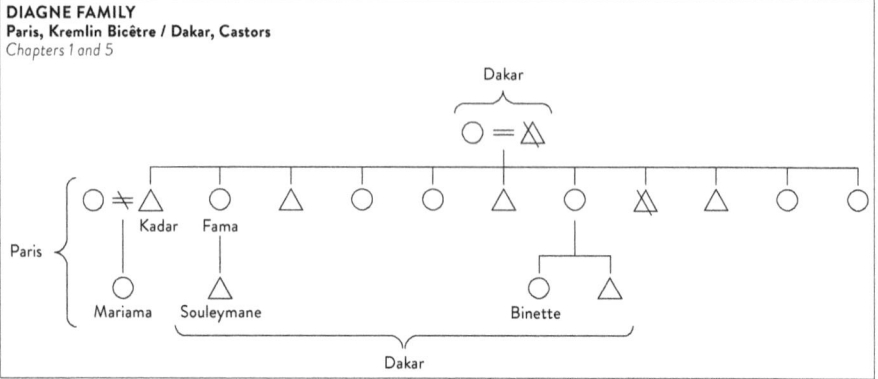

Dakar

Kadar  Fama

Paris

Mariama  Souleymane                                    Binette

Dakar

---

**SY FAMILY**
**Paris, 19ᵉ arrondissement / Dakar, Fann**
*Chapters 1 and 3*

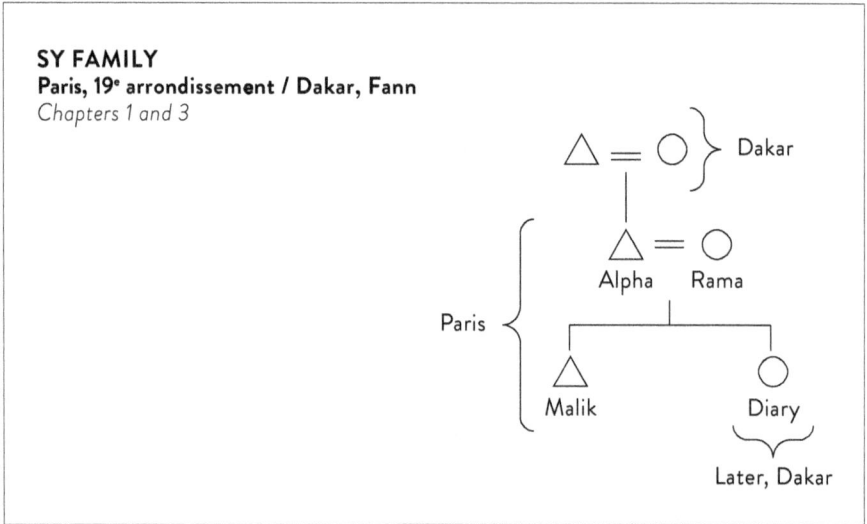

Dakar

Alpha  Rama

Paris

Malik                          Diary

Later, Dakar

**SÈNE FAMILY**
**Paris, 17ᵉ arrondissement / Dakar, Mermoz**
*Chapter 1*

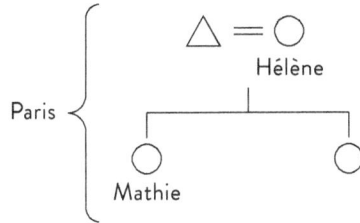

**SARR FAMILY**
**Paris, 14ᵉ arrondissement / Dakar, Baobab**
*Chapters 2 and 4*

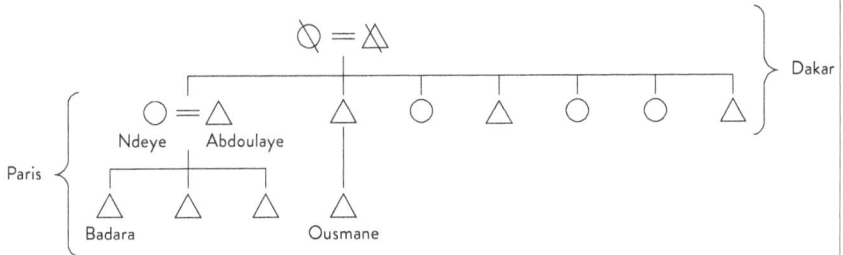

# NOTES

## Introduction

1. All names used in this book are pseudonyms, in accordance with research ethics requirements and to protect the privacy of my research participants.

2. I thank Bill Maurer for his (2009) invitation to "consider the possibilities" that "economic moralities" might afford. The semiotic approach to economic moralities that I develop here was born of my attempts to imagine such possibilities, using analytic tools at the intersections of economic and linguistic anthropology.

3. Formerly known as the Front national, this right-wing populist party has gained ground in local and national elections over the past decade as nationalist sentiment has grown in France and throughout Europe.

4. Most of the Senegalese adults I knew in Paris came from middle-class neighborhoods in Dakar like Mermoz, Sacré Cœur, Baobab, and other "SICAPs," while others came from middle-class households in working-class areas like Castors and Medina (see Antoine et al. 2004 for a description of middle-class areas in Dakar). SICAP refers to neighborhoods (like Liberté, Amitié, Baobab, Mermoz) constructed by the Société immobilière du Cap-Vert (SICAP) in the 1960s and 1970s, originally designed and still largely inhabited by middle-class families (Bugnicourt 1983, 32).

5. Referred to as *les professions intermédiaires* (intermediate professions) in French administrative terms, scholars typically associate these jobs with middle-class status in terms of income, education, and social status (Bosc 2014).

6. With degrees from French high schools in Dakar and diplomas from French universities (undergraduate or masters), the Senegalese adults in my study had formal educations that make them among the top 6.4 percent most educated in Senegal (ANSD 2014) and the top 16 percent most educated in France (Insee 2016).

7. The OECD reports that "amounting to USD 1644 million in 2014," remittances to Senegal "now exceed net ODA [Official Development Assistance] volumes (USD 1100 million in 2014), representing a sizeable amount of foreign exchange" (Delalande and Gaveau 2017, 3).

8. French rap songs like Doc Gynéco's 1996 "Les Filles Du Moove" or Youssoupha's 2007 "Les Apparences Nous Mentent," describe immigrants who have many children, then use state welfare funds to buy brand-name clothes and vacations in their country of origin (*au bled*).

9. "Doudou" was a recurrent character of an African woman that French actor Omar Sy (Senegalese father, Mauritanian mother) depicted in sketches on the *Services après-vente des émissions* comedy series on Canal+ from 2005 to 2012.

## Chapter 1

1. Taking a cue from my Senegalese interlocutors, I treat class and status as broadly interchangeable and inevitably intertwined, wealth useful for the status it confers, and vice versa (see also Ridgeway 2014).

2. I use the term "middle-class migrant" to question presuppositions that "migrants" are necessarily lower-class and precarious. I adopt the term migrant, rather than immigrant or emigrant, to emphasize the bi/multidirectionality of a person's movement (like transmigrant [see Glick Shiller 2004]). I use the term "immigrant" when speaking from the perspective of France's official immigration policy or to articulate perspectives voiced in French society and scholarship on "immigrants" in France.

## Chapter 2

1. The word *fraudeur* in French may be used for anyone who tries to cheat the system for personal benefit, whatever their nationality or ethnic origins, although Alioune's description focused specifically on the actions of African *fraudeurs*.

2. Aïda's criticism of the lack of hospitality she's found in France also came, paradoxically, at a dinner held (in France) in her honor. This apparent contradiction illustrates an idea I expand on in the next chapter, that Senegalese homes in France were often referred to and treated as private spaces, separate from "France" (see also Mouna Diallo's reflections in the Introduction about giving her daughter a "Senegalese education" at home).

3. To be fair, other Europeans, including the French (Mabilon 2022), also expressed shock. Hospitality in France, although not offered indiscriminately, is a social art and valued profession, regularly expressed through commensality and meals shared among family and friends (Fischler 2011).

4. Following Irvine, I define register as "a coherent complex of linguistic features linked to a situation of use" (Irvine 1990, 127), extending this to include other multimodal sign systems by referring to semiotic registers.

## Chapter 3

1. *Wesh* is a slang expression in French, derived from an Arabic salutation and used especially among Muslim youth.

2. In France, 4:00 p.m. is a time stereotypically associated with the *goûter*, children's afternoon snack, also called "*le petit quatre heure*" (the little four o'clock).

## Chapter 5

1. An earlier version of this chapter was published in the journal *Africa* (Yount-André 2018a).

2. The election of President Bassirou Diomaye Faye in 2024 marked the first time that the country has had a polygamous president, both first ladies living at the presidential palace. The president's public appearances with his two wives work to further legitimize polygamy in the political sphere, but the practice has overall become less common over the past thirty years (Dial 2014, 256).

3. Since the time of my fieldwork, the young people I worked with in France have gradually stopped using Facebook. Mariama, for example, still uses Instagram but stopped updating her Facebook profile years ago. Senegalese transnational families do overall remain, however, active on the site, but WhatsApp groups for individual families and Snapchat are also commonly used for connecting with family in Senegal and its diaspora.

# REFERENCES

Adida, Claire L., David D. Laitin, and Marie-Anne Valfort. 2010. "Identifying Barriers to Muslim Integration in France." *Proceedings of the National Academy of Sciences* 107, no. 52: 22384–90.

Agha, Asif. 2007. *Language and Social Relations*. No. 24. Cambridge: Cambridge University Press.

Agha, Asif, and Stanton Wortham. 2005. "Discourse Across Speech-Events: Intertextuality and Interdiscursivity in Social Life." *Journal of Linguistic Anthropology* 15, no. 1: 1–5.

Anderson, B. 2013. *Us and Them: The Dangerous Politics of Immigration Control*. Oxford: Oxford University Press.

ANSD (Agence National de la Statistique et de la Démographie). 2014. "L'Alphabétisation, Scolarisation, Niveau d'Instruction et Formation Professionnelle." In Rapport définitif RGPHAE 2013, 71–101. http://www.ansd.sn/ressources/rapports/Rapport-definitif-RGPHAE2013.pdf.

Antoine, Philippe Abdou Fall, Agnès Adjamagbo, Alioune Diagne, Fatou Dial, Laure Moguerou, and Amadou Lamine Ndiaye. 2004. *Crise, Passage à l'âge Adulte et Devenir de la Famille dans les Classes Moyennes et Pauvres à Dakar (Seconde Phase)*. Progress Report for CODESRIA, IRD-IFAN, Dakar 22.

Anving, Terese, and Ann-Mari Sellerberg. 2010. "Family Meals and Parents' Challenges." *Food Culture and Society* 13, no. 2: 200–14.

APS (Agence de Presse Sénégalaise). 2015. "Le secteur informel représente 41,6% du PIB (officiel)." Agence de Presse Sénégalaise. April 14.

Asad, Talal. 2003. *Formations of the Secular: Christianity, Islam, Modernity*. Redwood City, CA: Stanford University Press.

Austen, Ralph. 1993. "The Moral Economy of Witchcraft: An Essay in Comparative History." In *Modernity and its Malcontents*, edited by Jean Comaroff and John Comaroff, 129–66. Chicago: University of Chicago Press.

Babou, Cheikh Anta. 2021. *The Muridiyya on the Move: Islam, Migration, and Place Making*. Athens: Ohio University Press.

Bankston, C. L. 1998. "Youth Gangs and the New Second Generation: A Review Essay." *Aggression and Violent Behavior* 3, no. 1: 35–45.

Barou, Jacques. 2014. "Integration of Immigrants in France: A Historical Perspective." *Identities: Global Studies in Culture and Power* 21, no. 6: 642–57.

Barth, Fredrik. 1998 (1969). *Ethnic Groups and Boundaries: The Social Organization of Culture Difference*. Long Grove, IL: Waveland Press.

Beaud, Stéphane. 2011. "Par delà les choix scolaires: Les rapports de classes." *Revue française de pédagogie: Recherches en éducation* 175: 77–80.

Beaud, Stéphane, and Michel Pialoux. 2006. "Racisme ouvrier ou mépris de classe? Retour sur une enquête de terrain." In *De la question sociale à la question raciale? Représenter la société française*, edited by Éric Fassin, 72–90. Paris: La Découverte.

Bear, Laura. 2015. *Navigating Austerity: Currents of Debt along a South Asian River.* Redwood City, CA: Stanford University Press.

Bear, Laura, Karen Ho, Anna Lowenhaupt Tsing, and Sylvia Yanagisako. 2015. "Gens: A Feminist Manifesto for the Study of Capitalism." Theorizing the Contemporary, *Fieldsights*, March 30. https://culanth.org/fieldsights/gens-a-feminist-manifesto-for-the-study-of-capitalism

Berman, Elise. 2014. "Negotiating Age: Direct Speech and the Sociolinguistic Production of Childhood in the Marshall Islands." *Journal of Linguistic Anthropology* 24, no. 2: 109–32.

Berman, Elise. 2019. *Talking Like Children: Language and the Production of Age in the Marshall Islands.* Oxford: Oxford University Press.

Beyer, Caroline. 2012. "Étudiants étrangers: la circulaire Guéant à la vécu." *Le Figaro.* May 31. http://www.lefigaro.fr/formation/2012/05/31/09006-20120531ARTFIG00578-etudiants-etrangers-la-circulaire-gueant-a-vecu.php.

Beyer, Caroline. 2015. "L'affaire de la jupe ou les limites de la laïcité à l'école." *Le Figaro.* May 3. https://www.lefigaro.fr/actualite-france/2015/05/03/01016-20150503ARTFIG00145-l-affaire-de-la-jupe-ou-les-limites-de-la-laicite-a-l-ecole.php.

Bidet, Jennifer. 2021. *Vacances au bled: La double présence des enfants d'immigrés.* Paris: Raisons d'agir.

Bidou-Zachariasen, Catherine. 2004. "SYNTHÈSE Les classes moyennes: définitions, travaux et controverses." *Education et sociétés* 2: 119–34.

Bigot, Régis. 2009. *Les classes moyennes sous pression.* Crédoc Cahiers de Recerce no. 219. Paris: Crédoc.

Bledsoe, Caroline H. 1980. *Women and Marriage in Kpelle Society.* Redwood City, CA: Stanford University Press.

Bledsoe, Caroline H. 1990. "'No Success Without Struggle': Social Mobility and Hardship for Foster Children in Sierra Leone." *Man* 25, no. 1: 70–88.

Bledsoe, Caroline H., and Papa Sow. 2011. "Back to Africa: Second Chances for the Children of West African Immigrants." *Journal of Marriage and Family* 73, no. 4: 747–62.

Bloch, Maurice, and Jonathan Parry. 1989. "Introduction." In *Money and the Morality of Exchange*, edited by Jonathan Parry and Maurice Bloch, 1–32. Cambridge: Cambridge University Press.

Blum-Kulka, S. 1997. *Dinner Talk: Cultural Patterns of Sociability and Socialization in Family Discourse.* Mahwah, NJ: Erlbaum.

Bocoum, Seydou, Mousse Narou Mbengue, and Safietou Diagne Mododj. 1997. "L'Avare et le Pique-Assiette." In *Sidi et Rama: Lecture cours moyen 2e année.* Dakar: Ministère de l'éducation national du Sénégal.

Boehm, Deborah A. 2012. *Intimate Migrations: Gender, Family, and Illegality among Transnational Mexicans.* New York: New York University Press.

Boltanski, Luc. 1987. *The Making of a Class: Cadres in French Society.* Cambridge: Cambridge University Press.

Bonhomme, Julien, and Julien Bondaz. 2017. *L'offrande de la mort: Une rumeur au Sénégal.* Paris: CNRS.

Bosc, Serge. 2014. "Les Classes Moyennes: Une Notion protéiforme et Ambivalente." *Cahiers français: Les Classes Moyennes dans la Crise.* Paris: La Documentation Française.

Bourdieu, Pierre. 1974. "Avenir de classe et causalité du probable." *Revue française de sociologie* 15, no. 1: 3–42.

Bourdieu, Pierre. 1977. "The Economics of Linguistic Exchanges." *Social Science Information* 16, no. 6: 645–68.

Bourdieu, Pierre. 1979. *La Distinction: Critique sociale du jugement.* Paris: Éditions Minuit.

Bourdieu, Pierre. 1990. *The Logic of Practice.* Redwood City, CA: Stanford University Press.

Brodkin, Karen. 1998. *How Jews Became White Folks and What That Says About Race in America*. New Brunswick, NJ: Rutgers University Press.

Browne, Katherine E., and B. Lynne Milgram, eds. 2009. *Economics and Morality: Anthropological Approaches*. New York: Altamira.

Bruna, K. R., and K. Gomez, eds. 2009. *The Work of Language in Multicultural Classrooms: Talking Science, Writing Science*. New York: Routledge.

Bruner, J. S. 1978. "The Role of Dialogue in Language Acquisition." In *The Child's Conception of Language*, edited by A. Sinclair, R. Jarvella, and W. J. M. Levelt. New York NY: Springer.

Buggenhagen, Beth. 2011. "Are Births Just 'Women's Business'?: Gift Exchange, Value, and Global Volatility in Muslim Senegal." *American Ethnologist* 38, no. 4: 714–32.

Buggenhagen, Beth. 2012. *Muslim Families in Global Senegal: Money Takes Care of Shame*. Bloomington: Indiana University Press.

Buggenhagen, Beth. 2013. "Islam's New Visibility and the Secular Public in Senegal." In *Tolerance, Democracy, and Sufis in Senegal*, edited by Mamadou Diouf, 51–72. New York: Columbia University Press.

Bugnicourt, Jacques. 1983. "Dakar without Bounds." In *Reading the Contemporary African City*, edited by B. B. Taylor, 27–42. Singapore: Concept Media/Aga Khan Award for Architecture.

Carr, E. Summerson, and Michael Lempert. 2016. *Scale: Discourse and Dimensions of Social Life*. Oakland: University of California Press.

Carrier, James G. 2018. "Moral Economy: What's in a Name." *Anthropological Theory* 18, no. 1: 18–35.

Carsten, Janet. 1995. "The Substance of Kinship and the Heat of the Hearth: Feeding, Personhood, and Relatedness among Malays in Pulau Langkawi." *American Ethnologist* 22, no. 2: 223–41.

Carter, D. M. 1997. *States of Grace: Senegalese in Italy and the New European Immigration Minneapolis*: Minneapolis: University of Minnesota Press.

Castles, Stephen. 1986. "The Guest-Worker in Western Europe—An Obituary." *International Migration Review* 20, no. 4: 761–78.

Cavanaugh, Jillian R., and Shalini Shankar, eds. 2017. *Language and Materiality: Ethnographic and Theoretical Explorations*. Cambridge: Cambridge University Press.

Chafer, T. 2003. "France and Senegal: The End of the Affairs?" *SAIS Review* 23: 155–67.

Chauvel, Louis. 2006. *Les classes moyennes à la dérive*. Collection république des idées. Paris: Seuil.

Chauvel, Louis. 2023. "Squeezing the Western Middle Class: Precarization, Uncertainty and Tensions of Median Socioeconomic Groups in the Global North." In *Handbook of Post-Western Sociology: From East Asia to Europe*, edited by Laurence Roulleau-Berger, Peilin Li, Seung Kuk Kim, and Shujiro Yasawa, 495–509. Leiden: Brill.

Coe, Cati. 2011. "What Is Love? The Materiality of Care in Ghanaian Transnational Families." *International Migration* 49, no. 6: 7–24.

Coe, Cati. 2013. *The Scattered Family: Parenting, African Migrants, and Global Inequality*. Chicago: University of Chicago Press.

Coe, Cati. 2020. "Social Class in Transnational Perspective: Emotional Responses to the Status Paradox among Ghanaian Migrants." *Africa Today* 66, no. 3: 160–78.

Coe, Cati, and Julia Pauli. 2020. "Migration and Social Class in Africa: Class-Making Projects in Translocal Social Fields." *Africa Today* 66, no. 3: 2–19.

Coe, Cati, Rachel R. Reynolds, Deborah A. Boehm, Julia Meredith Hess, and Heather Rae-Espinoza, eds. 2011. *Everyday Ruptures: Children, Youth, and Migration in Global Pperspective*. Nashville, TN: Vanderbilt University Press.

Cole, Jennifer. 2011. "A Cultural Dialectics of Generational Change: The View From Contemporary Africa." *Review of Research in Education* 35, no. 1: 60–88.

Cole, Jennifer. 2014. "Producing Value among Malagasy Marriage Migrants in France." *Current Anthropology* 55, no. S9: S85–S94.

Cole, Jennifer. 2016. "Giving Life: Regulating Affective Circuits among Malagasy Marriage Migrants in France." In *Affective Circuits: African Migrations to Europe and the Pursuit of Social Regeneration*, edited by J. Cole and C. Groes. Chicago: University of Chicago Press.

Cole, Jennifer, and Deborah Lynn Durham, eds. 2008. *Figuring the Future: Globalization and the Temporalities of Children and Youth*. Santa Fe, NM: School for Advanced Research Press.

Cole, Jennifer., and C. Groes, eds. 2016. *Affective Circuits: African Migrations to Europe and the Pursuit of Social Regeneration*. Chicago: University of Chicago Press.

Collins, Patricia Hill. 2002. *Black Feminist Thought: Knowledge, Consciousness, and the Politics of Empowerment*. London: Routledge.

Comaroff, John L., and Jean Comaroff. 1981. "The Management of Marriage in a Tswana Chiefdom." In *Essays on African Marriage in Southern Africa*, edited by Eileen Jensen Krige and John L. Comaroff. Cape Town: Juta.

Comoretto, Géraldine. 2015. "Le goûter de 16h30 comme symbole du patrimoine alimentaire enfantin? Analyse des transactions non marchandes dans deux cours de récréation (France)." *Anthropology of Food* 9.

Conklin, Alice L. 1997. *A Mission to Civilize: The Republican Idea of Empire in France and West Africa, 1895–1930*. Redwood City, CA: Stanford University Press.

Copans, Jean. 2020. "Have the Social Classes of Yesterday Vanished from Africanist Issues or Are African Societies Made up of New Classes? A French Anthropologist's Perspective." *Review of African Political Economy* 47, no. 163: 10–26.

Crenshaw, Kimberley. 1991. "Mapping the Margins: Intersectionality, Identity Politics, and Violence Against Women of Color." *Stanford Law Review* 43, no. 6: 1241–99.

Croff, Amadou. 2019. *Janga Wolof Translator Phrases Book*. https://jangawolof.org/orthography/.

Courtin, Nicolas and Darbon, D. 2012. "Les diasporas africaines constituent-elles une classe moyenne en délocalisation partielle ou par procuration?" *Afrique contemporaine* 244: 118–19. https://doi.org/10.3917/afco.244.0118.

Daffé, G., and M. C. Diop. 2004. "Senegal: Institutional Aspects of Trade and Industry Policy." In *The Politics of Trade and Industrial Policy in Africa: Forced Concensus?*, edited by C. C. Soludo, O. Ogbu, and H. -J. Chang. Trenton, NJ: Africa World Press, Inc.

Darbon, D., and C. Toulabor. 2011. *Quelle(s) classe(s) moyenne(s) en Afrique?* Document de Travail 118. Paris: Agence Française de Développement.

Das, Veena. 2015. "What Does Ordinary Ethics Look Like?" In *Four Lectures on Ethics: Anthropological Perspectives*, by Michael Lambek, Veena Das, Didier Fassin, and Webb Keane, 53–125. London: HAU Books.

Daudens, Florent. 2012. "Les jeunes Français se ruent vers le Québec." *ICI Radio Canada*. December 1. http://ici.radio-canada.ca/nouvelles/societe/2012/12/01/005-immigration-pvt-francais.shtml.

Déchaux, J. H. 2003. "La parenté dans les sociétés occidentales modernes: Un éclairage structural." *Recherches et Prévisions* 72, no. 1: 53–63.

Delalande, Guillaume, and Valérie Gaveau. 2018. "Senegal's Perspective on TOSSD." *OECD Development Co-operation Working Papers* 43. https://doi.org/10.1787/4144f82a-en.

Demossier, Marion. 2010. *Wine Drinking Culture in France: A National Myth or a Modern Passion?* Cardiff: University of Wales Press.

Di Leonardo, Micaela. 1987. "The Female World of Cards and Holidays: Women, Families, and the Work of Kinship." *Signs: Journal of Women in Culture and Society* 12, no. 3: 440–53.

Di Leonardo, Micaela. 1998. *Exotics at Home: Anthropologies, Others, and American Modernity.* Chicago: University of Chicago Press.

Dial, Fatou Binetou. 2008. *Mariage et divorce à Dakar.* Paris: Karthala.

Dial, Fatou Binetou. 2014. "Divorce, remariage et polygamie à Dakar." In *Le mariage en Afrique: Pluralité des formes et des modèles matrimoniaux,* edited by Richard Marcoux and Philippe Antoine, 250–65. Québec: Presses de l'Université du Québec.

Diop, Abdoulaye-Bara. 1985. *La famille wolof.* Paris: Karthala.

Diop, Birago. 1977. *L'os de Mor Lam.* Nouvelles Éditions Africaines. https://www.biragodiop .com/bibliographie/78-oeuvre/125-l-os-de-mor-lam.html#:~:text=Son%20 d%C3%A9sir%20de%20se%20trouver,Il%20meurt.

Diouf, Jean. 2003. *Dictionnaire wolof-français et français-wolof.* Paris: Karthala Editions.

Dubet, François, and Marie Duru-Bellat. 2006. "Déclassement, quand l'ascenseur social descend." *Le Monde.* January 23. http://www.lemonde.fr/societe/article/2006/01/23/declasse ment-quand-l-ascenseur-social-descend_733638_3224.html.

Duguet, Emmanuel, Noam Leandri, Y. l'Horty, and Pascale Petit. 2007. "Discriminations à l'embauche: Un testing sur les jeunes des banlieues d'ile de France." *Centre d'Analyse Stratégique WP.*

Dumont, Louis. 1980 (1969). "Homo Hierarchicus." *Social Science Information* 8, no. 2: 69–87.

Duranti, A. 1992. "Language in Context and Language as Context: The Samoan Respect Vocabulary." In *Rethinking Context: Language as an Interactive Phenomenon,* edited by A. Duranti and C. Goodwin, 77–101. Cambridge: Cambridge University Press.

Duranti, A., E. Ochs, and B. Schieffelin, eds. 2012. *The Handbook of Language Socialization.* West Sussex: John Wiley and Sons.

Durham, Deborah. 2000. "Youth and the Social Imagination in Africa: Introduction to Parts 1 and 2." *Anthropological Quarterly* 73, no. 3: 113–20.

Durham, Deborah. 2004. "Disappearing Youth: Youth as a Social Shifter in Botswana." *American Ethnologist* 31, no. 4: 589–605.

Duru-Bellat, Marie. 2006. *L'inflation scolaire: Les désillusions de la méritocratie.* Paris: La République des Idées.

Ebin, V. 1993. "Les commerçants mourides à Marseille et à New York." In *Grands commerçants d'Afrique de l'Ouest,* edited by E. Grégoire and P. Labazée, 101–23. Paris: Karthala.

Ehrenreich, Barbara. 1989. *Fear of Falling: The Inner Life of the Middle Class.* New York: Pantheon.

Ervin-Tripp, Susan. 1976. "'Is Sybil There?': The Structure of Some American English Directives." *Language in Society* 5, no. 1: 25–67.

Ervin-Tripp, S. M., J. Guo, and M. D. Lampert. 1990. "Politeness and Persuasion in Children's Control Acts." *Journal of Pragmatics* 14, no. 2: 307–31.

European Commission. 2005. *Communication from the Commission to the Council, the European Parliament, the European Economic and Social Committee and the Committee of the Regions: A common agenda for integration; Framework for the integration of third-country nationals in the European Union.* COM 389 final, September 1. Brussels: EU Commission. http://eur-lex.europa.eu/LexUriServ/LexUriServ.do?uri=COM:2005:0389:FIN :EN:PDF.

European Union. 2010. *Charter of Fundamental Rights of the European Union. Official Journal of the European Union C83.* Vol. 53. Brussels: European Union.

Evaldsson, A.-C., and B. Tellgren. 2009. "'Don't Enter—It's Dangerous': Negotiations for Power and Exclusion in Preschool Girls' Play Interactions." *Educational and Child Psychology* 26, no. 2: 9–18.

Evans-Pritchard, E. E. 1940. *The Nuer: A Description of the Modes of Livelihood and Political Institutions of a Nilotic People.* Oxford: Oxford University Press.

Fall, A. S. 2007. *Bricoler pour survivre: Perceptions de la pauvreté dans l'agglomération urbaine de Dakar.* Paris: Éditions Karthala.

Fall, A. S., and C. Guèye. 2005. *Urbain-Rural—L'hybridation en marche.* Dakar: Enda-Tiers Monde.

Fall, P. D. 2010. "Sénégal: Migration, marché du travail et développement." In *Faire des Migrations un Facteur de Développement: Une Étude sur l'Afrique du Nord et l'Afrique de l'Ouest,* edited by the Organisation Internationale du Travail. Dakar: L'Institut international d'études sociales.

Fassin, Didier. 2005. "Compassion and Repression: The Moral Economy of Immigration Policies in France." *Cultural Anthropology* 20, no. 3: 362–87.

Fassin, Didier. 2009. "Moral Economies Revisited." *Annales: Histoire, Sciences Sociales* 64, no. 6: 1237–66.

Fassin, Didier, and Jean-Sébastien Eideliman, eds. 2014. *Économies morales contemporaines.* Paris: La Découverte.

Fassin, Didier, and Éric Fassin. 2006. "Conclusion: Éloge de la complexité." In *De la question sociale à la question raciale,* edited by Didier Fassin and Éric Fassin, 249–59. Paris: La Découverte.

Felouzis, Georges, and Joëlle Perroton. 2005. *L'apartheid scolaire: Enquête sur la ségrégation ethnique dans les collèges.* Paris: Seuil.

Ferguson, James. 2006. *Global Shadows: Africa in the Neoliberal World Order.* Durham, NC: Duke University Press.

Ferguson, James. 2013. "Declarations of Dependence: Labour, Personhood, and Welfare in Southern Africa." *Journal of the Royal Anthropological Institute* 19, no. 2: 223–42.

Ferguson, James. 2015. *Give a Man a Fish: Reflections on the New Politics of Distribution.* Durham, NC: Duke University Press.

Fernando, Mayanthi L. 2014. *The Republic Unsettled: Muslim French and the Contradictions of Secularism.* Durham, NC: Duke University Press.

Ferré, N. 1997. "La production de l'irrégularité." In *Les lois de l'inhospitalité,* edited by D. Fassin, A. Morice, and C. Quiminal, 47–65. Paris: La Découverte.

Fischler, Claude. 1999. *Du vin.* Paris: Odile Jacob.

Fischler, Claude. 2011. "Commensality, Society and Culture." *Social Science Information* 50, no. 3–4: 528–48.

Fischler, Claude, and Estelle Masson. 2008. *Manger: Français, Européens et Américains face à l'alimentation.* Paris: Odile Jacob.

Foley, Ellen E. 2009. *Your Pocket Is What Cures You: The Politics of Health in Senegal.* Newark, NJ: Rutgers University Press.

Fortes, Meyer. 1969. *Kinship and the Social Order: The Legacy of Lewis Henry Morgan.* Chicago: Aldine Publishing Company.

Fortes, Meyer. 1984. "Age, Generation, and Social Structure." In *Age and Anthropological Theory,* edited by David I. Kertzer and Jennie Keith, 99–122. Ithaca, NY: Cornell University Press.

Foutoyet, S. 2009. *Nicolas Sarkozy ou la Françafrique décomplexée.* Brussels: Tribord.

Fox, Robin. 1967. *Kinship and Marriage: An Anthropological Perspective.* Cambridge: Cambridge University Press.

Freeman, G. P. 1989. "Immigrant Labour and Racial Conflict: The Rôle of the State." In *Migrants in Modern France: Population Mobility in the Later 19th and 20th Centuries,* edited by P. E. Ogden and P. E. White. London: Unwin Hyman.

Gal, Susan. 2005. "Language Ideologies Compared." *Journal of Linguistic Anthropology* 15, no. 1: 23–37.

Gal, Susan. 2013. "Tastes of Talk: Qualia and the Moral Flavor of Signs." *Anthropological Theory* 13, no. 1–2: 31–48.

Gal, Susan, and Judith Irvine. 1995. "The Boundaries of Language and Disciplines: How Ideologies Construct Difference." *Social Research* 62: 967–1001.

Gal, Susan, and Judith T. Irvine. 2019. *Signs of Difference: Language and Ideology in Social Life*. Cambridge: Cambridge University Press.

Gamble, David. 1957. *The Wolof of Senegambia: Together with Notes on the Lebu and the Seerer*. London: International African Institute.

Geertz, Clifford. 1973. *The Interpretation of Cultures: Selected Essays*. New York: Basic Books.

Geisser, Vincent. 2010. "Islamophobia: A French Specificity in Europe?" *Human Architecture: Journal of the Sociology of Self and Knowledge* 3, no. 2: 39–46.

Gershon, I. 2010. "Breaking Up is Hard to Do: Media Switching and Media Ideologies." *Journal of Linguistic Anthropology* 20, no. 2: 389–405.

Geschiere, Peter. 1997. *The Modernity of Witchcraft: Occult in Postcolonial Africa*. London: University Press of Virginia.

Geschiere, Peter, and Francis Nyamnjoh. 1998. "Witchcraft as an Issue in the 'Politics of Belonging': Democratization and Urban Migrants' Involvement with the Home Village." *African Studies Review* 41, no. 3: 69–91.

Gibson, J. 1979. *The Ecological Approach to Visual Perception*. London: Houghton Mifflin.

Gibson-Graham, Julie-Katherine. 1996. "Querying Globalization." *Rethinking Marxism* 9, no. 1: 1–27.

Gillis, J. R. 1996. *A World of Their Own Making: Myth, Ritual, and the Quest for Family Values*. Cambridge, MA: Harvard University Press.

Girard, Youssef. 2008. "Assimilation et séparatisme dans le mouvement nationaliste algérien au milieu des années 1930." In *Histoire politique des immigrations (post)coloniales France, 1920–2008*, edited by Ahmen Boubeker and Abdellali Hajjat. Paris: Éditions Amsterdam.

Giret, Jean-François, and Philippe Lemistre. 2004. "Le déclassement à l'embauche des jeunes: vers un changement de la valeur des diplômes?" *Brussels Economic Review* 47, no. 3: 483–503.

Glick Schiller, Nina. 2004. "Transnationality." In *A Companion to the Anthropology of Politics*, edited by David Nugent and Joan Vincent, 448–68. Oxford: Blackwell.

Goffman, Erving. 1967. "On face-work." In *Interaction Ritual: Essays on Face-to Face Behavior*, 5–45.

Goffman, E. 1979. "Footing." *Semiotica* 25, no. 1–2: 1–29.

Goodwin, Marjorie Harness. 1990. *He-Said-She-Said: Talk as Social Organization among Black Children*. Bloomington: Indiana University Press.

Goodwin, Marjorie Harness. 2008. *The Hidden Life of Girls: Games of Stance, Status, and Exclusion*. New York: John Wiley and Sons.

Goodwin, Marjorie, and Amy Kyratzis. 2007. "Children Socializing Children: Practices for Negotiating the Social Order among Peers." *Research on Language and Social Interaction* 40, no. 4: 1–11.

Goodwin, Marjorie, and Amy Kyratzis. 2012. "Peer Language Socialization." In *The Handbook of Language Socialization*, edited by A. Duranti, E. Ochs, and B. Schieffelin, 365–90. Chichester: Wiley-Blackwell.

Goody, Esther N. 1973. *Contexts of Kinship: An Essay in the Family Sociology of the Gonja of Northern Ghana*. Cambridge: Cambridge University Press.

Gregory, Chris A. 1982. *Gifts and Commodities*. London: Academic Press.

Gregory, Chris A. 1997. *Savage Money: The Anthropology and Politics of Commodity Exchange*. Amsterdam: Harwood Academic.

Grysole, Amélie. 2018. "Private School Investments and Inequalities: Negotiating the Future in Transnational Dakar." *Africa* 88, no. 4: 663–82.

Grysole, Amélie, and Doris Bonnet. 2020. "Introduction au thème. Observer les mobilités sociales: l'investissement migratoire des familles." *Politique africaine: Mobilités de classe* 159, no. 3: 7–32.

Gudmundson, Liv. 2019. *Under Pressure: The Squeezed Middle Class.* Paris: OECD.

Gueye, A. 2002. "Les intellectuels sénégalais en France." In *Le Sénégal contemporain*, edited by M. C. Diop. Paris, Karthala.

Guimont, F. 1997. *Les étudiants africains en France, 1950–1965.* Paris: L'Harmattan.

Gulløv, E., C. Palludan, and I. Wentzel Winther. 2015. "Engaging siblingships." *Childhood* 22, no. 4: 506–19.

Gumperz, J. J. 1982. *Discourse Strategies.* Cambridge: Cambridge University Press.

Gumperz, J. J. 1992. "Contextualization Revisited." In *The Contextualization of Language*, edited by P. Auer and A. di Luzio, 39–53. Amsterdam: John Benjamins.

Guyer, Jane I. 1993. "Wealth in People and Self-Realization in Equatorial Africa." *Man* 28, no. 2: 243–65.

Guyer, Jane I. 2004. *Marginal Gains: Monetary Transactions in Atlantic Africa.* Chicago: University of Chicago Press.

Guyer, Jane I., and S. M. Eno Belinga. 1995. "Wealth in People as Wealth in Knowledge: Accumulation and Composition in Equatorial Africa." *The Journal of African History* 36, no. 1: 91–120.

Habib, Jacky, and Malaka Gharib. 2022. "#SwedenGate sparks food fight: Why some countries share meals more than others." *NPR.* June 7. https://www.npr.org/sections/goatsandsoda /2022/06/07/1102930419/-swedengate-sparks-food-fight-why-some-countries-share-meals -more-than-others.

Hale, Thomas A. 2009. "The Manifeste des Quarante-Quatre, Francophonie, la francafrique and Africa: From the Politics of Culture to the Culture of Politics." *International Journal of Francophone Studies* 12, no. 2–3: 171–201.

Hale, T. 2011. "'Liberation' and Colonialism in the Project of Francophonie Continuity and Change in Francophone Africa." Panel presentation at the African Studies Association Annual Conference, Washington, DC, November 19.

Hamilton, Kimberly, Patrick Simon, and Clara Veniard. 2004. "The Challenge of French Diversity." *Migration Policy Institute.* November 21. http://www.migrationpolicy.org/article /challenge-french-diversity.

Hamza, Assiya. 2012. "Moving on from Sarkozy's Immigration Policies." *France 24.* July 27. http://www.france24.com/en/20120727-new-french-immigration-initiatives-signal-break -sarkozy-policies-france-manuel-valls-interior-minister.

Hanks, William. 1990. *Referential Practice: Language and Lived Space among the Maya.* Chicago: University of Chicago Press.

Hann, Chris. 2018. "Moral(ity and) Economy: Work, Workfare, and Fairness in Provincial Hungary." *European Journal of Sociology* 59, no. 2: 225–54. doi10.1017/S000397561700056X.

Hannaford, Dinah. 2017. *Marriage Without Borders: Transnational Spouses in Neoliberal Senegal.* Philadelphia: University of Pennsylvania Press.

Hannaford, Dinah. 2018. "Easy Access: New Dynamics in Long-Distance African Intimacies." *Africa* 88, no. 4, 645–62. doi:10.1017/S0001972018000402.

Hardy, Georges. 1917. *Une conquête morale: L'enseignement en A.O.F.* Paris: Armand Colin.

Hargreaves, A. G. 2007. *Multi-Ethnic France: Immigration, Politics, Culture and Society,* New York: Routledge.

Harris, Marvin. 1968. *The Rise of Anthropological Theory.* New York: Thomas Y. Cowell Company.

Hashim, Iman, and Doctor Dorte Thorsen. 2011. *Child Migration in Africa.* New York: Bloomsbury Publishing.

Hazard, B. 2004. "Entre le pays et l'outre pays: 'Little Italy' dans le Bisaku (Burkina Faso)." *Journal des Africanistes* 74: 249–74.

He, A. W. 2003." Linguistic Anthropology and Language Education: A Comparative Look at Language Socialization." In *Linguistic Anthropology of Education*, edited by S. Wortham and B. Rymes, 93–121. Westport, CT: Praeger.

Héas, S., D. Bodin, K. Amossé, and S. Kerespar. 2004. "Football féminin: 'c'est un jeu d'hommes.'" *Cahiers du Genre* 36, no. 1: 185–203. https://doi.org/10.3917/cdge.036.0185.

Heiman, Rachel, Carla Freeman, and Mark Liechty, eds. 2012. *The Global Middle Classes: Theorizing through Ethnography*. Santa Fe, NM: School for Advanced Research Press.

Herzfeld, Michael. 1980. "Honour and Shame: Problems in the Comparative Analysis of Moral Systems." *Man* 15, no. 2: 339–51.

Herzfeld, Michael. 1992. *The Social Production of Indifference: Exploring the Symbolic Roots of Western Bureaucracy*. 1st ed. London: Routledge. https://doi.org/10.4324/978 1003135029.

Herzfeld, Michael. 2012. "Afterword: Reciprocating the Hospitality of These Pages." *Journal of the Royal Anthropological Institute* 18, no. S1: S210–17.

Hirtzmann, Ludovic. 2013. "Les Français s'exilent de plus en plus au Québec." *Le Figaro*. January 1. http://www.lefigaro.fr/international/2013/01/01/01003-20130101ARTFIG00150-les -francais-s-exilent-de-plus-en-plus-au-quebec.php.

Hondagneu-Sotelo, Pierrette and Ernestine Avila. 1997. "'I'm Here, but I'm There': The Meanings of Latina Transnational Motherhood." *Gender and Society* 11, no. 5: 548–71.

Howard, Kathryn. 2007. "Kinterm Usage and Hierarchy in Thai Children's Peer Groups." *Journal of Linguistic Anthropology* 17, no. 2: 204–30.

Hull, Matthew S. 2012. *Government of Paper: The Materiality of Bureaucracy in Urban Pakistan*. Oakland: University of California Press.

Hunleth, Jean. 2011. "Beyond On or With: Questioning Power Dynamics and Knowledge Production in 'Child-Oriented' Research Methodology." *Childhood* 18, no. 1: 81–93.

Hymes, D. 1972. "Models of the Interaction of Language and Social Life." In *Directions in Sociolinguistics: Ethnography of Communication*, edited by J. J. Gumperz and D. Hymes, 35–71. New York: Holt, Rinehart, and Winston.

Insee. 2015. *Taux de chômage en 2015*. Paris: Institut national de la statistique et des études économiques. http://www.insee.fr/fr/themes/tableau.asp?reg_id=0andref_id=NATnon03337

Insee. 2016. *Niveau d'Éducation de la Population*. France, *Portrait Social*. Paris: Insee Références.

Irvine, Judith. 1974. "Strategies of Status Manipulation in the Wolof Greeting." In *Explorations in the Ethnography of Speaking*, edited by Richard Bauman and Joel Sherzer, 167–91. Cambridge: Cambridge University Press.

Irvine, Judith. 1989. "When Talk Isn't Cheap: Language and Political Economy." *American Ethnologist* 16, no. 2: 248–67.

Irvine, Judith. 1990. "Registering Affect: Heteroglossia in the Linguistic Expression of Emotion." In *Language and the Politics of Emotion*, edited by C. Lutz and L. Abu-Lughod, 126–61. Cambridge: Cambridge University Press.

Irvine, Judith. 1996. "Shadow Conversations: The Indeterminacy of Participant Roles." In *Natural Histories of Discourse*, edited by Michael Silverstein and Greg Urban, 131–59. Chicago: University of Chicago Press.

Irvine, Judith. 2001. "Style as Distinctiveness: The Culture and Ideology of Linguistic Differentiation." In *Style and Sociolinguistic Variation*, edited by Penelope Eckert and John R. Rickford, 21–43. Cambridge: Cambridge University Press.

Irvine, Judith. 2005. "Knots and Tears in the Interdiscursive Fabric." *Journal of Linguistic Anthropology* 15, no. 1: 72–80.

Irvine, Judith. 2008. "Subjected Words: African Linguistics and the Colonial Encounter." *Language and Communication* 28, no. 4: 323–43.

Irvine, Judith, and Susan Gal. 2000. "Language Ideology and Linguistic Differentiation." In *Regimes of Language: Ideologies, Polities, and Identities*, edited by Paul V. Kroskrity, 35–84. Santa Fe, NM: School of American Research Press.

Iteanu, André. 2005. "A Perfect Individual." In *Youth, Otherness and the Plural City*, edited by Mette Andersson, Yngve Lithman, and Ove Sernhede, 107–38. Göteborg: Daidalos.

Iteanu, André. 2013. "The Two Conceptions of Value." *HAU: Journal of Ethnographic Theory* 3, no. 1: 155–71.

James, Allison, and Alan Prout. 1990. *Constructing and Reconstructing Childhood: New Directions in the Sociological Study of Childhood.* Oxford: Routledge.

James, A., and A. James. 2008. *Key Concepts in Childhood Studies.* London: SAGE.

Janbon, Antoine, and Quentin Wallon-Leducq, dirs. 2004. *Vivre ensemble, en France* (film). Paris: ANAEM (Agence Nationale de l'Accueil des Etrangers et des Migrations).

Jardin, Antoine. 2016. "Banlieues, le berceau du terrorisme?" *Sciences Humaines.* February 2. http://www.scienceshumaines.com/banlieues-le-berceau-du-terrorisme_fr_35800.html.

Johnson-Hanks, Jennifer. 2006. *Uncertain Honor: Modern Motherhood in an African Crisis.* Chicago: University of Chicago Press.

Jones, Emilia Ene. 2013. "Discrimination à l'embauche des jeunes en Île-de-France: Un diplôme plus élevé compense-t-il une origine maghrébine?" *Economie et statistique* 464, no. 1: 173–88.

Kane, A. 2001. "Financial Arrangements Across Borders: Women's Predominant Participation in Popular Finance, from Thilogne and Dakar to Paris; A Senegalese Case Study." In *Woman and Credit: Researching the Past, Refiguring the Figure*, edited by B. Lemire, R. Pearson, and G. Campbell. Oxford: Berg.

Kane, Ousmane. 2011. *The Homeland Is the Arena: Religion, Transnationalism, and the Integration of Senegalese Immigrants in America.* Oxford: Oxford University Press.

Karrebæk, Martha Sif. 2012. "'What's in Your Lunch Box Today?': Health, Respectability, and Ethnicity in the Primary Classroom." *Journal of Linguistic Anthropology* 22, no. 1: 1–22.

Keane, Webb. 2003. "Semiotics and the Social Analysis of Material Things." *Language and Communication* 23, no. 3: 409–25.

Keane, Webb. 2007. *Christian Moderns: Freedom and Fetish in the Mission Encounter.* Oakland: University of California Press.

Keane, Webb. 2008. "Market, Materiality and Moral Metalanguage." *Anthropological Theory* 8, no. 1: 27–42.

Keane, Webb. 2010. "Minds, Surfaces, and Reasons in the Anthropology of Ethics." In *Ordinary Ethics: Anthropology, Language, and Action*, edited by Michael Lambek, 64–83. New York: Fordham University Press.

Keane, Webb. 2013. "Secularism as a moral narrative of modernity." *Transit: Europäische Revue* 43: 159-170.

Keane, Webb. 2016. *Ethical Life: Its Natural and Social Histories.* Princeton, NJ: Princeton University Press.

Kett, Joseph F. 1977. *Rites of Passage: Adolescence in America, 1790 to the Present.* New York: Basic Books.

Kocka, Jürgen. 1981. "Class Formation, Interest Articulation, and Public Policy: The Origins of the German White-Collar Class in the Late 19th and Early 20th Century." In *Organizing Interests in Western Europe: Pluralism, Corporatism, and the Transformation of Politics*, edited by Susan Berger, 63–81. Cambridge: Cambridge University Press.

Koikkalainen, Saara. 2011. *Free Movement in Europe: Past and Present. Migration Information Source*, Online Journal of the Migration Policy Institute. April 21. http://www.migrationpolicy.org/article/free-movement-europe-past-and-present.

Kopytoff, Igor. 1971. "Ancestors as Elders." *Africa* 41, no. 2: 129–42.

Kopytoff, Larissa. 2015. "French Citizens and Muslim Law: The Tensions of Citizenship in Early Twentieth-Century Senegal." In *The Meaning of Citizenship*, edited by Richard Marback. Detroit: Wayne State University Press.

Kramer, Karen. 2005. "Children's Help and the Pace of Reproduction: Cooperative Breeding in Humans." *Evolutionary Anthropology Issues News and Reviews* 14, no. 6: 224–37. doi:10.1002/evan.20082.

Kremer-Sadlik, Tamar. 2019. "Ordinary Ethics and Reflexivity in Mundane Family Interactions." *Ethos* 47, no. 2: 190–210.

Kroeker, Lena. 2018. "Middle-Class Approaches to Social Security in Kenya." In *Middle Classes in Africa: Changing Lives and Conceptual Challenges*, edited by Lena Kroeker, David O'Kane, and Tabea Scharrer, 273–92. London: Palgrave Macmillan.

Kroeker, Lena, David O'Kane, and Tabea Scharrer. 2018. *Middle Classes in Africa: Changing Lives and Conceptual Challenges*. London: Palgrave Macmillan.

Kroskrity, Paul. 2000. *Regimes of Language: Ideologies, Polities, and Identities*. School of American Research Advanced Seminar Series. Santa Fe, NM: School of American Research Press.

Kulick, Don. 1992. *Language Shift and Cultural Reproduction: Socialization, Self, and Syncretism in Papua New Guinean Village*. Studies in the Social and Cultural Foundations of Language 14. Cambridge: Cambridge University Press.

Kulick, Don, and Bambi B. Schieffelin. 2004. "Language Socialization." In *A Companion to Linguistic Anthropology*, edited by Alessandro Duranti, 349–68. Chichester: Wiley-Blackwell.

Kusimba, Sibel. 2020. "Embodied Value: Wealth-In-People." *Economic Anthropology* 7, no. 2: 166–75.

Lambek, Michael. 2010. *Ordinary Ethics: Anthropology, Language, and Action*. New York: Fordham University Press.

Lamont, Michèle. 1992. *Money, Morals, and Manners: The Culture of the French and the American Upper-Middle Class*. Chicago: University of Chicago Press.

Lamont, Michèle. 2004. "Immigration and the Salience of Racial Boundaries Among French Workers." In *Race in France*, edited by H. Chapman and L. L. Frader. New York: Berghahn Books.

Lamont, Michèle, and Virág Molnár. 2002. "The Study of Boundaries in the Social Sciences." *Annual Review of Sociology* 28, no. 1: 167–95.

Lancy, David F. 2012. "The Chore Curriculum." In *Working and Learning Among Africa's Children*, edited by Gerd Spittler and Michael Bourdillion, 23–57. Berlin: Lit Verlag.

Latour, Bruno. 1993. *The Pasteurization of France*. Cambridge, MA: Harvard University Press.

Launay, Robert. 2006. "Practical Joking." *Cahiers d'Etudes Africaines* 46, no. 4: 795–808.

Laurent, Samuel. 2014. "Laïcité à l'école: L'arnaque de Marine Le Pen sur les cantines." *Le Monde: Les Décodeurs*. April 7.

Lê, Jérôme, Odile Rouhban, Pierre Tanneau, Cris Beauchemin, Mathieu Ichou, and Patrick Simon. 2022. "En dix ans, le sentiment de discrimination augmente, porté par les femmes et le motif sexiste." *Insee Première* 1911: 1–4.

Le Monde. 2009. "La première génération qui aura moins que la précédente." *Le Monde*. March 10. https://www.lemonde.fr/societe/article/2009/03/10/la-premiere-generation-qui-aura-moins-que-la-precedente_1165887_3224.html.

Le Monde avec AFP. 2024. "Élection présidentielle au Sénégal: En France la diaspora soulagée d'aller au vote." *Le Monde*. March 21. https://www.lemonde.fr/afrique/article/2024/03/21/election-presidentielle-au-senegal-en-france-la-diaspora-soulagee-d-aller-au-vote_6223230_3212.html.

Ledel, Johannes. 2022. "Stingy Swedes? Viral tale spotlights Swedish cultural quirk." *The Edition*. June 8. https://edition.mv/judiciary/24905.

Lee, Benjamin, and Edward LiPuma. 2002. "Cultures of Circulation: The Imaginations of Modernity." *Public Culture* 14, no. 1: 191–213.

Leins, Stefan. 2018. "Stories of Capitalism." In *Stories of Capitalism: Inside the Role of Financial
Analysts.* Chicago: University of Chicago Press.

Lentz, Carola. 2016. "African Middle Classes: Lessons from Transnational Studies and a Research Agenda." In *The Rise of Africa's Middle Class: Myths, Realities and Critical Engage-
ments,* edited by Henning Melber, 17–53. London: Zed Books.

Lentz, Carola. 2020. "Doing Being Middle-Class in the Global South: Comparative Perspectives
and Conceptual Challenges." *Africa* 90, no. 3: 439–69.

Lévi-Strauss, Claude. 1945. "L'Analyse structurale en linguistique et en anthropologie." *Word,
Journal of the Linguistic Circle of New York* 1, no. 2: 1–21.

Logan, Amanda L. 2016. "'Why Can't People Feed Themselves?': Archaeology as Alternative Ar-
chive of Food Security in Banda, Ghana." *American Anthropologist* 118, no. 3: 508–24.

Mabilon, Léa. 2022. "La polémique du #Swedengate: Cette tradition suédoise qui interdit qux
enfants invites chez lerus amis de diner à la tale familiale." *Madame Figaro.* June 16.
https://madame.lefigaro.fr/societe/actu/la-polemique-du-swedengate-cette-tradition
-suedoise-qui-interdit-aux-enfants-invites-chez-leurs-amis-de-diner-a-la-table-familiale
-20220613.

Maher, Stephanie. 2017. "Historicising 'Irregular' Migration from Senegal to Europe." *Anti-
Trafficking Review* 9: 77–91.

Maira, Sunaina, and Elisabeth Soep. 2005. "United States of Adolescence? Reconsidering US
Youth Culture Studies." *Young* 12, no. 3: 245–69.

Mamdani, Mahmood. 2005. *Good Muslim, Bad Muslim: America, the Cold War, and the Roots of
Terror.* New York: Harmony Books.

Manning, P. 2012. *Semiotics of Drink and Drinking.* New York: Continuum.

Martin, G. 1995. "Continuity and Change in Franco-African Relations." *Journal of Modern African Studies* 33: 1–20.

Mary, Kevin. 2010. "Entre la forteresse europe et l'amerique d'obama." *Hommes et Migrations*
1286–7: 124–33.

Maurer, Bill. 2006. "The Anthropology of Money." *Annual Review of Anthropology* 35: 15–36.

Maurer, Bill. 2009. "Moral Economies, Economic Moralities: Consider the Possibilities!" In *Economics and Morality: Anthropological Approaches,* edited by K. E. Browne and B. L. Milgram. New York: Altamira.

Maurin, Louis, Patrick Savidan, Nina Schmidt, Valérie Schneider. 2015. *Rapport sur les inégalli-
tés en France.* Tours: Observatoire des inégalités.

Mauss, Marcel. 1928. *Parentés à plaisanteries.* Melun: Imprimerie Administrative.

Mauss, Marcel. 2002 (1950). *The Gift: The Form and Reason for Exchange in Archaic Societies.*
London: Routledge.

Mbembe, Achille. 2011. "Provincializing France?" *Public Culture* 23, no. 1: 85–119.

Mbodj-Pouye, Aïssatou. 2016. "Fixed Abodes: Urban Emplacement, Bureaucratic Requirements, and the Politics of Belonging among West African Migrants in Paris." *American
Ethnologist* 43, no. 2: 295–310.

Mbodj-Pouye, Aïssatou. 2023. *An Address in Paris: Emplacement, Bureaucracy, and Belonging in
Hostels for West African Migrants.* New York: Columbia University Press.

McLaughlin, Fiona. 2001. "Dakar Wolof and the configuration of an urban identity." *Journal of
African Cultural Studies* 14, no. 2: 153–72.

Melber, Henning, ed. 2016. *The Rise of Africa's Middle Class: Myths, Realities and Critical En-
gagements.* London: Bloomsbury Publishing.

Melly, C. 2011. "Titanic Tales of Missing Men: Reconfigurations of National Identity and Gendered Presence in Dakar, Senegal." *American Ethnologist* 38, no. 2: 361–76.

Mercer, Claire. 2014. "Middle Class Construction: Domestic Architecture, Aesthetics and Anxieties in Tanzania." *Journal of Modern African Studies* 52, no. 2: 227–50.

Mercer, Claire. 2020. "Boundary Work: Becoming Middle Class in Suburban Dar es Salaam." *International Journal of Urban and Regional Research* 44, no. 3: 521–36.

Mercer, Claire, and Charlotte Lemanski. 2020. "The Lived Experiences of the African Middle Classes: Introduction." *Africa* 90, no. 3: 429–38.

Metcalf, B. D., ed. 1996. *Making Muslim Space in North America and Europe*. Berkeley: University of California Press.

Miers, Suzanne, and Igor Kopytoff, eds. 1977. *Slavery in Africa: Historical and Anthropological Perspectives*. Madison: University of Wisconsin Press.

Miller, D., E. Costa, N. Haynes, T. McDonald, R. Nicolescu, J. Sinanan, J. Spyer, S. Venkatraman, and X. Wang. 2016. *How the World Changed Social Media*. London: UCL Press.

Minni, Claude, and M. Okba. 2014. "Emploi et chômage des descendants d'immigrés en 2012." *Dares analyses* 23.

Montgomery, Heather. 2008. *An Introduction to Childhood: Anthropological Perspectives on Children's Lives*. New York: John Wiley and Sons.

Morgan, David. 1996. *Family Connections: An Introduction to Family Studies*. Cambridge: Polity.

Moya, Ismaël. 2017. *De l'argent aux valeurs: femmes, économie et société à Dakar*. Nanterre: Société d'ethnologie.

Mudde, Cas. 2013. "Three Decades of Populist Radical Right Parties in Western Europe: So What?" *European Journal of Political Research* 52, no. 1: 1–19.

Muehlebach, Andrea. 2012. *The Moral Neoliberal*. Chicago: University of Chicago Press.

Munn, Nancy D. 1992. *The Fame of Gawa: A Symbolic Study of Value Transformation in a Massim (Papua New Guinea) Society*. Durham, NC: Duke University Press.

Murphy, Michelle. 2017. *The Economization of Life*. Durham, NC: Duke University Press.

Murphy, William. 1980. "Secret Knowledge as Property and Power in Kpelle Society: Elders versus Youth." *Africa: Journal of the International African Institute* 50, no. 2: 193–207.

Murphy, William P., and Caroline H. Bledsoe. 1987. "Kinship and Territory in the History of a Kpelle Chiefdom (Liberia)." In *The African Frontier: The Reproduction of Traditional African Societies*, edited by Igor Kopytoff, 123–47. Bloomington: Indiana University Press.

Nahoum-Grappe, Véronique. 1991. *La Culture de l'Ivresse*. Paris: Quai Voltaire.

Nallet, Clélie. 2012. "Trajectoires d'émergence: 'Classes moyennes' d'Addis Abeba entre prospérité et précarité." *Annales d'Éthiopie* 27, no. 1: 207–25.

Ncube, Mthuli, and Charles Leyeka Lufumpa. 2015. *The Emerging Middle Class in Africa*. New York: Routledge.

Ndiaye, Pap. 2008. *La condition noire: Essai sur une minorité française*. Paris: Calmann-Lévy.

Ndiaye, Papa Oumar. 2020. "Les étudiants sénégalais en France et le travail salarié: Le 'petit boulot' comme clé de lecture d'une migration en crise?" *Journal of international Mobility* 8, no. 1: 143–66.

Ndoye, Fatou. 2001. *Evolution des styles alimentaires à Dakar*. Cirad: Enda-Graf.

Neveu Kringelbach, H. 2016. "The Paradox of Parallel Lives: Immigration Policy and Transnational Polygyny Between Senegal and France." In *Affective Circuits: African Migrations to Europe and the Pursuit of Social Regeneration*, edited by J. Cole and C. Groes. Chicago: University of Chicago Press.

Newell, Sasha. 2005. "Migratory Modernity and the Cosmology of Consumption in Côte d'Ivoire." In *Migration and Economy: Global and Local Dynamic*, edited by L. Trager, 163–90. Walnut Creek, CA: AltaMira Press.

Newell, Sasha. 2012. *The Modernity Bluff: Crime, Consumption, and Citizenship in Côte d'Ivoire*. Chicago: University of Chicago Press.

Ngugi, Wa Thiong'o. 1986. *Decolonizing the Mind*. London: James Curry.

Nieswand, Boris. 2011. *Theorising Transnational Migration: The Status Paradox of Migration*. New York: Routledge.

Nieuwenhuys, Olga. 1996. "The Paradox of Child Labor and Anthropology." *Annual Review of Anthropology* 25: 237–51.

Noiriel, Gérard. 2007. *A quoi sert "l'identité nationale"?* Paris: Éditions Agone.

O'Brien, D. C. 1998. "The Shadow-Politics of Wolofisation." *Journal of Modern African Studies* 36, no. 1: 25–46.

O'Brien, D. C. 2008. "A City That Keeps a Country Going: In Praise of Dakar." *Journal of Postcolonial Writing* 44, no. 1: 5–14.

Ochs, Elinor. 1988. *Culture and Language Development*. Cambridge: Cambridge University Press.

Ochs, Elinor. 1992. "Indexing Gender." In *Rethinking Context: Language as an Interactive Phenomenon*, edited by Alessandro Duranti and Charles Goodwin, 335–58. Cambridge: Cambridge University Press.

Ochs, Elinor, and Lisa Capps. 1996. "Narrating the Self." *Annual Review of Anthropology* 25: 19–43.

Ochs, Elinor, and Lisa Capps. 2001. "A Dimensional Approach to Narrative." In *Living Narrative: Creating Lives in Everyday Storytelling*. Cambridge, MA: Harvard University Press.

Ochs, Elinor, and Lisa Capps. 2009. *Living Narrative: Creating Lives in Everyday Storytelling*. Cambridge, MA: Harvard University Press.

Ochs, Elinor, and Carolina Izquierdo. 2009. "Responsibility in Childhood: Three Developmental Trajectories." *Ethos* 37, no. 4: 391–413.

Ochs, Elinor, and Tamar Kremer-Sadlik. 2007. "Introduction: Morality as Family Practice." *Discourse and Society* 18, no. 1: 5–10.

Ochs, Elinor, and Tamar Kremer-Sadlik. 2013. *Fast-Forward Family: Home, Work, and Relationships in Middle-Class America*. Oakland: University of California Press.

Ochs, Elinor, and Bambi Schieffelin. 2009. "Language Acquisition and Socialization: Three Developmental Stories and Their Implications." In *Linguistic Anthropology: A Reader*, edited by Alessandro Duranti. Chichester: Wiley-Blackwell.

Ochs, Elinor, and Bambi Schieffelin. 2012. "The Theory of Language Socialization." In *The Handbook of Language Socialization*, edited by Alessandro Duranti, Elinor Ochs, and Bambi Schieffelin, 1–21. West Sussex: John Wiley and Sons.

OECD. 2017. *A Recipient Perspective on TOSSD: The Case of Senegal*. Paris: OECD.

OFII (Office Français de l'Immigration et de l'Integration). 2015. "Qui sommes nous?" http://www.ofii.fr/qui_sommes-nous_46/index.html?sub_menu=1. Accessed June 20, 2015.

Olwig, K. F. 1999. "Narratives of the Children Left Behind: Home and Identity in Globalised Caribbean Families." *Journal of Ethnic and Migration Studies* 25, no. 2: 267–84.

Ong, Aihwa. 1987. *Spirits of Resistance and Capitalist Discipline: Factory Women in Malaysia*. Albany, NY: SUNY Press.

Orellana, Marjorie Faulstich, and Jennifer F. Reynolds. 2008. "Cultural Modeling: Leveraging Bilingual Skills for School Paraphrasing Tasks." *Reading Research Quarterly* 43, no. 1: 50–65.

Orellana, Marjorie Faulstich, Jennifer Reynolds, Lisa Dorner, and María Meza. 2003. "In Other Words: Translating or 'Paraphrasing' as a Family Literacy Practice in Immigrant Households." *Reading Research Quarterly* 38, no. 1: 12–34.

Osseo-Asare, Fran. 2005. *Food Culture in Sub-Saharan Africa*. Santa Barbara, CA: Greenwood Publishing Group.

Ossman, Susan, and Susan Terrio. 2006. "The French Riots: Questioning Spaces of Surveillance and Sovereignty." *International Migration* 44, no. 2: 5–21.

Oya, C. 2006. "From State Dirigisme to Liberalisation in Senegal: Four Decades of Agricultural Policy Shifts and Continuities." *European Journal of Development Research* 18, no. 2: 203–34.

Packer, Beth D. 2019. "Moral Agency and the Paradox of Positionality: Disruptive Bodies and Queer Resistance in Senegalese Women's Soccer." In *Routledge Handbook of Queer African Studies*, edited by S. N. Nyeck, 129–41. London: Routledge.

Pan, B. A., R. Y. Perlmann, C. E. and Snow. 1999. "Food for Thought: Dinner Table as a Context for Observing Parent-Child Discourse." In *Methods for Studying Language Production*, edited by L. Menn, and N. B. Ratner. Mahwah, NJ: Lawrence Erlbaum.

Panizzon, Marion. 2008. "Labour Mobility: A Win-Win-Win Model for Trade and Development: The Case of Senegal." *National Center for Competency in Research Working Paper 7.*

Pâris, Marie. 2014. "'Ruée vers l'Ouest': Le Québec, c'est vraiment l'eldorado?" *L'Obs: Rue89.* February 15. http://rue89.nouvelobs.com/blog/quebecoscope/2014/02/15/ruee-vers-louest-le -quebec-cest-vraiment-leldorado-232314.

Parmentier, Richard. 1994. *Signs in Society: Studies in Semiotic Anthropology.* Bloomington: Indiana University Press.

Parreñas, Rhacel Salazar. 2001. "Mothering from a Distance: Emotions, Gender, and Intergenerational Relations in Filipino Transnational Families." *Feminist Studies* 27, no. 2: 361–90.

Paugh, Amy, and Carolina Izquierdo. 2009. "Why Is This a Battle Every Night? Negotiating Food and Eating in American Dinnertime Interaction." *Journal of Linguistic Anthropology* 19, no. 2: 185–204.

Pauli, Julia. 2022. "Never Enough: Neoliberalizing Namibian middleMiddle-Class Marriages." *Africa* 92, no. 2: 191–209.

Peebles, Gustav (@GustavPeebles). 2022. "Far better for an anonymous state to hold the tethers of debt, distributing them "rationally" instead of via patronage. If I feed your kid, then you're going to feel enthrall to me; next time around, you're liable to add a dessert to the damned dinner that I served." Twitter (now X), June 1, 2022. https://x.com/GustavPeebles /status/1532085581383073795.

Peirce, Charles S. 1955. *Philosophical Writings of Peirce.* New York: Dover Publications.

Perry, D. L. 1997. "Rural Ideologies and Urban Imaginings: Wolof Immigrants in New York City." *Africa Today* 44, no. 2: 229–59.

Pettit, Matthew. 2023. "Life with the Maladie Alcoolique: Conceptions of Drinking and Abstinence in a French Mutual-Aid Group." PhD diss., University of Toronto.

Peugny, Camille. 2009. *Le déclassement.* Paris: Grasset.

Picut, Gaëlle. 2014. "Les immigrés diplômés davantage touché par le déclassement." *Le Monde.* December 1. http://www.lemonde.fr/emploi/article/2014/12/01/les-immigres-diplomes -davantage-touches-par-le-declassement_4532341_1698637.html#AWdigmY35528BtFy .99.

Pinçon, Michel, and Monique Pinçon-Charlot. 2010. *Sociologie de paris.* Paris: La Découverte.

Piot, Charles. 1999. *Remotely Global: Village Modernity in West Africa.* Chicago: University of Chicago Press.

Piquemal, Marie. 2015. "Laïcité: 'Pourquoi intervenir ici? On s'en sort plutôt bien.'" *Libération.* October 8. http://www.liberation.fr/france/2015/10/08/pourquoi-intervenir-ici-on-s-en -sort-plutot-bien_1399601.

Piquet, Caroline. 2014. "Visualisez si vous êtes riche, aisé, 'moyen,' 'populaire' ou pauvre." *Le Figaro.* April 16. http://www.lefigaro.fr/social/2014/04/16/09010-20140416ARTFIG00110-tes -vous-riche-pauvre-ou-appartenez-vous-a-la-classe-moyenne.php.

Pochard-Casablanca, Pascal. 2015. "En France, trois fois plus d'actes islamophobes en 2015." *RFI.* December 31. http://www.rfi.fr/france/20151230-france-trois-fois-plus-actes-islamo phobes-2015-antisemite-antireligieux.

Polanyi, Karl. 1944. *The Great Transformation: Economic and Political Origins of Our Time*. New York: Rinehart.

Portes, A., and R. G. Rumbaut. 2001. *The Story of the Immigrant Second Generation: Legacies*. New York: Russell Sage Foundation.

Portes, A., and M. Zhou. 1993. "The New Second Generation: Segmented Assimilation and Its Variants." *Annals of the American Academy of Political and Social Science* 530, no. 1: 74–96.

Quiminal, C., and Timera, M. 2002. "1974–2002: Les mutations de l'immigration ouest-africaine." *Hommes et Migrations* 1239: 19–32.

Rabain, Jacqueline. 1979. *L'enfant du lignage: Du sevrage à la classe d'âge chez les Wolof du Sénégal*. Paris: Payot.

Radcliffe-Brown, Alfred R. 1940. "On Joking Relationships." *Africa* 13, no. 3: 195–210.

Radcliffe-Brown, Alfred R., and Daryll Forde. 1950. *African Systems of Kinship and Marriage*. London: Routledge.

Raissiguier, Catherine. 2003. "Troubling Mothers: Immigrant Women from Africa in France." *Jenda: A Journal of Culture and African Women Studies* 4.

Raissiguier, Catherine. 2010. *Reinventing the Republic: Gender, Migration, and Citizenship in France*. Redwood City, CA: Stanford University Press.

République Française. 2007. *Rapport au Parlement: Les orientations de la politique de l'immigration; Premier rapport établi en application de l'article 1er de la loi du 26 novembre 2003*. Paris: République Française.

Riccio, Bruno. 2001. "From 'Ethnic Group' to 'Transnational Community?'": Senegalese Migrants, Ambivalent Experiences, and Multiple Trajectories." *Journal of Ethnic and Migration Studies* 27, no. 4: 583–99.

Riccio, Bruno. 2005. "Talkin' about Migration—Some Ethnographic Notes on the Ambivalent Representation of Migrants in Contemporary Senegal." *Wiener Zeitschrift für kritische Afrikastudien* 8: 99–118.

Ridgeway, Cecilia L. 2014. "Why Status Matters for Inequality." *American Sociological Review* 79, no. 1: 1–16.

Riesman, Paul. 1992. *First Find Your Child a Good Mother*. New Brunswick, NJ: Rutgers University Press.

Robbins, Joel. 2008. "Rethinking Gifts and Commodities: Reciprocity, Recognition, and the Morality of Exchange." In *Economics and Morality: Anthropological Approaches*, edited by Katherine E. Browne and B. Lynne Milgram, 43–58. Lanham, MD: AltaMira Press.

Rosa, Jonathan. 2019. *Looking Like a Language, Sounding Like a Race*. Oxford: Oxford University Press.

Rosaldo, Michelle Z. 1980. *Knowledge and Passion: Ilongot Notions of Self and Social Life*. Cambridge: Cambridge University Press.

Sahlins, Marshall. 1972. *Stone Age Economics*. New York: Aldine de Gruyter.

Sahlins, Marshall. 2013. *What Kinship Is—And Is Not*. Chicago: University of Chicago Press.

Salem, G. 1981. "De la brousse sénégalaise au Boul' Mich: Le système commercial mouride en France." *Cahiers d'Études Africaines* 21: 267–88.

Sargent, C. F. and S. Laranché-Kim. 2006. "Liminal Lives: Immigrant Status, Gender, and the Construction of Identities Among Malian Migrants in Paris." *American Behavioral Scientist* 50, no. 1: 9–26.

Schieffelin, Bambi B. 1990. *The Give and Take of Everyday Life: Language, Socialization of Kaluli Children*. Cambridge: Cambridge University Press.

Schieffelin, Bambi B., Kathryn A. Woolard, and Paul V. Kroskrity, eds. 1998. *Language Ideologies: Practice and Theory*. Oxford Studies in Anthropological Linguistics. Oxford: Oxford University Press.

Schielke, Samuli. 2012. "Surfaces of Longing: Cosmopolitan Aspiration and Frustration in Egypt." *City and Society* 24, no. 1: 29–37.

Schmalzbauer, Leah. 2001. "Searching for Wages and Mothering from Afar: The Case of Honduran Transnational Families." *Journal of Marriage and Family* 66, no. 5: 1317–31.

Schmitz, J. 2006. "Migrants ouest-africains: Miséreux, aventuriers ou notables?" *Politique Africaine* 109.

Schwartzman, Helen B. 1976. "The Anthropological Study of Children's Play." *Annual Review of Anthropology* 5: 289–328.

Schwartzman, Helen, ed. 2012. *Transformations: The Anthropology of Children's Play*. New York: Springer.

Scott, James C. 1976. *The Moral Economy of the Peasant: Rebellion and Subsistence in Southeast Asia*. New Haven, CT: Yale University Press.

Scott, Joan Wallach. 2007. *The Politics of the Veil*. Princeton, NJ: Princeton University Press.

Sen, Amartya. 1981. *Poverty and Famines: An Essay on Entitlement and Deprivation*. Oxford: Oxford University Press.

Shankar, Shalini, and Jillian R. Cavanaugh. 2012. "Language and Materiality in Global Capitalism." *Annual Review of Anthropology* 41: 355–69.

Shingler, Benjamin. 2014. "Montreal's French invasion: Why immigrants from France are moving en masse." *The Globe and Mail*. October 14. http://www.theglobeandmail.com/news/national/montreals-french-invasion-why-immigrants-from-france-are-moving-in-en-masse/article21085397/.

Shipton, Parker. 2007. *The Nature of Entrustment: Intimacy, Exchange, and the Sacred in Africa*. New Haven, CT: Yale University Press.

Silberman, Roxane, and Irène Fournier. 1999. "Les enfants d'immigrés sur le marché du travail: Les mécanismes d'une discrimination sélective." *Formation emploi* 65, no. 1: 31–55.

Silverstein, Michael. 1976. "Shifters, Linguistic Categories, and Culture Description." In *Meaning in Anthropology*, edited by Keith H. Basso and Henry A. Selby, 11–56. Albuquerque: University of New Mexico Press.

Silverstein, Michael. 1985. "The Functional Stratification of Language and Ontogenesis." In *Culture, Communication and Cognition: Vygotskian Perspectives*, edited by James V. Wertsch, 205–35. Cambridge: Cambridge University Press.

Silverstein Michael. 1993. "Metapragmatic Discourse and Metapragmatic Function." In *Reflexive Language: Reported Speech and Metapragmatics*, edited by J. Lucy, 32–58. New York: Cambridge University Press.

Silverstein, Michael. 2003. "Indexical Order and the Dialectics of Sociolinguistic Life." *Language and Communication* 23, no. 3: 193–229.

Silverstein, Michael. 2005. "Axes of Evals: Token Versus Type Interdiscursivity." *Journal of Linguistic Anthropology* 15, no. 1: 6–22.

Silverstein, Michael, and Greg Urban. 1996. *Natural Histories of Discourse*. Chicago: University of Chicago Press.

Silverstein, Paul. 2005. "Immigrant Racialization and the New Savage Slot: Race, Migration, and Immigration in the New Europe." *Annual Review of Anthropology* 34: 363–84.

Simon, Patrick. 2003. "French Integration Policy: Old Goals in New Bottles?" *Migration Information Source*, Online Journal of the Migration Policy Institute. January 1. http://www.migrationpolicy.org/article/french-integration-policy-old-goals-new-bottles.

Simon, Patrick. 2008. "The Choice of Ignorance: The Debate on Ethnic and Racial Statistics in France." *French Politics, Culture and Society* 26, no. 1: 7–31.

Simon, Patrick, and Mohamed Madoui. 2011. "Le marché du travail à l'épreuve des discriminations." *Sociologies Pratiques* 2: 1–7.

Southall, Roger. 2016. *The New Black Middle Class in South Africa*. Martlesham: Boydell and Brewer.

Spronk, R. 2012. *Ambiguous Pleasures: Sexuality and Middle-Class Self-Perceptions in Nairobi*. New York: Berghahn Books.

Stoller, Paul. 2002. *Money Has No Smell. The Africanization of New York City*. Chicago: University of Chicago Press.

Strathern, Marilyn. 1988. *The Gender of the Gift: Problems with Women and Problems with Society in Melanesia*. Berkeley: University of California Press.

Sweet, Nikolas. 2023. "Talk on the Move: Articulating Mobility in West Africa." *Journal of Ethnic and Migration Studies* 49, no. 13: 3511–28. doi:10.1080/1369183X.2021.1924050.

Swigart, Leigh. 1992. "Practice and Perception: Language Use and Attitudes in Dakar." PhD diss., University of Washington.

Swigart, Leigh. 1994. "Cultural Creolisation and Language Use in Post-Colonial Africa: The Case of Senegal." *Africa: Journal of the International African Institute* 64, no. 2: 175–89.

Swigart, Leigh. 2001. "The Limits of Legitimacy: Language Ideology and Shift in Contemporary Senegal." *Journal of Linguistic Anthropology* 10, no. 1: 90–130.

Tall, S. M. 2002. "L'émigration internationale sénégalaise." In *La société sénégalaise entre le local et le global*, edited by M. C. Diop. Paris: Karthala.

Ténédos, Julien. 2006. *L'Économie domestique: Entretien avec Florence Weber*. Paris: Aux lieux d'être.

Terray, E. 1999. "Le travail des étrangers en situation irréglière ou la délocalisation sur place." In *Sans-papiers: l'archaïsme fatal*, edited by M. Chemillier-Gendreau, J. Costa-Lascoux, and E. Terray, 9–34. Paris: La Découverte.

Terray, E. 2008. "L'État nation vu par les sans papiers." *Actuel Marx* 2, no. 44: 41–52. doi:10.3917/amx.044.0041.

Terrio, Susan J. 2009. *Judging Mohammed: Juvenile Delinquency, Immigration, and Exclusion at the Paris Palace of Justice*. Redwood City, CA: Stanford University Press.

Terrio, Susan J. 2010. "The Production of Criminal Migrant Children: Surveillance, Detention, and Deportation in France." In *Children and Migration: At the Crossroads of Resiliency and Vulnerability*, edited by Marisa O. Ensor, 79–96. London: Springer.

Tetreault, Chantal. 2008. "La Racaille: Figuring Gender, Generation, and Stigmatized Space in a French Cité." *Gender and Language* 2, no. 2: 141–70.

Tetreault, Chantal. 2015. *Transcultural Teens: Performing Youth Identities in French Cités*. New York: John Wiley and Sons.

Thomas, D. 2007. *Black France: Colonialism, Immigration, and Transnationalism*. Bloomington: Indiana University Press.

Thompson, Edward P. 1971. "The Moral Economy of the English Crowd in the Eighteenth Century." *Past and Present* 50: 76–136.

Thorsen, D. 2006. "Child Migrants in Transit: Strategies to Assert New Identities in Rural Burkina Faso." In *Navigating Youth, Generating Adulthood: Social Becoming in an African Context*, edited by C. Christiansen, M. Utas and H. E. Vigh. Uppsala: Nordiska Afrikainstitutet.

Tichit, Christine. 2014. "The Onset of Social Class Tastes among Children of Migrants in France: Competing Food Patterns in the Context of Migration." ISSI Visiting Scholar Working Paper Series 2013-14.01. http://escholarship.org/uc/item/8r8073p6.

Tsing, Anna. 2013. "Sorting Out Commodities: How Capitalist Value is Made Through Gifts." *HAU: Journal of Ethnographic Theory* 3, no. 1: 21–43.

Vujasinovic, Marko. 2017. "Est-Ce La Fin Du CDI?" *Forbes*. June 7. https://www.forbes.fr /management/fin-du-cdi-rh/.

Wallerstein, Immanuel. 1965. "Elites in French-Speaking West Africa: The Social Basis of Ideas." *Journal of Modern African Studies* 3, no. 1: 1–33.

Weber, Florence. 2008. *Le travail au noir: Une fraude parfois vitale?* Paris: Rue d'Ulm.

Weiner, Annette. 1992. *Inalienable Possessions: The Paradox of Keeping While Giving*. Berkeley: University of California Press.

Whitehouse, Bruce. 2012. *Migrants and Strangers in an African City: Exile, Dignity, Belonging*. Bloomington: Indiana University Press.

Whyte, David, and Jörg Wiegratz. 2016. "Neoliberalism, Moral Economy and Fraud." In *Neoliberalism and the Moral Economy of Fraud*, edited by David Whyte and Jörg Wiegratz. London: Routledge.

Wilder, G. 2005. *The French Imperial Nation-State: Negritude and Colonial Humanism Between the Two World Wars*. Chicago: University of Chicago Press.

Wittgenstein, Ludwig. 2009. *Philosophical Investigations*. Translated by G.E.M. Anscombe, P.M.S. Hacker, and Joachim Schulte. Malden, MA: Wiley-Blackwell.

Woolard, Kathryn A. 2020. "Language Ideology." In *The International Encyclopedia of Linguistic Anthropology*, edited by J. Stanlaw, 1–21. New York: Wiley and Sons Limited. https://doi.org/10.1002/9781118786093.iela0217.

Woolard, Kathryn A., and Bambi B. Schieffelin. 1994. "Language Ideology." *Annual Review of Anthropology* 23: 55–82.

World Bank. 2023. "Personal remittances, received % of GDP—Senegal." World Bank Group: Data. https://data.worldbank.org/indicator/BX.TRF.PWKR.DT.GD.ZS?locations=SN

Wortham, Stanton E. F. 1996. "Mapping Participant Deictics: A Technique for Discovering Speakers' Footing." *Journal of Pragmatics* 25, no. 3: 331–48.

Yount, Chelsie and Stefan Leins. nd. "Introduction: Economic Moralities: Value Claims on the Future." *Journal of Cultural Economy*.

Yount-André, Chelsie. 2016. "Snack Sharing and the Moral Metalanguage of Exchange: Children's Reproduction of Rank-Based Redistribution in Senegal." *Journal of Linguistic Anthropology* 26, no. 1: 41–61.

Yount-André, Chelsie. 2017. "Indexing Integration: Hierarchies of Belonging in Secular Paris." *Journal of the Anthropological Society of Oxford* 9, no. 1: 43–64.

Yount-André, Chelsie. 2018a. "Gifts, Trips, and Facebook Families: Children and the Semiotics of Kinship in Transnational Senegal." *Africa* 88, no. 4: 683–700.

Yount-André, Chelsie. 2018b. "Empire's Leftovers: Eating to Integrate in Secular Paris." *Food and Foodways* 26, no. 2: 124–45.

Yount-André, Chelsie. 2020a. "Investir dans plusieurs classes sociales: Enfance transnationale et accueil des enfants de la diaspora à Dakar". *Politique Africaine* 159: 83–104.

Yount-André, Chelsie. 2020b. "Strategic Investments in Multiple Middle Classes: Morals and Mobility Between Paris and Dakar." *Africa Today* 66, no. 3–4: 89–112.

Yount-André, Chelsie. 2022. "Material Care and Kinship on Trips to Dakar: Proximity via 'Pluriparentalité' in Transnational Senegalese Families. *Journal des Africanistes* 92, no. 1: 78–100.

Yount-André, Chelsie, and Yanga Zembe. 2023. "Consuming Inequities: Vegetarianism, Climate Crisis, and Political Upheaval in Post-Apartheid South Africa." *Anthropology of Food* 17. https://doi.org/10.4000/aof.14021.

Zaloom, Caitlin. 2019. *Indebted: How Families Make College Work at Any Cost*. Princeton, NJ: Princeton University Press.

Zelizer, Viviana. 1985. *Pricing the Priceless Child: The Changing Social Value of Children*. Princeton, NJ: Princeton University Press.

Zelizer, Viviana. 2000. "The Purchase of Intimacy." *Law and Social Inquiry* 25, no. 3: 817–48.

Zelizer, Viviana. 2005. "Circuits within Capitalism." In *The Economic Sociology of Capitalism*, edited by Victor Nee and Richard Swedberg, 289–322. Princeton, NJ: Princeton University Press.

Zuckerman, Charles. 2020. "'Don't Gamble for Money with Friends': Moral-Economic Types and Their Uses." *American Ethnologist* 47, no. 4: 432–46.

Zuckerman, Charles. 2022. "When Ethics Can't Be Found: Evaluative Gaps in Ordinary Life." *Cultural Anthropology* 37, no. 3: 450–85.

# INDEX

# ACKNOWLEDGMENTS

My thanks for this book must begin in Senegal—Dakar, Mermoz—where I was first hosted as a student and "daughter" in 2005, and to where I have repeatedly returned in the twenty years since, making those kinship relations gradually more material with each return. To Emilie Diang Cissoko, Marie Hélène Lopes Ndiaye, and Karim Ndiaye, thank you for making Mermoz my home and me a part of your family. In Dakar, I thank ACI Baobab for organizing these first connections and Professors Abdou Salam Fall and Rokhaya Cisse at the University of Dakar, who have hosted me at Camp Jérèmy/LARTES since 2008.

Most of the Senegalese families in Paris and Dakar, whose stories fill these pages, I cannot mention here by name, as I am bound to anonymity by institutional ethics requirements. To those who took part in the fieldwork on which this book is based, it has been a privilege to take part in your family life, to share your food, watch you(r children) grow up, and to puzzle through transnational family-making together.

The book itself began as doctoral research at Northwestern, in co-tutelle with the École des hautes études en sciences sociales (EHESS) in Paris. At the EHESS, I thank Claude Fischler, who taught me to see food as a total social fact, such that I might develop an approach that examines food sharing to understand children's socialization into economic moralities. At Northwestern, Caroline Bledsoe taught me to ask questions like an Africanist and to be leery of jargon. Bill Murphy, meanwhile, introduced me to Peircean semiotics and Michael Silverstein's metapragmatics. Together, they taught me, as they have their own children, to always "look closer" (thanks to Kara, my age-mate, for this phrasing). Caroline's lessons came by way of parable. Margin notes and offhand comments became magic beans I puzzled over, sometimes for years. These chapters come from puzzling Caroline inspired, which I answered with the tools of linguistic anthropology.

At Northwestern, I thank Helen Schwartzman, who taught me to pay attention to children and pay childlike attention, and Robert Launay, for his lessons on kinship (in African families and francophone anthropology alike) and for helping me weave together anthropology in Paris and Chicago. Much gratitude goes to Karen Tranberg Hansen for introducing me to economic anthropology and the term "economic moralities." At Northwestern, I also thank my colleagues Matilda Stubbs, Jean Hunleth, Arturo Marquez, Florent Souvignet, Morgan Hoke, Douglas Smit, Livia Garofalo, Beth Derderian, Nazli Özkan, Vanessa Watters, Elisa Lanari, Ryan Lash, and Jessica Pouchet for reading drafts and listening to the many talks that became these pages.

My time in Chicago was marked by my introduction to linguistic and semiotic anthropology at the University of Chicago Semiotics Workshop, Language in Culture courses, and Michicagoen conferences where I was fortunate to receive mentorship and feedback from Sue Gal, Costas Nakassis, Justin Richland, Judy Irvine, Michael Silverstein, Summerson Carr, and Webb Keane, and from colleagues like Janet Connor, Mike Prentice, Sandhya Narayanan, and Nikolas Sweet. I especially thank Meghanne Barker and Chip Zuckerman for reading so many drafts of these chapters. At Northwestern, I thank Shalini Shankar for urging me see the materiality of language. Collaborations with Jillian Cavanaugh and other scholars of food and language, including Amy Paugh, Martha Karrebæk, and Kate Riley, were instrumental in helping me develop the semiotic theories of food sharing articulated here.

Presenting these chapters to audiences in Paris was a process that fundamentally shaped my reflections on francophone West Africa and immigration in France. I thank colleagues in France for the discussion and debate, especially Amelie Grysole, Ismaël Moya, Jean Schmitz, Pietro Fornasetti, Jennifer Bidet, Florence Weber, Beth Packer, Aïssatou Mbodj-Pouye, and Delphine Sall. I thank Marie Lachambre for correcting my French, in every single paper and article that presents a French version of the ideas developed here.

I am also grateful to a network of Africanist scholars of transnational kinship and class-mobility, in the United States and Europe, with whom I have collaborated to develop these theories on migration and middle-class mobility. I thank Julia Pauli, Jennifer Cole, Christian Groes, Dinah Hannaford, Bruno Riccio, Anaïs Ménard, Branwyn Poleykett, Dick Powiss, and Emma Bunkley. An extra special thanks to Pamela Feldman-Savelsberg and Cati Coe, whose support throughout the book-writing process was so helpful, kind, and caring. Your feedback, poignant and patient, helped me clarify the book's key arguments.

This book has also benefitted from the feedback of many mentors and colleagues I met during my postdoctoral research. I especially thank the Just Remit Project team at Leiden University and the Impact Hau team at the University of Bologna. I thank PIs Matthew Hoye and Marc Brightman (respectively) for their generous support of follow-up fieldwork in Dakar, book writing and revision, and for cosponsoring a workshop on "Economic Moralities" at Leiden in 2023, which allowed me to develop and articulate ideas that I have presented in most depth in this book. I thank Caitlin Zaloom, Deborah James, Bill Maurer, and Erik Bähre for their participation in this workshop. I especially thank Stefan Leins, my co-organizer and coeditor, for his support in developing the approach to economic moralities presented here. I thank my colleagues with whom I have collaborated on these projects and all those who were kind enough to give me comments on drafts: Oiara Bonilla, Giulia dal Maso, Claudia Campisano, Benjamin Eyre, Chris Mizes, Stefan Voicu, Riccardo De Cristano, Natalia Gómez Muñoz, Ketevan Gurchiani, Nikki Mulder, Alice Pearson, Sarah-Jane Phelan, Kevin Yildirim, Ainur Begim, Sean Field, Johannes Lenhard, Martina Abisso, Audrey Soula, Duff Morton, John Mathius, and Nishita Trisal.

I would like to thank the two anonymous reviewers and my editor, Elisabeth Maselli, at Penn Press for her generous answers to my many questions. I thank Erin Greb for the maps of Dakar and Paris and Stephanie Agenais for the beautiful kinship diagrams and tables. I thank my *jàngalekat* Ndeye Oulimata Diop for correcting my Wolof transcriptions. Many thanks to my research assistant in Dakar, Raïssa Minkilane, for her help with research and book revisions. I thank Ndeye Mane Sall for her friendship, support, and constant willingness to help me fact-check via WhatsApp, define terms, translate from Wolof, explain expressions, and generally help me make sense of life in Senegal and its diaspora.

I thank my family for supporting my studies, research, and travels, however crazy my life—stretched now between three continents—must now seem to those back in Missouri. Thanks to my brother Tyler Yount and to my father Kevin Yount for his comments on the book in full. I am especially grateful to my mom, Barbara Fawver, for carefully copyediting the whole book at multiple stages, always at the last minute. I thank my great-aunt, Jackie Heitman Grindstaff Varner, for her comments as a librarian and a Heitman sister—one of the seven who make up the Missouri matriarchy that was the site of my own childhood kinship making. These pages were written in loving memory of my grandma, Donna Heitman Yount.

This book is dedicated to my daughter Marguerite, who kept me close company during her babyhood as I wrote the earliest versions of these chapters and who has grown to become my key informant on childhood in France. Becoming a mother in my own "host country" as I wrote these pages fundamentally changed my ability to grasp the moral and material stakes of being a parent with family networks spread across continents.

Fieldwork and writing for this project were supported by the Wenner-Gren Foundation, the Chaire Unesco World Food Systems, Northwestern University's Department of Anthropology, Buffett Center, Program of African Studies, and French Interdisciplinary Group, as well as the Institut interdisciplinaire d'anthropologie du contemporain. This project has also received funding from the European Research Council under the European Union's Horizon 2020 research and innovation program (grant agreement No. 949628).

www.ingramcontent.com/pod-product-compliance
Lightning Source LLC
Chambersburg PA
CBHW030332270326
41926CB00010B/1592